Just a Country Lawyer

Just a Country Lawyer

A Biography

of Senator Sam Ervin

by PAUL R. CLANCY

Indiana University Press   Bloomington   London

Library of Congress Cataloging in Publication Data
Clancy, Paul R   1939–
   Just a country lawyer.
   Bibliography: p. 301
   1. Ervin, Samuel James, 1896–   I. Title.
E840.8.E74C55   328.73′092′4   [B]   73-16528
ISBN 0-253-14540-6.

CONTENTS

ILLUSTRATIONS FOLLOWING PAGE 118

PREFACE

THE FIRST TIME I saw Sam Ervin was in July, 1970. He was standing beside a precarious tower of books in the U.S. Senate chamber, arms waving, shouting to puzzled spectators in the galleries about how a certain godawful legislative proposal known as the D.C. Crime Bill was full of more unconstitutional provisions than a mangy hound dog has fleas.

It was a fascinating performance. Here was this aging southern filibusterer, who had so stubbornly resisted civil rights legislation, fighting for the rights of muggers and dope pushers in the black ghettos of Washington. It was another lost cause for Ervin because, in this case, too many would-be liberals had gone into hiding at the first whisper of law-and-order by the Nixon Administration.

When I interviewed Ervin shortly after, he described himself as a "true liberal," who believed in the ultimate worth and dignity of men and women. Given his prior record, I had some misgivings, but soon became convinced that he was a man who, given the chance, could reconcile many of the divergent and conflicting viewpoints in this country.

Although I had no earthly idea of doing it myself, I thought someone ought to write a book about Ervin. I soon discovered that many who had either covered him or worked for him had, at one time or another, hoped to be able to do just that. Sam Ervin, so in tune with the past and yet in many ways also with the present, so brimming over with the folklore of his homeland and memories of his youth, seemed a compelling subject.

I harbored the idea for nearly three years and became more and more convinced of its validity as I followed his unbelievably varied activities in the Senate. A newspaper editor could have assigned someone full time to cover what was happening with Ervin and his committees and end up with more interesting copy than one who had dispatched a whole team to the White House.

Hardly a day would pass when the Constitutional Rights Subcommittee did not discover some outrageous new scheme being hatched by either the government or private industry to trample on the rights of American citizens. Stopping by to see Marcia MacNaughton or Larry Baskir at the subcommitee office was a sure way of getting my pockets stuffed with stories and ideas for stories. Bob Smith, Ervin's legislative aide, always had some reading on the crosscurrents in the Senate and the intellectual winds that blow across American politics. Rufus Edmisten would hold forth at the drop of a hat on the intrigues of the Senate and of North Carolina politics. Along with former Constitutional Rights chief counsels George Autry and Paul Woodard and aides Hall Smith and Pat Shore, these people were immensely helpful in providing insights into the career and character of Ervin, and for this I am very grateful.

Ervin had been building toward a collision with Richard Nixon, or someone like him, practically all his life, and it seemed, during the first few years of the new Administration, that there would be quite a crunch when it happened. If Ervin ever gained the levers of power, it might even be spectacular. It was a great bit of drama to observe and write about. By January, 1973, after Ervin had been appointed to head the Watergate Committee, the temptation to drop everything and try the book was irresistible. Of course no one knew—except perhaps those who took part in the White House cover-up—just how explosive the investigation would become or that, within six months, Sam Ervin would have undergone an apotheosis and Richard Nixon, like Humpty Dumpty, a great fall.

I am also greatly indebted to Ervin himself for giving me so much of his increasingly precious time and for dredging up so many memories, some of them painful, some pleasant, and some hysterically funny. Altogether, we talked for about thirty hours between April and October, most of the time in his library at home, but also while on trips to some political rally, or across his desk in Washington.

There are a great many Ervin buffs, not the least of whom are members of his family. His wife Margaret, his sisters Jean and Eunice, his brother Hugh, his daughters Leslie and Laura, his son Sam III, and grandson Jimmy, were all generous in sharing their memories of Ervin as a boy, young man, husband, father, and grandfather.

To Barbara, my wife, and Beth and Jenny, my daughters, who gave me encouragement and solitude when each was needed, I would like to express my thanks. This book is dedicated to them.

PAUL R. CLANCY

Washington, D.C.
January, 1974

Just a Country Lawyer

1. *The Right Man*

There is no truth existing which I fear,
or would wish unknown to the whole world.

THOMAS JEFFERSON

SAM ERVIN AWOKE on the morning of May 17, 1973, feeling rested, although still slightly under the weather. He had stood in the rain without hat or umbrella two days before on a college campus in Maine and caught cold. He dressed in one of his new blue shirts—his one concession to the vainglories of television—and a blue sport jacket, then went into breakfast with "Miss Margaret," his wife of nearly fifty years. She had prepared his usual hearty breakfast of orange juice, bacon and eggs, unbuttered toast, and coffee. For a man of seventy-six who had never taken very good care of himself, he felt chipper. Nevertheless, he was apprehensive, not for what the day or the coming year would bring to the country, but for himself. He dreaded what it would do to his own private world.

It was a cool, breezy morning with a promise of rain in the air as he emerged from his apartment building. He and his wife had lived in that modest, poorly heated place for almost twenty years because it was right in the center of Sam Ervin's universe. He could look directly across the street from his fourth-floor living-room window at the Supreme Court, that capricious guardian of the rights of man. Across the way, to the right, was the Capitol Building, where once—but no longer—the most powerful branch of government sat.

He strolled down the block and across Constitution Avenue

to his office, where he checked to make sure his wife and a friend from North Carolina would have front-row seats for the day's event. Then, to avoid the crowds that were swarming all over the third floor of the Old Senate Office Building, he took the back elevator to the basement, walked down the long corridor to the subway, and rode over to his special hideout in the Capitol. It was the one place in Washington—or in the world, for that matter—where no one, neither aides nor newsmen, could get to him.

While mobs jammed the rotunda downstairs from the hearing room and the phone in his office jangled incessantly, while everyone looked frantically for him, Sam Ervin lay back serenely in the Senate barber shop, freshly shaved, a warm towel swirled over his face. He was as relaxed as a baby, oblivious to the world outside, which, during the past few weeks, had gone slightly mad.

It would get worse. Much worse. The country would be swept with accusations and rocked with disillusionment. Disbelief would be followed by cynicism. The accusers would be vilified. The government would seem on the brink of tottering. But the system had withstood severe shocks in the past and had recovered. It would again. Jefferson had said there was nothing to fear from the conflict between truth and error. Courage was called for.

Ervin whooshed back from the Capitol on the front seat of the subway shuttle and retraced his steps to the elevators beneath his office. There he met Howard Baker, his Republican counterpart, who was on his way over to see Ervin, and they rode up together, exchanging pleasantries about basement corridors. They talked briefly in Ervin's book-crowded office, then walked down the long hallway together, the camera lights bobbing in front of them like moonlight on the waves. Ervin, nearly a foot taller than Baker, looked slightly menacing as he carried at the ready the colorful gavel made for the occasion by his friends the Cherokee Indians.

Ervin strode through a crowd of microphone holders, as if they weren't there, into the cavernous, ornate Senate Caucus Room, setting off an expectant twitter among the spectators and reporters who filled the room to overflowing. The room, which had echoed with charges and denials in times past, was awash with light. But none of those sensational investigations approached the potential for high-level scandal that this one held. Ervin knew. He had been there to see them unfold. Now, as the Watergate hearings began, four top Administration officials had been fired or told to resign, two former cabinet members had been indicted, and the President of the United States had accepted the responsibility, although not the blame, for it all.

And this silver-maned old man, whose voice quivered and twanged as he spoke of the "black cloud of distrust" hanging over the nation, who seemed surprisingly tall as he stood to swear in the first witness, who gave us a quick lesson in the rules of evidence, seemed quite ready, if not altogether willing, to sit in judgment.

Sam J. Ervin, Jr., despite an impressive record of both accomplishment and mischief in the United States Senate, had managed to stay out of the national spotlight until the issue of presidential campaign abuses became a full-blown national scandal. He had a reputation as a constitutional seer and storyteller, but those who had fought him on major issues thought his appreciation for the Constitution ended in the 1930's and his stories not very funny. He had never attained the power of most of the southern warlords.

Yet in a few short weeks, this self-proclaimed country lawyer with his bottomless barrel of aphorisms from Shakespeare, the Bible, and the North Carolina mountains, became a national symbol of decency and fairness in politics, the embodiment for many of wisdom, a genuine American folk hero. He was a real live replica of our Uncle Sam, but more human, more compassionate than the original—"the real thing," as the members of his fan club proclaimed.

It was partly the media exposure that created the Ervin image—with all of that air time he could have been colorless and nasty and still have become a national figure—but much more than that was going on. The country needed a man like Ervin. Somewhere, in the midst of Vietnam, drug trips, and Watergate, the bottom had fallen out of the national moral conscience. It was not the time for a modern, now-generation Clark Kent to appear with a plastic smile and a new line of instant remedies. The country, with young people in fact leading the way, was unmistakably looking for a grandfatherly figure, and found one, for a time at least, in this fallible, but seemingly incorruptible man.

What a contrast to those clear-eyed, baby-faced types in pin-striped suits who casually testified in unaccented voices that they had agreed to commit bribery, perjury, and obstruction of justice! And then came the heavies, the top aides to the President and members of the cabinet, "team players" who, while they were "clicking away on all eight cylinders," arrogantly and cynically asserted that certain portions of the Constitution were out of date. Or, as they liked to put it, "inoperative." After all, they said, they were working for a cause—to keep "the enemy" from winning the election. To save the king. In so doing, they willingly, almost methodically, abdicated their own ethical and moral standards. Tragically, they brought the office of the presidency to one of its lowest points in history. Within months after Richard Nixon's second inauguration, the almost unthinkable subject of impeachment was being discussed openly.

What had happened to our sense of outrage? Had we become so numbed by the assaults on our trust and conscience; had concern for inflation and order so overshadowed pride in our country's institutions that we were willing to shrug at a direct threat to our system of free elections? On behalf of, if not with the approval of, the President himself? Senator Sam gave it all back to us.

Watching him pursue a witness or scowling at one in a

pantomime of outrage was like holding up a mirror to our own consciences. We had long grown accustomed to seeing our public officials with their masks on, but Ervin was different. That rough sea of a face, with the nervous eyebrows flying like the wings of a hawk, the hound-dog cheeks quivering, the lips racing, and the sparkling eyes darting, seemed to be responding to some inner critical mass of moral indignation. Shock, outrage, pleasure, fatigue, compassion. From time to time the crooked fingers would fly to his face as if to bring it back under control. The mind raced faster than the lips and often he would fall flat on a word. But to one who had watched smooth-tongued liars for weeks, a verbal pratfall was refreshing.

Early in the hearings, Ervin was listening with arms folded as a former aide in the Committee for the Re-election of the President confessed that he agreed to lie to federal investigators, the grand jury, and the federal court, all because he wanted to be known as a "team player." Ervin was looking right at the witness, but his mind seemed to be far away. Sixty years before, on one of those idyllic spring days in Chapel Hill, a bony old philosophy professor had told his students that there were higher loyalties than those imposed by groups or even by self-interest. To Ervin, the Watergate debacle demonstrated an abysmal absence of any such ethical values.

The witnesses were respectable family men, many of them, never in trouble with the law, never before in the position of having to apologize for their conduct. And now this. Indictments would follow. Doors to their futures would be closed. And no one would be there to thank them when they had paid the penalty. From out of his student days a Shakespearean quotation came tumbling into Ervin's mind as if he had committed it to memory at lunchtime instead of half a century earlier. Cardinal Wolsey could have been speaking of Nixon when he said

> Had I but serv'd my God with half the zeal
> I serv'd my king, he would not in mine age
> Have left me naked to mine enemies.

Ervin always had a bit of folklore, a story, a line of poetry, or a biblical maxim for just about every subject he encountered. Though basically a shy person, he never ran from a good "stowry." To Ervin, a story that happened to fit the occasion—and sometimes even one that didn't—was worth an hour or more of argument. A story could be a devastating weapon in the courtroom or in public debates in Congress. He had introduced the Senate to poor old arthritic Cousin Ephraim Swink in his first speech nearly twenty years before, shattering the pomposity and bluster of a demagogue.

But that was a long time ago. Long enough for the climate of fear that had paralyzed the country in the fifties to wear off. Long enough for a Senate career, which had seemed to wander off the tracks for so long in pursuit of a lost cause, finally to reach fruition and power.

His stories and sayings had never been so effective in the Senate. Sam Ervin used to be that lovable old fellow who quoted from the Bible and the Constitution, and his colleagues, sure they had the votes to beat him, indulged him affectionately. But when those oft-heard parables and interminable lectures were utilized for obstruction and delay, he was not so lovable. In some quarters he was laughed at and in others cursed. Or worse, he was dismissed as irrelevant. The Constitution, along with the Founding Fathers who wrote it, suffered the same fate.

But during the long months of the Watergate hearings in 1973, when Ervin recited the Constitution to witnesses, the words, lilting with the cadences of the North Carolina mountains, sounded as though they had been forged in an eighteenth-century blacksmith's shop, still glowing with the heat of revolution. He helped set off a constitutional revival in the United States.

One of the things that shocked Ervin the most was the White House's "enemies list." Like the lists bandied about by the old witch-hunting committees of Congress, this one contained the names of journalists, politicians, entertainers, and businessmen whose only offense had been to speak or publish their honest convictions. To a man who drank the spiritual wine of the First Amendment from the tables of Madison and Jefferson and knelt at the altar of civil liberties, that was nothing short of tyranny over the mind of man. It was a worse crime than murder or pillage because without liberty democracy dies.

As he told students at Davidson College just before the hearings began, "Our greatest possession is not the vast domain; it's not our beautiful mountains, or our fertile prairies, or our magnificent coastline. It's not the might of our Army or Navy. These things are of great importance. But in my judgment the greatest and most precious possession of the American people is the Constitution."

The very idea that the White House had approved and apparently put into operation a comprehensive plan for domestic surveillance, including illegal wiretapping and burglary, was incomprehensible to Ervin. It struck at the heart of the Fourth Amendment, the right of people to be "secure in their persons, houses, papers and effects, against unreasonable searches and seizures."

The right to privacy was sacred with Ervin. A lot of people paid lip service to it while letting the government and private industry pry into their most intimate thoughts and habits. Ervin considered lie detectors "twentieth-century witchcraft," computers dehumanizing, and bugging devices the very essence of villainy. One of the gravest threats to freedom was the overzealous judge or legislator who gave policemen the power to trample on constitutional rights. As he told the California Bar Association in September, 1971, "I cling to the abiding conviction that it is better for lawmakers to permit some wrongdoers to escape than it is for them to sacrifice upon the altar of fear and doubt the age-old boast of Anglo-American law that every man's home is his castle."

The same high-sounding phrases were used, however, in fighting open housing and public accommodations legislation.

To Ervin there was no paradox or inconsistency. One man's pursuit of happiness should not take away from another his right to be a thorough-going sob. He didn't think it naive to assume that reform would come about through the application of good will instead of force.

Equal rights for all; special rights for none. That was the essence of the old Sam Ervin. Liberals disagreed with him in the 1960's and loved him in the 1970's. It was all the same to him. When Ervin spouted his favorite passages of the Constitution during the furious debates with the Administration or at the Watergate hearings, he was a fundamentalist preacher laying down the Ten Commandments. Thou shalt not bug without a court order. Thou shalt not withhold information from Congress or the courts concerning crimes. Period.

Politicians have always gone around invoking the name of the Founding Fathers, with the usual result of bringing a glaze to the eyes of their listeners. The Founding Fathers were too straightlaced for the computer age, too alarmist for the consensus generation. But Ervin, born in the era of the horse and buggy and kerosene lamp, the descendant of a long line of Scotch-Irish settlers who fought for their independence, spoke with the authority of an age that was closer to the origins of the Republic. He brought back Jeffersonian liberalism, placing greater trust in individuals than governments, believing, as those who wrote the Constitution believed, that the powers of the state must be vigilantly kept in check by the rights of free men, and when in doubt the balance must be tipped toward freedom. He often seemed to qualify as one of the Founding Fathers themselves, or at least as their chosen delegate to the twentieth century.

He memorized their instructions at an early age. Whether the government was responding to threats to national security, crime waves, subversive activities, violent protests, or leaks to the press, the warnings came straight from the quilled pens of his spiritual ancestors.

Benjamin Franklin: "They that can give up essential liberty to obtain a little temporary safety deserve neither liberty nor safety."

Daniel Webster: "Good intentions will always be pleaded for every assumption of authority—it is hardly too strong to say that the Constitution was made to guard the people against the dangers of good intentions."

James Madison: "It is proper to take alarm at the first experiment on our liberties. We hold this prudent jealousy to be the first duty of citizens, and one of the noblest characteristics of the late Revolution."

William Pitt, the younger: "Necessity is the plea for every infringement of human freedom. It is the argument of tyrants; it is the creed of slaves."

When used to fight civil rights legislation or consumer protection laws or to defend the filibuster, the fine phrases sounded hollow to those eager for reform. But when employed to defend a vigorous press, protect criminal suspects from law-and-order justice, expose the Army for snooping on civilians, or uphold the rights of protestors, they rang with vitality. Against the law-and-order pronouncements of the Nixon Administration, they sounded downright radical.

The Watergate episode was for Ervin the perfect example of what can go wrong when government becomes too powerful. It begins to view constitutional freedoms as threats to its power and it needs to know—by whatever means, legal or otherwise—what its opponents, and those it believes to be its opponents, are doing and thinking.

Ervin did not just happen along when the Watergate investigation began. He was not, as columnists said, selected from Central Casting to fill the role of Wise Old Judge. He had been slaving away in the Senate for two decades on precisely the issues that were raised by the scandal. It seemed uncanny, but he was standing—by virtue of his seniority, his committee positions, his knowledge of the Constitution and love of history, his judicial experience and reputation for fairness, his disdain for political pressure, and his old-fashioned ideas of morality—right in Richard Nixon's path. He was the right man for the times, a rare happening in political history. The clash seemed almost inevitable or, as Ervin's Presbyterian forebears might have suspected, predestined.

The differences between Nixon and Ervin were vast. Their personalities, political backgrounds, and temperaments were essentially opposite. The two men had said very little about each other before their clash, though it was obvious from their indirect comments that there was very little mutual respect. Though Nixon once referred to Ervin as "a great constitutional lawyer," he was obviously not referring to Ervin's views on the powers of the President's office because he promptly disagreed with the senator on that score. It was apparent from Nixon's comments about the investigation that he thought Ervin was out to get him.

Ervin never had a very high opinion of Nixon, not since he heard that the former congressman and senator began his political career by deliberately smearing others. During an interview, he said he thought Nixon's problem stemmed from his inability to trust others. He saw in Nixon an enemy to civil liberties. It was no coincidence that Ervin came into his own as a respected leader of the Senate during Nixon's presidency. By that time the old battles were over and the new ones were just beginning.

As chairman of the Constitutional Rights Subcommittee, he was in a unique position to counter Nixon's moves to throttle the press, engage in domestic surveillance, and invade the homes of criminal suspects without warrants and jail them without trials; as chairman of the Separation of Powers Subcommittee, he launched probes of the President's attempts to take away the spending power of Congress, withhold information through "executive privilege," and reactivate the moribund Subversive Activities Control Board in order to harass controversial groups.

It was because of his leadership in these areas that the Senate turned to him in the winter of 1972 to launch one of the most intensive investigations of political corruption in history. Because of Nixon, all the issues Ervin had been grappling with behind the scenes for many years were coming to a flash point in a single explosion: Watergate.

Presiding over that monstrous tale of espionage and intrigue was an unpleasant and wearying job. For Ervin American history had reached a low point when the respected and dignified office of the President could fall by its own hand into disrespect and humiliation.

There was growing pressure on Ervin as the hearings got under way to spare the President at any cost, regardless of whether the facts showed that he took part in the Watergate planning or cover-up. Many of the people who took this position argued that the system would be torn apart, the country's reputation tarnished, the economy weakened, and the executive crippled. But Ervin had more faith than his critics that a country built on truth could stand the truth.

"I'm not afraid to go wherever it may lead," he said during a lengthy interview in the midst of the hearings. At that point, he truly did not know where it would lead. "A lot of people say, well the government is coming to a standstill and you'd better be careful about how much truth you find out; you don't want to wreck the government. They say if you find the truth is leading too close to the President, you must suppress the truth because it's necessary to have a stable government.

"In reply to that, I would say that I don't think you can found a government on the suppression of truth; I don't think a government or an institution of that nature will endure very long."

Ervin has always been a student of history, which, as English historian James Froude said, "is a voice forever sounding across the centuries the laws of right and wrong." George Washington warned in his farewell address that the occupants of public office have a love for power and a proneness to abuse it. Lord Acton said toward the end of the last century that power corrupts and absolute power corrupts absolutely. About the same time, Rudyard Kipling was describing how freedom was wrenched "inch and ell and all" from the king. Ervin, who went to war with Kipling's verses ringing in his ears, rolled the lines off his tongue as though reciting the Pledge of Allegiance: "So they brought us freedom, not at little cost, wherefore must we watch the king, lest our gain be lost."

The four years before Watergate had, for Ervin, been devoted to precisely that: watching the king.

North Carolinians took part as much as anybody else in the second coronation of Richard Nixon, and they were defensive about Nixon. Some of Ervin's old conservative friends gave him a bad time about all his moralizing. They must have found it galling to have this old cherub sitting there quoting the Scriptures when everybody knew all politicians were corrupt. The trouble with Ervin was that it was difficult to find anything wrong with him, unless you counted diluting good bourbon whiskey with "ginge'ale." There had to be something wrong with a politician who returned unspent political funds, 20 cents on the dollar.

Ervin caught a lot of hell for going after Nixon, even if that happened to be where the truth led. He had never had to do any serious campaigning for any office, not for his seat in the North Carolina General Assembly, his judgeships, his brief experiment in the House after World War II, or for the Senate. Because of Watergate it appeared that if he decided to run for yet another term in the Senate, he would have to face the first real campaign of his career. That did not mean that he would behave any differently. Anybody, in Sam Ervin's book, who had to spend his way into public office did not deserve to hold the office. Most of his friends and virtually everyone in his family were telling him not to run again, to return to the home from which he had been gone so long. His wife wanted to be back in Morganton with her grandchildren. And for him it really would not be like retiring. His library at home contained thousands of books. He could read and write and go back into the courtroom as a practicing attorney, the thing he loved to do most in the world.

Ervin had always managed to get back home. As a lawyer and circuit-riding judge he would fight the twisting mountain roads to return, even for half a weekend, to the place where he was born and raised, to the home surrounded by memories of his boyhood. He would eagerly immerse himself in the easy, unhurried life of the town and emerge refreshed and renewed.

He did not seek peace of mind by cruising down some freeway in a purring machine. Instead he turned inward. He had an uncanny ability to shut out the outside world. Things could be exploding all around him, as they were with Watergate, and he could sit in his library and turn all his attention to John Paul Jones or to his distant relatives, the Huguenots, both of which he studied while at home in the spring of 1973.

But the fall recess was a nightmare. Seemingly the entire national press corps converged on his hometown under orders to bring back Sam Ervin–at-home stories. Politicians and lawyers and promoters and constituents, not to mention the overwrought committee staff members, called him mercilessly from dawn till evening, when he finally flicked the specially installed switch that turned off his phone. He hated to deactivate the phone, but it gave him no peace. People who claimed that God had told them the answer to Watergate chose the hours after midnight to call. (He told them he couldn't accept as evidence what they claimed God had said because it was hearsay.)

There was no peace in the place where he had always been able to find it before.

But still he pursued it.

You could find him on those August mornings at the barber shop or the post office, or walking down the main street of

Morganton with a rumpled suit on his arm, headed for the cleaners. Everybody in town seemed to know Sam Ervin—he had spent all his life there—and many of them would stop to chat with him as if he were really still one of them. And it did seem that way. Something about the smallness of the town and the way the mountains cozy up to it give the place a feeling of intimacy. Women and children would turn to watch as the tall, round-shouldered man with drooping chins and snow-white hair glided by.

There was something about him. He was not forbidding. His face was too gentle for that. But distant. Preoccupied. He was not cut out to be a celebrity. He told one of his daughters in the midst of the hearings that he would rather be unheralded, unwept, and unsung. You could see in his eyes the hunger to be left in peace, to be treated like everyone else, and not to be reminded that he could never again be blessedly alone.

On one of his trips downtown he descended the hill to a rectangular red brick building on the south side of the square. It was still called the Ervin Building, even though he sold it years ago. His office is there, right across from the old gray courthouse —just about as far away as his apartment in Washington is from the Supreme Court: so he can keep an eye on it. It is directly across the square from the spot where his father built his law office around the turn of the century. They shared a thriving law practice there for fifteen years.

He thudded heavily up the wooden stairs to the second floor. A small paper sign taped on the inside of the glass part of the door said, simply, "Senator Sam Ervin." The unlocked door swung open—most of the lawyers in town use the office as a library—releasing the deep musty aroma of books inside. Ervin went back to his narrow, book-walled office and thumbed through a volume of U.S. Supreme Court opinions as the mid-morning sun, pouring through the windows, glanced off its pages.

He was doing a little homework during the Senate recess in

preparation for the certain legal confrontation with President Nixon. Could the Senate compel Nixon to produce evidence that bore directly on his own guilt or innocence and that of his closest aides? No one knew for sure. But Ervin's reading of the law and history convinced him that the President should come forward. If the courts ruled the other way, Ervin felt—with only slight overdramatization—the Republic would be lost.

In parts of the country that had been scarred and blighted by change, and in Washington, where reality was often difficult to find or even imagine, collapse of the system seemed quite possible in those explosive days of 1973. But it seemed safe in that slow-moving, unchanging town in the quiet South Mountains of North Carolina, where evidence of a boyhood lived at the turn of the century could still easily be found: the courthouse itself, where Ervin had watched his father match wits with his fellow members of the bar; the red brick schoolhouse just off the square, where he had entered the first grade seventy years before; the tall, white frame house in which he had grown up, sitting just across the side street from his own home.

Everything was in place. He could look around and see life, as he liked to say, steady and whole; know where he had come from, and, knowing that, where he was going.

2. *Time to Live*

"LIKE ULYSSES," SAM ERVIN SAID in a Senate speech in late 1959, "all of us are a part of all we have met." Ervin found part of himself in his father, a lawyer of the old school. "He implanted in my youthful heart a love of law and a hate of tyranny. All the things I have met since the days of my youth have intensified this love and this hate."

He might have included among the things he has met the dead as well as the living, for Ervin had always lived in the balance between the present and the past, keeping his sights on where man has been as well as on where he thought man was going, and listening to voices of old friends—unmet but dear.

The study of family history is not just a hobby with men like Ervin. It is more like a passion. It places them in time. It gives them a fix on themselves in man's long journey through history and whispers to them that theirs is a noble tradition. These forces turned on the gyroscopes that have guided this inner-directed man through praise and scorn, triumph and disaster, with equal amounts of disdain.

His own personal set of forefathers helped push back the frontier in the new world, fought in the Revolution as well as in the Civil War, and sang sweet, sorrowful poetry.

His ancestors, most of them Scotch-Irish Presbyterians, were persecuted for their religious beliefs. They migrated from Ulster to Belfast and finally sailed in 1732 to the coast of South Carolina. Anyone who would immigrate in those days was given land in that vast, moss-draped swampland.

"All of them came to America to obtain the simple right to bend their own knees and raise their own voices to their own God in their own way," Ervin said on another occasion. "I believe their experience had some relation to the creation of my abiding conviction that religious liberty is the most precious of all freedoms."

That band of Scotch-Irish settlers, as well as many other Scotch-Irish from Virginia who flooded the valleys of North Carolina, had been treated so badly by the King of England that they were, almost to a man and woman, ready for revolution.

James Ervin, the first of the lot, planted himself in Williamsburg County, South Carolina. He was, as a local historian described him, "of accepted nobility of character and Christian exaltations." He died in 1776, leaving "ten slaves and other property." His son John, who owned a plantation and twenty-nine slaves, fought against the British with the Swamp Fox, General Francis Marion. As Colonel John Ervin's great-grandson Sam Ervin wrote in a family history almost two centuries later, "Needless to say, the atrocities committed by the foe had filled the hearts of Marion's men with an undying hatred for the British and the Tories and a thirst for vengeance."

Three quarters of a century later the Ervins opposed John C. Calhoun's doctrine of nullification. But once the Civil War began, many of them fought against the Yankees and paid with their lives.

John Witherspoon Ervin, teacher, newspaper publisher, and incurably romantic poet, went out to fight the Union soldiers at Dingles Mill in Clarendon County. It was one of the last skirmishes of the war; in fact, the South had already surrendered. Three of his sons were wounded fighting in the war. His youngest son, Samuel James Ervin, was ten years old when the war ended.

The psychological wounds the boy suffered were just as severe as the physical ones his brothers sustained. The war cut his boyhood short. It deprived him of an education. It placed his parents in grinding poverty. And it cut the South off from the Union. It came between him and everything he ever loved, he said many years later.

His father never woke up to the fact that the South had fought a war and lost. Unable to support his family, he felt "broken down in spirit, body and mind." He said in his journal he was "utterly incapable of exertion." But the sight of his uncomplaining wife slaving away to keep the family alive caused him "to gather up all my manhood and make a trial to secure her from suffering."

Armed with quills plucked from a neighbor's goose, with paper he squirreled away while collecting the Confederate war tax in Clarendon County, and with ink his wife concocted from barks gathered in the woods, John Witherspoon Ervin began writing, primarily for newspapers. It was an exertion which "aroused me completely from my lethargy and despondency. I had become myself again."

But faced with an empty cupboard one evening, he set off for the swamp to catch the family's dinner. On his way, however, he met his pastor, who conveyed to him a seventy-five dollar check for winning a newspaper story contest. "I felt like a beggar who had suddenly been metamorphosed into a capitalist."

His poems, some of which were collected by his grandchildren and bound in a blue folder, were saturated with sentimentality. He said of England:

> From that island we drew the rich Saxon blood
> That indignantly stirs at wrong,
> And feels for the noble, the pure and the good
> A love everlasting and strong.

He looked somewhat like his grandson Sam: tall, with deep blue eyes, light brown hair, and fair complexion. He was a nature lover of keen intellect and deeply religious nature—not at all cut out to withstand the vicissitudes of Reconstruction. His generation never felt the full impact of the war, but the sons and daughters of that era had to, as the saying went, get down and root hog or die.

His young son Samuel James picked up the burden. Before he passed from the scene at the age of eighty-nine, he sat down in his rocking chair and told Jean, his youngest daughter, about his boyhood struggles. She took it down with a pencil in a schoolgirl notebook as fast as she could write.

"Potter [the Union commander] burned the courthouse and the school buildings," he said. "Father and Dr. Preleau were working in the woods so Potter couldn't find them. I was ten and took their lunch in a basket because I could pretend to be picking berries and be unnoticed by Potter. I imitated a man's voice and said, 'Surrender, you rebels!' They drew their pistols on me and then laughed when they saw who I was."

His father, he said, "tried to make a living teaching school. Nobody had any money to pay him with. He was a man who could never collect anything. A few could have paid him something. Taylor Stukes could have paid him in corn but never did. He gave father a silver watch in appreciation.

"There was a new world when the war was over. I had big ears. I listened to a Negro talk to my father about the people in authority in Clarendon County, saying if there is anyone of these fellows who is an enemy to the good white folks, just tell me, I'll get rid of him. Father shamed him and told him that they could catch him and kill him and make the condition of the good white people even worse."

The boy helped out as best he could, taking to the swamps to shoot partridges, 'possums, squirrels, and doves, catching fish, and picking strawberries. He sold them to help his mother feed her eight children. "If any boy loved his mother, I did," he said.

"I've always been ashamed about one thing I did. When we lived in Paxville there was a beautiful white heron about six feet tall. The heron was eating frogs. I aimed with a rifle and shot the ball right through him. He flew to a tree and then got sick and fell down. He got ready for a fight. I broke a limb and beat him over the head. What possessed me to shoot such a beautiful bird as that I've never been able to understand." He also told of blinding an alligator with his rifle, wading into the mill pond, wrestling it to the bank, and beating it to death with a hoe.

The boy's love for his mother was what drove him then. "When I was ten or eleven, I hired out to pick cotton for Simon Richburg who married my aunt. I wanted to earn my money. I went with the grown Negroes with a big satchel on my back. We would stop for breakfast and dinner and stop in time to take cotton back to the barn and weigh it. I was paid about a half cent or a cent a pound. On Saturday, I'd go home and give the money to mother. I loved my mother. That is what distressed me so about poverty."

He remembered owning only one book as a boy, a paperback with pictures. He got it from a printer named Melvin Lucas in return for a string of fish he had caught.

The Ervin family struggled along for nine years after the war. John Witherspoon finally gave up writing and accepted an offer to teach in Morganton, North Carolina. By horse and buggy, the Ervins transported all their earthly possessions to that faraway village near the mountains. The year was 1874. Their son, Sam Ervin's father, was nineteen years old.

There were not many jobs those days in Morganton, but Samuel James found one with the post office. He carried the mail every day on foot over two miles to the railroad station and back. But other than that the job was not very demanding, and he soon began spending his spare time reading law books.

In the meantime, with the money he earned, he built a house for his parents and his sister at the end of a dirt road a little more than a mile from the town square. It was what was called a planter's house, with four rooms, two up and two down.

Education was a rare thing in those post–Civil War days. The education system in the South had virtually collapsed. The only sort of schooling available was offered by men like John Witherspoon Ervin. In the absence of a school, he taught classes in the family dining room.

In 1878, the old man's wife died, and he was left a forlorn figure who yearned for the "sweet wonderful one that never comes back to me."

> From the depths of a wounded heart I pray
> To the Lord that loved us much,
> Strength for my weary, lonely way
> And His gentle, healing touch.
> For my heart clings close to the tender love
> That walks by my side no more
> But beckons me now from her home above
> To her side on the heavenly shore.

John Witherspoon Ervin, the "saddest of all sadhearted men," was often ignored or forgotten in that busy household, as he sat alone, praying for the coming of night. He finally managed to bounce back from his romantic despondency and sing of other things, of thoughts he had stored up from youth, of his mother.

> Old things love I the best,
> The songs my mother used to sing
> As I sat by her knee,
> Still o'er my soul their magic fling—
> Sweeter than life to me.

His son had little time for sentimentality or even idle thoughts. He took the North Carolina bar exam in 1879, when he figured he had read enough law. That was how one became a lawyer in those days. Early in his career, when business was slow, he would sit down and read the seventy-odd volumes of State Supreme Court decisions, making notations in the margins. He must have had a prodigious memory, because for the rest of his life he was able to reel off those opinions and cite them chapter and verse. He became one of the state's most prominent lawyers.

His future bride, Laura Theresa Powe, lived across the road from the Ervin house. Both the Powes and the Ervins had migrated from the South Carolina low country to that small village in the shadow of the Blue Ridge Mountains, but by different routes. John Witherspoon Ervin and William E. Powe, Laura's father, had been born in the same town, Chester, South Carolina; and Samuel and Laura were in fact second cousins. Powe (pronounced "Po"), a Welshman and an Episcopalian, had lived in Salisbury, North Carolina, seventy miles to the east, for a generation. He acquired a large farm on the outskirts of Morganton in 1867, two years after the birth of his daughter. He brought his former slaves with him.

Laura Theresa Powe was a patient, shy person. She had very little formal education. When the local private academy was opened to girls on a limited basis she attended for two years. There was no library in the town, although the postmistress kept the works of Sir Walter Scott on a shelf in the post office for customers to borrow.

Those were lean years. Morganton was basically a rough frontier town settled by self-educated men and women who had survived the Civil War and its aftermath. The men still carried pistols. Once, when a mob of blacks was pursuing a young black man, Samuel drew his gun and said he'd kill every last one of them if they didn't leave him alone. Work was scarce, and in many ways women held the town together after the war. John Witherspoon once described the town as a "matriarchy."

When the Powes migrated to Morganton, a federal garrison was stationed there, an army of occupation. All the men who had participated in the war, including Laura's grandfather, Dr. William C. Tate, were disenfranchised. Tate had opposed secession until President Lincoln issued an order for North Carolina to supply troops to help put down the rebels. "If North Carolina had to fight in the war, it was better to fight on the side of its neighbors than more distant people," he is supposed to have said. He had four sons in the Confederate Army.

When Union troops occupied the town, a black officer came up to Tate and gave him what he considered an impudent order. "How I wanted to kill him," Tate told his grandchildren years later.

The Reconstruction Acts burned a permanent scar upon the soul of the South. Even in the middle of the twentieth century Sam Ervin considered them "the most monstrous legislation ever passed in American history." And to many southerners, including Ervin, the civil rights legislation of the early 1960's amounted to a Second Reconstruction. The post–Civil War period toughened the South's resistance and, in the words of W. J. Cash, left it with "a propensity to see in every notion coming out of the North a menace and an abomination; to view every idea originated by the Yankee or bearing the stamp of his acceptance as containing hidden within itself the old implacable will to coerce and destroy."

Laura Powe was a composed woman. Samuel Ervin was eccentric. He decided she would be a fitting bride when he noticed, during the tremors which were felt during the great Charleston earthquake, that she had the presence of mind to blow out all the candles in her parents' home before taking shelter. They were married in 1886 and proceeded to populate Morganton with ten offspring. Samuel James Ervin, Jr., was the fifth. He came into the world on September 27, 1896, shortly before William McKinley, a Scotch-Irishman from Canton, Ohio, beat William Jennings Bryan for the presidency.

It was the twilight of Reconstruction, a period remembered with more bitterness than the war itself and the fact of defeat. But it was evident that Ervin, a spare, French-looking man with pointed beard and swallowtail coat, had begun to make a go of things after breasting the grim tide that drowned so many others. He had arrived in the town twenty-six years earlier with his mother and his romantic, helpless father. The instinct for survival ran hot in his veins, and he not only eked out an existence but began to prosper through the worst of times.

During the week in which Sam, Jr., was born, a small notice appeared in the *Morganton Herald*, a weekly newspaper: "S. J. Ervin, attorney-at-law, Morganton, N.C. Practices in all the courts of the State where his services might be required, and special attention given to all business." But another advertisement in the same newspaper stated the economic problem in large type: "Notice!! If you want *further credit* at the hardware store, come in and PAY WHAT YOU OWE."

Eighteen ninety-six was also the year the U.S. Supreme Court said it was perfectly legal to have separate-but-equal facilities for blacks and whites. "If one race be inferior to the other socially, the Constitution of the United States cannot put them on the same plane," the Court said, shutting the door so tight that it would not be opened again for more than half a century. It is a striking coincidence that the boy born at the dawn of court-sanctioned segregation would go to the Senate in 1954, when that doctrine was nullified. But he did not accept it without a fight.

When Sam, Jr., was born, black Republican rule was rapidly coming to an end all over the South as states found it very simple to deprive Negroes of the right to vote. In North Carolina the cry for "white supremacy" was unmistakably clear. It was not something that was whispered in back rooms. It was discussed openly, complete with the rationalization that it was really good for blacks: literacy tests would impress on them the need for an education.

On January 11, 1900, when Sam was three years old, the *Morganton Herald* carried a virulent letter on its front page from Thomas M. Huffman, a resident of nearby Hickory. Huffman said—and the newspaper took its hat off to him for saying it—that blacks were "in every sense of the word unfitted for the intelligent exercise of the ballot. The Democratic position upon the race issue is concisely embodied in the proposition that North Carolina is a white man's state and must be governed by white men," he said.

In August of the same year North Carolina overwhelmingly passed a constitutional amendment that made blacks—and only blacks—pass a literacy test as a requirement for registering to vote. It worked like a charm. One-party Democratic rule began, a system that would enable men like Sam Ervin to stay in the Senate as long as they pleased.

On a cold winter evening many years later, Sam's younger sister Eunice was taken by her father to a program of Negro spirituals given by a local choir. It was a rare outing for the senior Ervin, who detested social affairs. Eunice recalled her father saying "they were doing this to help themselves and we should do everything we could to support them."

The young girl was impressed with the soulful music and the theatrics of Felix Fleming, the choir director, who would spin around on his heel. Every time he did, the choir responded by singing louder. How dramatic Fleming's white hair looked against his black skin, the young girl thought. She whispered to her father that he looked like one of the footmen in *Alice in Wonderland*.

After the concert her father told her that he remembered Felix Fleming when he was a young man. Ervin had gone to the polling place and saw Fleming arrive, leading a band of blacks carrying sticks. Ervin said he told Fleming, "I know there is a white man at this polling place who has sworn to kill you before he allows you to vote." Fleming, her father said, stood around the polling place with his companions all day and then left without ever attempting to go inside.

Ervin's father resented efforts to deprive blacks of the franchise. He told his son that every man who was qualified should be given the right to vote. Ervin recalled that his father "had an abhorrence, and I think I acquired a lot of it by example, he had an abhorrence of people in official positions suppressing anybody. He used to tell me about one occasion when this officer very foolishly called on a black man to help arrest another white man. And the white man resisted and they had the Negro indicted instead of the white man. He was very much outraged by that."

But young Sam Ervin grew up very much unaware of racial problems. Though the town's character is quite southern in some respects, Morganton has always had a relatively small black population. Everyone knew his place. Blacks worked for white families year after year, knew them as benefactors, and were, as in the Ervin household, practically members of the family. But paternalism rested ultimately on fear and few ever tested its perimeters. "I knew about all the colored people in Morganton when I was growing up," Ervin said. "There were very close personal bonds between the races."

Life was unhurried and uncomplicated in 1900. In the same edition of the *Morganton Herald* that carried the "White Supremacy" headlines, the newspaper printed an editorial endorsement of S. J. Ervin for district judge, the only public office he ever sought: "Mr. Ervin is a native South Carolinian, who came to this town a mere lad, and reduced by the war to poor circumstances. By his own well-directed energies he has acquired a standing in his profession, in the community and in the church of which he may well be proud. He is really one of the best equipped lawyers in the state, a man of tireless energy, practical withal, of even temper and conservative in his views." The neighboring *Mitchell Mirror* said Ervin was "a high toned Christian gentleman."

S. J. Ervin was nominated at the Burke County convention, but lost the hotly contested nomination at the district convention 80½–51½. Later he took great pride in the fact that not one dollar of the people's money crossed his palm.

It probably had nothing to do with the lost judgeship, but Ervin carried through life a profound contempt for the judiciary because he felt he knew more law than anyone on the bench. Because of his awesome grasp of the law and his superior and forbidding appearance, lesser men avoided him. He had few close personal friends and as a result was often quite lonely.

He built a small law office building on a small hill across the square from the courthouse. From there he could cross the street and be up the spiral steps to the courtroom in about one minute. The brick, two-room building had seven large cement steps leading to a wide front porch and a center door. The front room housed his rolltop desk with dozens of pigeon holes, and in the back room there was a golden oak bookcase with a glass front. He would have nothing to do with telephones. He also spurned that other newfangled invention, the automobile, walking briskly down the long clay road from home every morning. He would never, even in his late seventies, accept a ride.

The office was heated by fireplaces in front and back. It was said that old man Ervin, who became increasingly agitated with federal policies, would build a fire every morning and, while it was starting up, keep warm by reading his newspaper.

On the right side of the building there was a snug little alleyway shaded by an oak tree. On hot summer days he would sit out there in his rocking chair reading his law books or writing on his long legal pads.

Ervin had a masterful command of the language, but did not overact as many lawyers in his day were prone to do. Court was the only theater in town, and lawyers sometimes did so much shouting in the stone courthouse that youngsters passing by the square on the way home from school could hear them.

There is a still-honored southern tradition of grand rhetoric, which Sam, Jr., inherited. It goes back to the days when vilifying the Damn Yankees was a regional pastime, complete with exquisite phrases, biblical quotations, and exaggerated gestures. It is a fine art, which southern politicians continue to dominate. One of Ervin's few indulgences was peppering the state's major newspapers with letters to the editor whenever the spirit moved, and that was often. When North Carolina was considering the Prohibition Amendment, he fired off this classic to the *Greensboro Daily News*:

> No law prescribing what a man shall eat or drink or wherewithall he shall be clothed has ever been obeyed and none ever shall be.

The only hope of the evolution of humanity is through the exercise of self control on the part of each one of us and whether we will drink wine that maketh glad the hearts of men or water wherewith the wild asses do quench their thirst is for each of us to decide. It is not a matter for control by legislative enactment and those who foolishly deem that it is are mere visionary dreamers who build their houses upon the sand.

This letter contains the same kind of flourishes his son became fond of using. In another letter he blasted the anti-saloon leagues in the forty-eight states, which were headed by ministers of the gospel. "Oh religion, what crimes are done in thy name!" he lamented. He dictated his letters, pacing up and down the porch, to whichever daughter was nearest at hand. They were neatly typed, characteristically signed "Lex" (the law), and mailed off.

The senior Ervin would not go anywhere that the practice of law or the Lord's business didn't call him to. He detested social visits and paid a formal call on his mother-in-law only once a year. He called her "Mrs. Powe" and she called him "Mr. Ervin."

He rarely carried on about God or religion; but, in his own way, he believed. "He never could understand how anybody who looked at the universe and saw the order and beauty in it could fail to believe in God," one of his grandsons said. Every Sunday, without fail, he marched all ten of his children off to Sunday school and church, the girls in their long dresses, fancy bows, and Gibson Girl hair, the boys in knickers and long black stockings, wearing white collars with lace that fell halfway down their backs.

Ervin and three other lawyers in town were elders in the First Presbyterian Church and, true to their profession, they argued constantly among themselves about nearly everything. His wife, a patient woman, finally threatened to take all ten children out of the church if they didn't stop their bickering, and take them to her Episcopal Church. It would have meant a serious depopulation of the tiny church and, for the time being at least, the fighting stopped.

Though a church elder, Ervin was not pious. When the different church bells chimed on Sunday mornings, each with its own sound, he would sing out in tune with the bells, "Apostolic succession (Episcopal), "Predestination" (Presbyterian), "Immersion" (Baptist), and "Saved by grace" (Methodist). For years he stoically sat and listened to Reverend Hollingsworth, one of the early preachers, take him to task for teaching his children to play cards. The minister could think of little else to talk about save card playing and dancing.

Ervin was not an affectionate man. He rarely played with his children, and individual relationships with them were difficult. With his full-bearded Prince Albert appearance, his crusty manners, and fierce determination, Ervin maintained a rather forbidding exterior, but in the judgment of his son Sam, he was a very compassionate man.

He was a circuit-riding lawyer, which meant that he was gone for weeks at a time, traveling by horseback or train from town to town. But he set an example of rectitude that the children knew, even without his presence, they must follow. "My father and mother," said Hugh Tate Ervin, two years younger than Sam, "when it came to raisin' children, they gave us a purpose in life. My father used to say, 'Never tell a lie. Even if it damages you, always tell the truth.' We fairly followed out their raisin', that's the truth. Anybody that's a politician that can say that is quite a man."

The character that Ervin wanted to hand down to his vast brood of sons and daughters was summed up in advice he once gave his grandsons. He told them in a letter that their Ervin ancestors "were all men of courage and of high character and, I believe, they were all gentlemen. In my judgment they would have died before doing anything dishonorable. After all, good character should always be the main aim and purpose of life."

"My father was such a powerful personality," Eunice said. "He didn't believe in aristocracy in the same terms as my mother did. I think he believed in a spiritual aristocracy based on the development of character. He wanted to be sure that in the development of his children, no one would ever do a dishonest thing. We grew up with the concept that the law of the land and all its ramifications constituted a sort of invisible palace in which we all lived, and the law of the land was a great creation of a great many people."

As a young boy, Sam had the privilege of going to Washington with his father. Ervin took him to the Supreme Court, showed him the busts of the great jurists of the past, and said in a tone of reverential awe, "The Supreme Court will abide by the Constitution though the heavens fall." It was the Constitution of the Founding Fathers in its original form, interpreted according to its original intent.

Ervin's mother was a genteel southern lady who calmly and patiently bore her children—Laura, 1888; Catharine, 1890; Margaret, 1892; Edward, 1894; Sam, 1896; Hugh, 1898; Joseph, 1901; Eunice, 1903; John, 1906; and Jean, 1909—suffered with them, ministered to them, and sheltered them from hard work. She assumed the major responsibility for their upbringing and passed on her sunny, forgiving disposition to her second son. Sam's attitude toward women reflected the reverential respect he paid to his mother.

"She was very charitable in her judgment of people," Sam said. "She always told me there's a lot of good in everybody and she said the most foolish thing a person does is try to reform another. You can't reform other people, but you can try to call out the best qualities in them and try to see they exercise those. You can get a lot of good out of people that some people think are bad. She had the capacity to love sinners while hating sin."

As the family grew larger, the Ervins added rooms to the sides and back of the house, like birds building a nest. It grew to be a sizable homeplace, with six bedrooms and two living rooms. There were about eighteen acres running down the hill in back, plenty of room for a good-sized garden. Later it sprouted a tennis court and a baseball diamond.

The town in which young Sam Ervin grew up had fewer than 4,000 inhabitants. Green mountain peaks and ridges towered over it, and the only buildings poking through the treetops were church spires. It looks very much the same today. It sustained a few small industries—a tannery, some cotton and hosiery mills, and a woodworking plant.

For a place so close to the mountains, Morganton has an unusually mild climate, caused by a belt of warm air that plays over its mountain slopes. The climate exempted the region from that fearful scourge—consumption. "If the thousands in the New England and Middle States, who tremble as they feel the premonitory symptoms of lung trouble, could be made to realize that in the balmy atmosphere of Caldwell, Burke and Polk counties nature has provided a restorative that will prove efficacious to many, if not all, they will come in scores to hear the testimony of those whose vital energies have been restored to their normal condition by a sojourn of a few years in and around Morganton," said the Hon. Alphonzo Calhoun Avery in 1890. The newspaper rhapsodized in 1920, "Truly mother nature has treated Burke County as a favored child."

Except for the weather, Morganton had few comforts in the early part of the century. It took years for S. J. Ervin to get the city fathers to extend street lights as far as his home at the outskirts of town.

Sam's earliest recollections were of riding in the family buggy behind their horse, Nellie, over rain-soaked clay roads.

Cars did not come on the scene until the end of the first decade. "We used to have an old fellow named John Garrison lived down there," Ervin said, pointing to the south from his home, which is right next to the old Ervin homeplace. "Had an old Harvester and when he got out and cranked it up you could hear it being cranked all over town, practically. It had high wheels that were very good for these ruts but it wouldn't pull much up the hill. So when he got to a steep hill he'd turn it around and back it uphill."

With so many brothers and sisters and cousins across the street the Ervin children always had plenty of companions. Their father's nieces and nephews from South Carolina came to spend the summer in the cool mountains. Jack Starrett, young Sam's first cousin, was playing with one of Sam's younger brothers when a fight broke out, and he went home hollering. Ervin told the story during one of the endless civil rights debates in 1960:

"When he got home, his mother, my aunt, asked him what the trouble was.

" 'Well, I tell you, mother,' he said, 'I have just been over at the Ervins', and I just don't think none of those Ervins is fittin' to be angels.' "

Ervin's grandmother on his mother's side had been born about a mile outside the city and knew everyone in town. Sam Ervin recalled her: "I 'member as a child fourteen or fifteen years old I'd go over there and she'd sit there and rock and say she was just waitin' for the Old Mahster—that's what so many southern people called the Lord—Old Mahster to call her home.

"And people would pass and she'd say there's so-and-so's son or daughter, referring back to some childhood friend of hers. So she told me much about the people of this county and much of the history and things that got me interested at a very early age.

"There was an old railroad. My grandmother used to tell me the railroad'd got four miles east of Morganton at the time of the outbreak of the Civil War and was not extended any further until after it was over. She said she went on the first train ride that ran from up here down to Salisbury. It was a great event. It was the first time she'd ever seen a train."

Every once in a while someone would find a strain of gold in the county, not exactly strike it rich, but find enough to turn some men into dreamers. One summer a pegleg named Moses asked the Ervins for permission to pan for gold in the stream that ran through a pine grove at the back of their property. He spent the whole summer there, and when he finished he paid them ten dollars for the use of their stream.

The children walked the same mile their father walked to his office, and a bit more, going to school. The building was constructed in 1903 and was, for those days, quite a structure. It still stood in 1973, two stories of red brick worn smooth, but was destined to come down to make way for a new county office building. Its last tenants were the Blue Ridge Community Action agency and the Regional Health Council of Eastern Appalachia.

Blacks in those days went to separate, one- and two-teacher schools.

Baseball was an insatiable craze for young Sam Ervin and for virtually every other boy in Morganton. Just about every street in town had its own team. Sam played catcher for the "Sandy Flat" team, and for years he kept the notebooks he had crammed with the scores of all the games. Businesses all over town, even the post office, closed on weekday afternoons when the big games were played.

It was a serious strain on a young boy's finances to pay for a dollar-and-a-quarter baseball, and sometimes the batters would hit the team right in the piggy bank by losing the ball in the honeysuckle vines. "In those days," as Ervin told it, "Joe Jackson [who later played for the Chicago Black Sox] was playing on a cotton mill team down in Greenville, South Carolina. He was a left-handed hitter and he had an awful clout. They had a big swamp in right field and about every time he came to bat he knocked the ball in the middle of the swamp. They had to fire him because it was too much of an expense to the team."

When the boys got tired of baseball, they wore out the knees of their long socks playing marbles, or swam in nearby Catawba River or Lake James—a half mile across and back. "Those were great days, really," Ervin smiled. "You had time to live." He knew just about everybody in town, "even where all the cats and dogs belonged."

The Ervins raised chickens, cows, and pigs, and almost all the vegetables they ate. At Christmastime they received such delicacies as oranges, apples, raisins, and sometimes candy. But otherwise everything was homegrown, most of it by their father, who loved his gardening second only to his law practice. Practically the only chore the children performed regularly was helping him with the garden. It was viewed as a great privilege to be able to follow behind his hoeing with the seeds. They were also taught to milk the cow, carry firewood into the house, and clean the chimneys in the constantly smoky kerosene lamps.

Ervin claimed that he helped with the gardening, but his reputation among the other members of the family was that of a loafer. "Papa would call us to help in the garden and all would come but Sam," Hugh claimed. "Mamma'd say, 'Leave Sam alone; he's studyin'.' " Then he said with a laugh, "Sam made out he couldn't learn to milk the cow."

Most of the major household chores were performed by servants. "We had a cook, Betty Powell, who was an Amazon," according to Sam. "About six-foot-three inches tall. Black. She had some younger daughters come up and help her work. She was almost a member of the family."

For the Ervin children, survival was not, as it had been for their parents, one of their constant concerns. Things were taken care of for them, and they were left free to develop their individual talents and personalities. They were rarely corrected. Their mother ran the house with the help of a cook, a nurse, and, every Monday, a washwoman.

"We had stoves in every room," Hugh said. "In the fall, Miles Tanner came here about the first chilly spell and started cutting wood. That old darky'd cut wood all winter long, cut it up and then split it. The boys would bring it into each room and then we had to go and build the fires." Standing by those wood stoves, Sam Ervin laughed, "you could freeze on one side and burn up on the other."

They took baths in tin tubs with water heated on the wood stove. Unheated parts of the house could get so cold in the winter they did everything they could to avoid baths. The hallways could get like icebergs.

Things slowed down in the winter. The children did not have the horse and buggy at their disposal and had to go everywhere on their own power. Which meant they didn't go far.

Having missed a formal education himself, their father had a strong desire to see his children properly schooled. He was the first chairman of the Morganton Graded School system when it was founded in 1903, Sam's first year in school. A small plaque placed in the building in 1906 bears his name among the trustees. "I'm going to educate my children and leave them a world to live in," he would say.

His second son, Sam, was an above-average student, extremely good in history and reading but turned off by science and math. And, though normally well behaved, he had a certain gift for mischief. "I used to have to answer the roll call every morning with a quotation from the scriptures. On one occasion I had just looked through the Bible and I found a verse that said, 'I have more understanding than all my teachers.' And so I answered the roll call the next morning with that. Of course, the class was hilarious. And the teacher kept me in, said there was no such verse in the Bible. And I showed it to him. I've forgotten where it is now. I think it's King Solomon that said that. I pointed it out to him, and he said, 'Well, you didn't say it in the right spirit of reverence.'" The story, told seventy years later, provoked gleeful laughter, as though the puckish deed had just been done.

Sam's father told him that if he ever got a whipping at school he could look forward to the same thing at home ("They backed up the teachers in those days"). But his father was not much on whippings. When he was a boy his own father had once hit him a few licks with a switch and then thrown it away. And once, only once, when young Sam was asked to do something by his father and refused, he got the same. "I got an awful whippin'. Finally, my mother had to come and make him stop."

As stern and forbidding as Sam's father seemed to be, he was protective toward his children, almost to a fault. Whenever one of them was lost, he'd go to the well and call down to make sure the child had not fallen in. He never got used to the idea of his daughters staying out late. A sure signal that it was time to be home was when Mr. Workman, the keeper of the town powerhouse, stopped playing his trombone. The powerhouse was right in the center of town and one could hear him playing every night until 11 P.M. When he stopped, all young girls knew they'd better be home. If the Ervin girls were late, their father would go out looking for them with his lantern.

If those were years of bliss, they were also years of tragedy. Edward, the oldest boy, caught a bad case of whooping cough when he was a small child and then developed a gasping asthmatic condition. There was no medical help for it, and the boy spent his nights sitting in a straight chair, every breath an agony. "I think we all learned compassion from him," Eunice said. He died when he was thirty-nine.

Despite the benign climate, Margaret, four years older than Sam, died of tuberculosis when she was nineteen. Before it was diagnosed, one lung was gone, and she was given no hope of recovery. Her parents felt it would be cruel to send her away, so she spent her last months in her bedroom, with no one permitted to see her except her mother. When she died, her mother took all her personal belongings out to the yard and burned them.

The Ervins had an apple orchard out back. One day, Joseph, then just six years old, climbed one of the trees and fell. Sam was there when it happened, saw his brother lose his grip and fall, bouncing from limb to limb, and then land on his hip on the ground. The injury culminated eventually in a bone disease that drove him to suicide at the height of a promising political career.

Catharine, who had entranced her younger brother with her reading of poetry, contracted Hodgkin's disease and died when she was fifty. Dr. James King Hall of Richmond, husband of her older sister Laura, wrote to the family at the time of her death, assessing what the years of joy and sorrow had done to the Ervins. "They are brave people; self-sustaining, courageous, always looking forward and upward, and unwilling to be overwhelmed by the events of the moment."

Sam's mother, serene and reticent, kept her grief to herself. One day she scratched a few lines on a small scrap of paper: "The only way to live is to live in the circumstances which are about you, whatever they are, and recognize that they are life—for you, for me, for the world of this day. This is the inheritance into which we were born."

When she died, on June 14, 1956, almost ninety-one years after her birth, the *Morganton News-Herald* called her "a grand matriarch of a devoted family." "Upon her children, who possessed surpassing intellectual talents, she bestowed a warmth of motherly devotion and endowed them with the capacity for humor and a downright humanness to complement their heritage from her late husband for vigorous spirit, serious study, and a bent for achievement."

The Ervin house was almost always filled with the smell of something cooking. Tremendous quantities of bread were baked at one time. A three-legged pot of beans always bubbled on the wood stove. Sometimes there was the enchanting smell of pickles being made.

Polly Powell, who inherited the cooking job from her mother, used to complain that the ants in the kitchen were young "Mr. Sam's fault." As a boy he would take flour from the kitchen and put it around the edges of all the ant hills so the occupants would have something to eat. Once, when a buzzard landed in the yard with a broken wing, he fed it and nursed it back to health.

He was a skinny lad, like his father. And his mother fretted over that constantly: how to get "Samuel"—she called all her children by their full names—to gain weight. She tried unsuccessfully to fatten him up by feeding him raw eggs. As a youth he was tall and thin. He looked like the incarnation of a 1920's Norman Rockwell drawing, with protruding Adam's apple and bowl-shaped haircut. He was awkward and shy but self-assured, and he found in everything a touch of humor.

His grandfather, the poet and schoolteacher who had fought the Yankees at Dingels Mill in another age, died in 1902. He had taught Sam to read at the age of four. "I don't remember so much his teaching, but when I didn't learn right quick he'd thump me on the head with his finger and say, 'Mighty thick, mighty thick.' That's the only conversation I recall having with him."

His father, who as a boy had traded a string of fish for his only book, had a sizable library at home, including virtually everything of Shakespeare, Dickens, Scott, and Kipling. Young Sam got a stiff dose of gallantry and romance, of heroic courage and steadfast loyalty. "One hour of life, crowded to the full with glorious action, and filled with noble risks, is worth whole years of those mean observances of paltry decorum," Sir Walter wrote.

His father loved reading poetry and encouraged young Sam to read; often it was poetry with a message, like Byron's tale of the Assyrian hordes, who, gleaming in purple and gold, descended on Palestine, only to be annihilated by the plague:

> The might of the Gentile, unsmote by the sword,
> Hath melted like snow in the glance of the Lord!

The boy used to draw and cut out paper soldiers in full uniform. Once when he was brooding, his mother asked him what was wrong. He complained that all the wars had been fought and he was afraid he'd never participate in one.

He also had a yearning for the sea. He didn't know why. Someone from the town had once gone to Annapolis and that became his ambition too. Had he not flunked the math exam for the Naval Academy he might have become an old sea dog instead of a lawyer, judge, and U.S. senator.

"A wanderer is man from his birth," Matthew Arnold said. "He was born on a ship on the breast of the river of time." Ervin memorized those lines from a sermon delivered by the new minister of the church. The town's healthful climate had attracted a northerner who fed the young man's hunger for poetic language. Carey E. Gregory, stricken with tuberculosis, found western North Carolina healing to his lungs and receptive to his ideas. He taught ethics, mostly, the good old moral values—hard work, generosity, right and wrong, the golden rule. He was not of the evangelistic, damnation-salvation school that held sway over so many Bible-belt churches.

"There's no royal road to learning," he said one day. And Sam, a young man about to go off to college, remembered. "He was a real scholar," Ervin said. "He had a great appreciation for fine literature. I owe a lot to him."

To those who did not know young Sam well, he frequently seemed to be going through life in a fog. He had the ability, even then, to crawl up inside his mind and hide. He was collecting, storing, sorting out, and evaluating knowledge. And, in so doing, he could shut out the rest of the world. Friends and family could go into his room when he was studying, even dust around his feet, and he wouldn't know it.

"He was the sort of person you liked very much because he had those qualities of a young person coming along," said Mrs. Gladys Tillet, a contemporary of Sam's who grew up in Morganton and was a friend to his sisters. "He was always serious but humorous. He was a very well-mannered person, very devoted to his mother. I think of him as always in a good humor.

"There were always lots of books in that family. You read books and you developed yourself. It was a very healthy, wholesome life. Everybody in town knew everybody else. In a little town like that it's one of the privileges of growing up. You learn so much about human nature. And so much about people."

Personal communication was a treasured thing in those days. People talked with each other and remembered stories about others in town and savored them. They listened and remembered. And they read and remembered.

Sunday afternoons after church families got together around the piano and sang hymns. Laura, the eldest sister, played and had a beautiful singing voice. Afterward the young people would get together with banjos. Sam, never very musically inclined, nevertheless had a fair second tenor voice.

His father read constantly and was rarely seen seated at a chair without a book in his hand. He read aloud to his wife in his rich, theatrical voice whenever she was in the same room. Rather than sit with nothing to do, she developed her knitting skills. In sixty years of marriage it seemed that the Ervins never ran out of things to talk about.

In 1910 or so, a marvelous new entertainment medium came to town—the silent picture show. For 10 cents one could see John Bunny, Foyle Finch, or Ben Turpin and, later, Charlie Chaplin.

"It was a delightful time to live," Ervin reminisced. "People were rarely in a hurry. We had a wag around town, Jim Wilson. Somebody . . . mentioned to Jim that President Wilson was looking for men of means and leisure to appoint as ambassadors to foreign countries. [Jim] said if it wasn't for that requirement about means he could find enough men of leisure right here to fill all the embassies of the world."

Stories about Ervin's youth have rarely found their way into public speeches. But on March 8, 1967, in talking about computers, he told the Senate about his first job. "It was right after I finished high school, and I was working with a construction crew. On the first day I was pushing a wheelbarrow and my boss called out and asked what I was doing.

"I replied, 'They told me to carry dirt in this wheelbarrow.'

"The boss said, 'You put that right down—you don't know anything about machinery.' "

Sam finished high school—at that time it went through the eleventh grade—and prepared to go on to the University of North Carolina, which was becoming a family tradition. Almost all the Ervin children went there or to some other college, accumulating a staggering number of years of tuition paid for by their father, who had never taken a college course.

The year was 1913, and Woodrow Wilson was in the White

House. Sam never forgot what Wilson said in a speech the year before: "Liberty has never come from the government. Liberty has always come from the subjects of it. The history of liberty is a history of the limitation of governmental power, not the increase of it. When we resist therefore the concentration of power, we are resisting the processes of death, because concentration of power is what always precedes the destruction of human liberties."

Before leaving for Chapel Hill, the studious, remote young man walked his sister Eunice to school on her first day in the first grade. He read a book all the way.

3. *Light and Liberty*

When the Lord appeared to Solomon in a
dream by night at Gideon and told Solomon
that he could have whatever he most desired,
Solomon did not choose fame or gold or
pleasure or power. He begged God for an
understanding heart and thereby proved
himself to be the earth's wisest son.

SAM ERVIN

UNIVERSITY OR FOUNDERS' DAY on any campus tends
to be a profoundly stuffy affair in which faculty members parade
in full academic regalia and alumni resurrect the spirits of
long-forgotten men who laid the first cornerstone. But on
October 12, 1973, Memorial Auditorium at the University of
North Carolina was jammed with students and guests who had
come to hear Sam J. Ervin, Jr., class of '17, impart the wisdom of
seventy-seven years.

"The world of the mind is an illimitable land whose
boundaries are as vast as the universe itself," said the old sage,
"and thought is calling us at all times to the undiscovered
countries lying beyond the next visible range of mountains."

The speech, although read in a crackling monotone, was the
best of Sam Ervin. He had written it partly during the Watergate
hearings and partly during the preceding weekend at home,
pulling together many of his richest observations on life, liberty,
and learning:

"Let books be your friends, for, by so doing, you can summon to your fireside in seasons of loneliness the choice spirits of all the ages. Observe mankind through the eyes of charity, for, by so doing, you will discover anew the oft forgotten fact that earth is peopled with many gallant souls. Study nature, and walk at times in solitude beneath the starry heavens, for, by so doing, you will absorb the great lesson that God is infinite and that your life is just a little beat within the heart of time. Cling to the ancient landmarks of truth, but be ever ready to test the soundness of a new idea. Accept whatever your mind finds to be true, and whatever your conscience determines to be right, and whatever your heart declares to be noble, even though your act in so doing may drive a hoary prejudice from its throne. And, above all things, meditate often upon the words and deeds of Him who died on Calvary for, by so doing, 'ye shall know the truth, and the truth shall make you free.' "

Then, looking up from his carefully chiseled words, his voice suddenly strong and lyrical, he challenged his audience, in the words of Tennyson:

> . . . Come, my friends,
> 'Tis not too late to seek a newer world.
> Push off, and sitting well in order smite
> The sounding furrows; for my purpose holds
> To sail beyond the sunset, and the baths
> Of all the western stars, until I die.

The old man, himself a child of the Victorian era and a product of its style and morality, received a tremendous ovation from his 20th-century listeners.

Sixty years before, almost to the day, the skinny, shy, callow youth had boarded the train in Morganton and discovered that illimitable land in Chapel Hill. The years conspired to put white hair and double chins, gnarled fingers and twitching eyebrows on his exterior, but there was no evidence that they had cooled the passions of his mind.

The memories of those high-spirited days were still fresh and vivid. The year 1913 was an exciting time to be at the University of North Carolina. Culturally and economically the South was beginning to stir, finally shrugging off the devastating effects of the Civil War and Reconstruction. And North Carolina, with much of its impetus coming from the University, was leading the way.

The traditions of the Old South were there and the best of them—the passion for liberty, the manners, the religious faith—seemed noble and right and at the same time in harmony with progress and social awakening. "The South," said George B. Tyndall in *The Emergence of the New South*, "stood between two worlds, one dying and the other struggling to be born." Ervin's earlier days in Morganton had been great ones for growing up, but these were electric days to be studying in Chapel Hill.

Albert Coates, who later became professor emeritus of the Law School and founder of the University's Institute of Government, was a student then and found, with some help from Wordsworth: "Bliss was it in that dawn to be alive, and to be young was very heaven! And we were young."

The campus was a meeting ground for the Old South and the New. The four hundred "gay-hearted boys" who left the shelter of its ancient oaks to take up arms against the North were not forgotten. In fact, the surviving veterans of the Civil War, those who would have received their degree as the class of 1861 had they not gone to war, finally got their diplomas in an emotional ceremony in 1911.

The school had a strong tradition of academic and religious freedom, which it preserved in later years in the face of tumultuous criticism. It was the nation's first public university when it opened its doors in 1795, and its graduates, it was said, would assemble and fight against any threat to the spirit of the motto, "Lux Libertas." The University was a tranquil, soothing place. With its rock walls, spreading oaks, and soft stone buildings, one could almost hear, as one author said, "the still, sad voice of humanity." And also its music.

There were few automobiles in Chapel Hill, few girls, and almost no drinking—unless it was smuggled moonshine or the quarts of whiskey that came down by train from Baltimore once a month. North Carolina had become bone dry in 1907, long before Prohibition. The campus was isolated on a hill surrounded by the dense woods of Orange County, and students rarely went anywhere on weekends. Instead, they stayed in the dormitories or lolled about around the Old Well and talked. They developed the campus bull session to a fine art.

They provided their own entertainment. They sang "Sweet Adeline" and defended the latest antics of the college's eccentric philosophy professor. They talked and debated. The only alternative was the movies at the Pickwick (where it was obligatory to buy a bag of peanuts and cover the floor several inches deep with shells). Or they stood out in front of the Paterson Drug Company and made crazy bets.

Ervin recalled someone saying, " 'I'll back you out [dare you] walking to Raleigh by way of Durham.' So we started out walking about 8 o'clock one night and walked all night, about thirty-eight miles. It was easier walking in those days because the roads were not paved, easier on your feet." Ervin and his buddies, tired and aching but triumphant, rode the train back the next morning.

Ervin was not a very luminous student, still suffering from a deep aversion for unpoetic subjects like math and physics. But he was serious, studious, and well liked. Albert Coates did not know him well then but said he was "a man who stood out. You were aware of him." His senior yearbook went a little overboard, perhaps, when it said of Ervin, "Everything he meets, responds, and at once a sympathetic friendship ensues. Like Midas, he has that magic touch which makes everyone he meets his friend; and consequently he is liked by all."

The University was an intimate place. There were only two hundred students in the freshman class of 1913, and Ervin knew all of them; in fact, he knew everyone at the University, faculty as well as students.

He became close friends with a sensitive, bright student named William B. Umstead, who taught Bible class in his Old East dormitory room. He invited Ervin to join, and the first time the class met Umstead asked him to lead the class in prayer. "I never had prayed in public in my life," Ervin recalled. "I never was so embarrassed. And so I said, 'Lord, help us. Amen.'"

After class, he told Umstead, "Bill, don't ever ask me to lead in prayer. I'm not accustomed to praying in public." And Umstead replied, "Well, I've heard some preachers pray for forty-five minutes and go into great detail with the Lord, but you've covered the subject about as completely and quickly as any person I've ever heard."

The world was still peaceful in the spring of 1914, and one day when the young man's mind was a thousand miles from the Latin classroom, he was called on to translate Horace's *Odes*. Ervin was not much of a Latin scholar, but he found that he could make up for it by sheer force of memory. When his instructor, Wilbur Hugh Royster—father of journalist Vermont Royster—called on him, the absent-minded student opened his book upside down and rattled off the entire translation from memory. Royster saw what was happening and made Ervin go to the front of the classroom without his book and continue "reading" his lesson.

"You ought to be ashamed of yourself," he scolded his student. "It'd be a whole lot easier to learn some Latin than it is to memorize all that English."

Ervin never did learn much Latin. But, as he has often said, adversity, like a toad, often wears a precious jewel in its head. It enabled him to develop his memory into a formidable talent. More than twenty years later, when Ervin was appointed to the bench, he received a congratulatory telegram from Royster. "If you can recite your charges to juries like you used to recite Horace's *Odes* to me," it read, "they will be verbatim correct."

At the end of his freshman year, Ervin went home to work in the tannery, go fishing, and get acquainted with the law. He went to his father's law office and began reading the classic work on English common law, *Blackstone's Commentaries*. And for good measure, he took on the voluminous *Ewell's Essentials of Equity*.

Before he returned to Chapel Hill in the fall of 1914, war had been declared in Europe. A new monstrosity, trench warfare, was discovered as the Germans were stopped at the first battle of the Marne. War was the chief topic of campus conversations for the next three years.

Ervin's teachers ranged from the colorless to the peculiar. John Manning Booker read poetry with a flourish, but he did so facing the wall at the back of the classroom. Daniel Huger Bacot was so humorless, the students decided to test him by tying up a cow in his classroom one night. Upon seeing the beast the next morning, the professor of literature said he was glad to see "the intellectual level of my audience has increased so much over previous lectures," and then proceeded to lecture for an hour without ever looking at the cow again.

There was the historian, J. G. de Roulhac Hamilton, who said that emancipation of the blacks brought "wonderful benefits" to the South; but he nevertheless argued that the Reconstruction Acts were so wicked that the actions of the Ku Klux Klan were justified. "The inherent evils of the movement are plain," Hamilton said in his book, *Reconstruction in North Carolina* (1914), "but it is an old adage that desperate diseases require desperate remedies."

It was a Machiavellian claim, just the sort of thing Ervin has condemned. But so wounded was the South by the imposition of black control that it was willing to shrug off the tactics of the Klan and the Redshirts. The state, Hamilton said, "had come into the hands of the class best fitted to administer government, and the supremacy of the white race and of Anglo-Saxon institutions was secure."

Much of Ervin's view of North Carolina's history came from

this intense southerner. During an interview, he vigorously defended Hamilton's theories: "The Union would have been reunited without grave difficulty at a very early period. In the North Carolina constitutional convention of 1865 they had amended the constitution so as to abolish slavery and repudiate the Confederate dead. But as a result of the Reconstruction Acts, all of the natural leaders were disenfranchised. They were denied the right to hold office. We had all the Negroes who were just released from slavery, that were in a state of ignorance, given control of the government along with some scalawags . . . and the legislature plundered our state for the aggrandizement of these men. They gave us a government of people who were totally incapable; they gave us judges who didn't know enough to get out of the legal rain; they just prostituted government for illegal purposes, and so you had these freedmen's courts set up in which southerners couldn't get justice in the hands of the law; and so sometimes you had to resort to vigilantes to get it; and that was what the Ku Klux were. The Ku Klux started out a pretty honorable thing, but of course any organization that operates in secret soon gets to be rather violent."

Reminded of his oft-stated condemnation of expediency, Ervin said, "Well, sometimes the ends are so damn bad, you have to take very drastic means."

The means included the blacks-only literacy test amendment; and Ervin, the man of great principle, could even buy that on pragmatic grounds. "I felt it was the only way you could get an electorate that could read and write." If the amendment had required all North Carolinians, blacks and whites, to pass a literacy test, he said, the whites would never have approved it; therefore Ervin and many of his generation learned to accept it as necessary. "When the fathers have eaten sour grapes and the children's teeth are on edge, they are likely to do things that aren't exactly right to recover from what they've undergone. Which is not exactly a southern attribute; it's sort of human."

Ervin became an avid student of history. Hamilton made it

plain to him that if he were to understand the fundamental principles of the Constitution, he must know what brought those principles into being. The state's libertarian history, even more than the Civil War, sunk in deeply. North Carolina refused in 1788 to ratify the U.S. Constitution until it was assured that a bill of rights would be passed "asserting and securing against encroachment the principles of civil and religious liberty, and the unalienable rights of the people."

Ervin also dug down into the fine details of local history in search of his own origins. He won several awards as a student for his essays. In one, "A Colonial History of Rowan County, North Carolina," he said the Scotch-Irish moved to the western part of the state under the influence of "the inviting nature of the climate and the soil, the peacefulness of the Catawba Indians, and the laxity of North Carolina laws . . . on the subject of religion."

His mother's people had originally migrated from Rowan County. In March of 1916, as the young student was doing research for his essay, he wrote excitedly home to his mother that he had discovered rare accounts of her mother's parents, "a prominent and well-to-do family" who built their home on a bluff overlooking the Yadkin River near Salisbury. In the same letter he asked his mother to send him ten dollars.

Ervin studied constitutional law under Lucius Polk McGehee, who was at times a highly nervous man. The students could tell when it was one of his difficult days by the habit he had of taking quick little puffs on his cigarette, jerking it rapidly out of his mouth each time. On those days they knew they'd better not cross him.

Ervin and his fellow students were once sitting on the steps of the law building, arguing such preposterous legal subjects as, "Can a man marry his widow's sister?" Ervin was feeling scholarly after having read Blackstone and asked if anyone knew what a "deodand" was. It is "a gift to God," a legal custom of ancient standing in which the instruments of crime were sold to help compensate the victim. Of course, Ervin was the only one who knew.

Beverly Royster, one of the students, bet Ervin five dollars—all Ervin had to his name—that he wouldn't have the nerve to ask McGehee. Just then they saw Dean McGehee coming across the campus "just puffin' in that nervous style."

"Bev, let's take down that bet," Ervin said.

"No, sir," said Bev.

"It was a class in constitutional law and a deodand had nothing to do with constitutional law and I was terribly afraid to ask Mr. McGehee. Then I got to thinkin', damn, it was my last five dollars and how much better it would be to have ten dollars instead of being totally broke.

"So about one half minute before the class was over I screwed up my courage to the stickin' point and I asked Dean McGehee what a deodand was. Well, he kept the class over about fifteen or twenty minutes. He knew more about deodands than even Blackstone had ever written about. And when he got through, he said, 'I want to commend you for not being content merely to study the lessons assigned you but doing some reading on your own.' "

Thanks to McGehee, Ervin developed the iron butt of a thorough, conscientious lawyer; it was his duty to his clients and to the court to put in the work and study necessary to serve the law. It was no field for a lazy man or one who was satisfied with shoddy work; and the principle flowed through all areas of life.

If many of Ervin's teachers were somewhat on the eccentric side, his philosophy professor, Henry Horace Williams, tended toward the bizarre. With his outlandish drawl and comic antics—he once wrapped a string around his nose—the old man with great bat ears and sunken cheeks turned out a generation of individual thinkers. Thomas Wolfe referred to him as "the Hegel of the cotton patch."

Early in the Watergate hearings, when former campaign

officials admitted to committing assorted felonies out of loyalty to the President, Ervin recalled that Williams had said again and again that one of life's most difficult tasks was choosing between conflicting loyalties. "He used to say it wasn't a choice between good and evil—a stark good, a clear good and evil—that tries men's souls. It was a choice between conflicting loyalties. He said every person can be compared to a small dot in the center of many concentric circles—that the circle nearest to the person might be his family, the next might be his community or his church or his political party or his friends. And he said that the time that people had the greatest difficulty was when two loyalties conflicted and they had to choose between the two loyalties."

Ervin studied ethics at the feet of this queer old gadfly and learned to question the logic of everything, even if it was nailed down by dogma and universal acceptance.

"This is principle, the universal," Williams said, standing, as he always did, in his classroom. "We call a principle in intelligence, truth; in emotion it is beauty; in action we call it righteousness. These three make up logic, as I see it. The individual studies in order to know; he acts; and he falls in love with beauty."

To Williams, as it would be to Ervin, "beauty is truth, truth beauty." Nothing, not even the danger of a temporarily ship-wrecked government, ought to stand in the way of truth. One must follow truth without fear, wherever it leads. Said Williams, in the midst of one of his many controversies, "If teaching the truth and living the truth shall cost me my job or my head, so be it. I can do no other."

In 1973, when former Attorney General John Mitchell testified that the constitutional "separation of powers" allowed President Nixon to withhold information, Senator Ervin rose up with full indignation and said, "Well, I don't believe there's anything in the Constitution that says the President should be separated from the truth."

Light and Liberty

In Williams' words, "Out of conflict comes truth. Truth is to be found at the end of a rocky road."

"He was a great teacher in that he never tried to teach you his thoughts," Ervin said. "He tried to teach you to think and to make your own conclusions, not to accept a thing merely because it is alleged to be so."

Floyd R. Crouse, one of the closest friends Ervin ever had—who went with him to Chapel Hill, to Harvard, and to the state legislature— saved his notes from Williams' class. He died while Ervin was in the Senate, but his notebooks from Harvard and the University of North Carolina remained stacked at his bedside in the mountain village of Sparta.

"It is natural for man to move along the three fundamental lines—truth, goodness and beauty," his neatly inked notes say. "These three things are universal. They are God. A man's life seeks God for the same reason that water seeks the ocean. That is where it came from."

If there was anyone who rivaled Williams for the title of most eccentric and most idolized by the students, it was a Presbyterian minister named W. D. Moss, "Parson Moss." He became "Preacher Reed" in Wolfe's *The Web and the Rock.* Williams and Moss were fast friends. As Robert Winston said of the two in his book, *Horace Williams, Gadfly of Chapel Hill,* "They delighted in each other so much so the public declared that when the old philosopher took snuff, the parson sneezed."

Ervin thought of Moss as "one of the most remarkable men I knew." He recalled that the parson once told a dying man that heaven "as near as I can figure out is like Chapel Hill in the springtime."

But Ervin's favorite story about Moss, one which caused him to grasp his sides with laughter, concerns Jonah, who is most noted in the Bible for having spent three days in a whale's belly. He was ordered to go to the city of Nineveh to preach the gospel, but didn't want to go. "Parson Moss said the reason Jonah didn't want to go to Nineveh was that in those days they had the idea that God lived in a locality and he didn't think Jehovah could be found in Nineveh. It was a sinful city and he didn't want to go any place where he didn't think God was." This is what Moss said, according to Ervin: "Now we laugh at the idea that God wasn't in Nineveh. But I notice that sometimes some of these businessmen in Chapel Hill go to Norfolk, Virginia, on a trip and they act as if they didn't think God was in Norfolk."

Ervin's natural love was English literature, and had Edwin A. Greenlaw, who taught him Shakespeare and composition, prevailed in his wishes for his young student, Ervin would have become an English teacher. Greenlaw urged Ervin to return to Chapel Hill and live the life of academia. He might have been perfectly content and probably become a distinguished man of letters, but Ervin had already set his sights on the law. But he kept in mind the advice of a Scottish lawyer by the name of Sir Walter Scott: "A lawyer without history or literature is a mechanic, a mere working mason; if he possesses some knowledge of these, he may venture to call himself an architect."

Ervin was not the campus politician that his brother Joe, who entered UNC a few years after he did, turned out to be. Sam was class historian, assistant editor of the *University Magazine*, permanent president of the class of 1917, and he was voted most popular in his class and "best egg." But his first try at running for an office was a disaster.

"I would have been editor of the *Daily Tar Heel* [the student newspaper]," he said, "but I made a mistake. They had about sixteen of us in nomination for the post of editor of *The Tar Heel*, and in those days I was more modest than I am now. I wouldn't vote for myself in preference to somebody else. So I voted for a boy named Jimmy Hoover from High Point, and Jimmy beat me—Jimmy was elected with eight votes and beat me by one. So ever since then I have always voted for myself."

Thomas Wolfe, the tall ungainly lad from Asheville, was two years behind Ervin at Chapel Hill. The two knew each other mainly through Sigma Upsilon, the campus literary society; and they had the western North Carolina mountains as common ground. Ervin recalled Wolfe as "normally a very taciturn person, but when he got with some friends he could speak almost as fluently as he wrote."

A typical Sigma Upsilon initiation assignment for an incoming member was to write an essay on why Edgar W. Turlington, an English teacher and member of the society, should take unto himself a wife. "There were some rich literary productions," Ervin said.

The young, golden-voiced president of the University, Edward Kidder Graham, made a dramatic chapel talk one spring. He went over the great moments in the fight for liberty: the Magna Carta, the Petition of Right, the Declaration of Independence, the Bill of Rights. The students had heard it all before and were restless, shuffling their feet. Graham stopped suddenly and, hacking at his wrist with the edge of his hand, said, "Young gentlemen, these are not empty phrases. Cut them and they bleed with the blood of men and women and little children." "We listened from then on," said Albert Coates.

Ervin has frequently quoted the statement on civil liberties published in Wolfe's notes: "So then, to every man his chance,— to every man, regardless of his birth, his shining, golden opportunity—to every man the right to live, to work, to be himself, and to be whatever thing his manhood and his vision can combine to make him—this, seeker, is the promise of America. I do not believe that the ideas represented by 'freedom of thought,' 'freedom of speech,' 'freedom of press' and 'free assembly' are just rhetorical myths. I believe rather that they are among the most valuable realities that men have gained, and that if they are destroyed men will again fight to have them."

Ervin's senior year began in the fall of 1916, a time of rising expectations and tensions. First there was the reelection of Wilson, who had brought about the "Americanization" of the Democratic Party in the South. The students had a rally in the chapel the night of the election. There was no radio yet but they were able to follow the returns by telegraph, reading out bulletins about every five minutes. For a long time it looked as though Charles Evans Hughes, the Republican nominee, was winning. "We went away that night thinking Wilson was defeated because that was the time they went around to serenade Charles Evans Hughes and his son came out and said, 'The President cannot be disturbed. He's asleep.' "

Wilson was reelected by a slim margin, largely on the slogan, "He kept us out of war."

But war seemed more and more inevitable. The Germans were pressing on toward Paris and sinking American merchant ships. It was a concern that weighed heavily on Ervin in the winter of 1916 and the spring of 1917.

On April 2, Wilson went to Congress and asked for a declaration of war so the world could be made "safe for democracy." Those were stirring words to the twenty-year-old student who considered Wilson one of the finest speakers ever to occupy the White House.

"We are but one of the champions of mankind," Wilson said. "We shall be satisfied when those rights have been made as secure as the faith and the freedom of nations can make them." The day had come when America "is privileged to shed her blood and her might for the principles that gave her birth and happiness and the peace which she has treasured." Ervin read the speech the following day. He was ready to shed his own blood if necessary.

War was declared on April 6.

President Graham declared to the assembled students that the country's task was larger than the American or French revolutions or indeed of the American Union itself. It would lead toward a "permanent peace" and world unity. "Our larger task is peace; our immediate task is war!" he said, as reported by the April 21 issue of *The Tar Heel*. "There is now no alternative for a Christian democracy. There will be no peace until the world is politically organized and it cannot be politically organized till the people truly rule. To this great common good we pledge our lives and our sacred honor."

War had become a holy cause and it was surely believed that, to the righteous warrior, death would not have its usual sting. *The Tar Heel* editors were almost rapturous about the idea of American soldiers, especially Carolina students, going into combat. "Their quest is like that of the Knights of the Round Table," they said on April 21. "They go to preserve democracy and its attendant blessings, to secure the rights of small nations, to make straight the ways of peace and to protect civilization. There is the noblest and purest of causes, most free from selfish motives and narrow prejudices."

Students were signing up for military training and volunteering by the hundreds. Ervin's father suggested that he at least wait until he was called. But he could not. Like the seniors who threw down their books and went off to war in 1861, Ervin volunteered. He was accepted for officer training at Fort Oglethorpe, Georgia. It was May, 1917, a month before graduation.

The previous summer Sam Ervin had met charming Margaret Bell of Concord, N.C., while she was visiting her aunt and uncle in Morganton. They had fallen rather seriously for each other, and she was excitedly looking forward to attending the commencement ball with him. But there was no commencement ball that spring or even a commencement. Ervin received his diploma in the mail while training in Georgia.

In July he sent a newsy letter home to "Papa," reporting the details of a typically busy day that had begun with reveille at 5:15 A.M. "After sweeping barracks, morning mess, etc.," he wrote on YMCA stationery, "we fell in line with full marching packs at 6:45 and hiked about three and a half miles where our battalion took up a defensive position. We were followed by the second battalion which attempted to dislodge us, but we were so well concealed that the 'enemy' would have been completely wiped out if in actual combat. I never realized before what complete protection khaki affords when there is a great deal of green around."

He said training would end in August and he would have about two weeks of leave before being called to active duty in September. "Of course, I would be delighted for you and Mamma to come to see me, if possible."

"I'm quite well," he concluded. "Love to all. Devotedly, Sam."

He sailed for France in September.

The following spring, Thomas Wolfe, then beginning to soar with extravagant rhetoric, wrote a poem for the *University Magazine* in which he outdid Wilson, Graham, and *The Tar Heel* editors:

> We have taken up the gauntlet,—we will answer blow
> for blow,
> We have sent your blood and iron, pay thou the cost,
> and go.
> All our hearts are filled with glory at the wonder
> that will be,—
> We have taken up the gauntlet and, thank God, men
> shall be free.

4. World War I

To judge from the history of mankind, we
shall be compelled to conclude that the
fiery destructive passions of war reign in
the human breast with much more powerful
sway than the mild and beneficent sentiments
of peace; and that to model our political
systems upon speculations of lasting tran-
quility, is to calculate on the weaker
springs of human character.

ALEXANDER HAMILTON

ONE DAY, IN THE SPRING OF 1919, when Jean Ervin was in the fourth grade, the principal appeared at the classroom door and beckoned to her. Would she rather stay and serve ice cream and cookies, he asked, or go home early; her brother was arriving on the 1:15 train.

The nine-year-old girl ran all the way home.

She did not know her brother Sam very well. He had been away at school for so long and had worked in the summers. She hardly remembered what he looked like.

Jean arrived home just before her brother did. The whole family and many of their neighbors were assembled on the front lawn of the big white house. A friend brought Sam home in his little two-seater, open-top Ford. Sam climbed out, tall and stiff-looking, very military, still dressed in uniform, with heavy leather leggings and a steel helmet under his arm. He was very thin, painfully erect, and walked with a slight limp.

What fun it was to examine his helmet, so heavy with its thick leather band inside. While Jean was playing with it, she discovered a piece of chocolate candy, hardened and mashed flat inside the leather band. War meant that when you rushed into battle you put your chocolate in your helmet and saved it for later.

The Ervins had heard very little from Sam after he sailed for France in September, 1917. Occasionally they had received letters from him with some French coins inside. But for almost five months after he was wounded their letters came back unopened. No one, including the American Army, seemed to know where he was.

The war was very remote to Jean, and was brought home only by family rituals. Her father had a victory garden, which he tended vigorously every day at the crack of dawn. At night he would get out his huge maps of Europe and spread them out on the table alongside *The New York Times*, placing pins in the maps and moving them back and forth to show where the latest Allied and German positions were.

San Ervin's family and closest friends knew very little about the horrors he encountered during the war. They knew that he had been wounded twice and had received citations for heroism, and that he had been moved from hospital to hospital and finally sent home long after the war had ended.

For months after he got home he was nervous and frequently unable to sleep at night. He would get out of bed and walk out to the back yard and smoke. He smoked heavily for years after the war. His family respected his long silences and his obvious desire not to talk about the war. Everyone could see that it had shaken him deeply.

One summer evening, Eunice, who was a teenager when he returned, was sitting in the living room reading—she and Sam were the literary wing of the family. She could hear the swing creaking on the porch and couldn't help but hear her father and brother talking.

"Sam, if you're willing, I wish you'd tell me about some of your war experiences," she heard her father say. And then Sam told his father about an incident in the trenches. Eunice heard him laugh nervously as he began, talking about the murderous gunfire that stranded some wounded men out in no-man's land, how he and another man volunteered to go out after them with a stretcher, how the other man was later killed, and how he went to visit the boy's father in South Carolina after the war.

But these were shadowy details. He never volunteered to talk about the war, and most people, including his wife, allowed him to keep his memories to himself. He was not one to talk about his own heroism. That was why, years after he returned, the townspeople were surprised to hear that young Sam Ervin was awarded the Distinguished Service Cross for extraordinary heroism.

On a spring day, many years later, when he was engaged in trench warfare of sorts with the White House, he sat in the library in his home and allowed the memories to come slipping back. He sipped a glass of slightly warm beer, walking occasionally to his shelves to find a time or location of one of the battles. And he remembered how it was.

After receiving his commission at Fort Oglethorpe, Lieutenant Ervin sailed with several hundred other soldiers from Halifax, Nova Scotia. They had to wait several days for a flotilla of transport ships, led by an old British cruiser, the *Victoria*, to arrive from Australia. The crew of the ship Ervin sailed on, the *Kroomland*, conducted funerals at the back of the ship for several Australian soldiers who had died on the rough voyage and consigned them to the deep.

There was nothing particularly ominous about these ceremonies to Ervin, who felt excited and, as he said, "young and foolish." There was no question about going; it was expected of him and he went. There were big celebrations in 1917 for the boys who went to war with Uncle Sam's Army.

One such event had taken place in his hometown on

September 3, marked, as the newspaper said, by solemnity and patriotism. There was a parade that began at the courthouse square, led by the Morganton Band. Uncle Sam (Waits Harbison) rode a decorated mule and Miss Liberty (Miss Bobbie Cobb) rode in the fire wagon decorated in the national colors. The young men, wearing "Burke's Boys" armbands, followed the band ahead of the Exemption Board, the Home Guards, the Red Cross, the Confederate veterans, the Boy Scouts, and several hundred school children. Ervin's father made a short speech on the school grounds, the band played several patriotic songs, and the crowd sang "America." The speeches "were charged with patriotic spirit and encouragement and with kind words for the boys who are leaving to fight our battles. The ladies of the Red Cross served a bountiful dinner to the soldiers and Confederate veterans. It was indeed a great celebration—one which will long be remembered." The boys knew what was expected of them.

Sam Ervin spent his twenty-first birthday at sea.

His unit landed at Liverpool after a placid voyage, then went by train to Southampton for the trip across the English Channel. The channel was notoriously rough and that night's journey to Le Havre was no exception. "Most everybody got seasick but me," said Ervin. "I'll never forget; they were lined up at the rail about three deep and some Englishman came dashing up, pushing folks aside and said, 'Say, caun't you give a poor fellow a chaunce?' "

In Le Havre, Ervin and a fellow North Carolinian, T. K. Cobb, sallied forth to dine on their first French meal. Of course they assumed that no one at the restaurant spoke anything but French, and Cobb's first challenge was to ask the waitress for some butter. First he drew a picture of a cow, and then began stropping a piece of bread with his knife. "Oh, you want some butter," said the waitress in perfect English.

Toward the end of November, Lieutenant Ervin was assigned to a training camp near Lyon, which he and his fellow southerners pronounced "Lion." After a couple of weeks, he was

World War I

detached to General Pershing's headquarters in Chaumont for several weeks, preparing tables of equipment.

Then, in the dead of winter, Ervin went into the trenches with his outfit, Company 1, 28th Infantry Regiment, 1st Division. He was totally without experience in handling troops and so, rather than delegating authority, he tried to do all the patrolling himself. His platoon was assigned to a deep hollow that was constantly filled with water. The men had no place to rest. The water turned to ice, and their feet cracked open and bled. As a result, Ervin became exhausted and sick, and collapsed in the trenches with a nasty pulmonary infection. "I oughta had gone to the hospital," he said, but instead he was sent to one of the villages behind the lines and placed in charge of billeting troops.

Finding lodgings for other soldiers was not exactly what Ervin had in mind when he volunteered for the Army. "I was very foolish in those days. I thought a soldier went to war to fight and I wanted to get assigned back to my combat unit." Besides, the billeting officers had to sleep in barns which, as Ervin put it, were filled with "cooties" (lice). There was no DDT then, and "about the whole American Army had cooties." Better to sleep in the open than in those barns.

Ervin badgered his superiors for a transfer but was turned down repeatedly. It looked as though his dashing career was at an end. As long as he was an officer he would be a billeting officer. So he did what he had to: he asked permission to resign his commission as a lieutenant and reenlist as a private. The Army agreed, giving him an honorable discharge and sending him back to the front.

Resigning his commission was a difficult decision. It meant something to be an officer: status, prestige, social standing. Beside, people wouldn't understand. He wrote dejectedly to Margaret, saying he did not know when he would return and, since he was now just a lowly private, maybe she had better just forget about him. Of course—as Ervin may have known—the letter had just the opposite effect. Margaret became more determined than ever to keep him as her beau.

At Christmastime he sent a letter to his oldest sister, Laura, asking if she would pick out "an appropriate gift" for Miss Margaret Bell, who was then a senior at Converse College in Spartanburg, South Carolina. The gift she received was a fancy parasol.

The war was looking grim for the Allies in the winter of 1917–18. The Germans were pushing toward Paris, and American troops had not yet engaged them. The American Expeditionary Force was still being organized. The Germans began a big push in March, driving the British back almost to the Channel. The Hun was at the gate, said Kipling, who inspired his countrymen to stand up and take the war with "iron sacrifice of body, will and soul." Naturally, that became one of Ervin's favorite verses.

In late March and early April the enemy began pushing back the French, forcing a salient in their lines that came to a point at the small village of Cantigny. The 28th Infantry was assigned to retake it.

On May 12, 1918, while he was in training, Ervin wrote a very personal letter:

Dearest Mamma:

Today is "Mother's Day," and according to orders from General Pershing it is to be most fittingly observed by each member of the Amixforce writing a letter to his mother. No order heretofore given has, in my humble opinion, contained so vast a store of true wisdom.

Humanity is not constructed in such a manner that it can realize, even to the slightest degree, the tremendous magnitude of the debt it owes to motherhood.

I feel, however, that the events of the past twelve-months have given me a far deeper insight into the true significance of things than I ever possessed before. And my hope and prayer is that I may be spared to come back in honor and safety in order that I may repay a small part of the great debt that I owe to you. No one can be under a greater obligation than I, for my mother is the most beautiful and self-sacrificing mother in the world.

You have spoken in several letters that words are insufficient for some things, and this is one of them. Only one's feelings can adequately express it.

I am quite well, and trust every one at home is the same. Will close, and please give my love to all.

Devotedly,
Sam

The attack was to take place at dawn on May 28. For several days before the American soldiers rehearsed behind the lines, in a place very much like Cantigny, carefully practicing for the battle. They were taking no chances on the first American performance of the war.

The Germans responded to all this preparation with a fierce amount of shelling. When they got back into the trenches, during the agonizing time before jumping off, they had to wait until midnight before eating. That was the only time the food detail could risk bringing it to them. One night they dined on "slumgullion," a very thick soup that might have been used as an offensive weapon if they had thought of it.

"A shell hit nearby and threw up this great clump of dirt right down in the mess kit of this boy named Williams from Pennsylvania, who stuttered all the time. But that was the only time he didn't stutter. He cussed a blue streak for a little while and then he said, 'Well, there's no use my cussin' because this thing's not going to matter a bit fifty years from now.' So as a result of that he gave me a little philosophy—not to worry too much about knowing things at the present moment."

Ervin, although well educated and well read, has always learned from real life, from people reacting to basic situations. He would rather take his cues from people and events than from books containing the collected wisdom of the ages.

He was put in charge of a carrying party to haul barbed wire and posts from which entanglements would be made. He remembered that night well because he and his party had to make frequent trips in and out of no-man's land. They worked all night while the rest of the unit rested at the American aid station, which was set up behind a cliff. A huge cave had been dug into the cliff, and the white chalky earth, which underlay that part of the country, had been hauled out and spread over the ground. It gave the entire area a weird, ghostly look. And lying on that phosphorescent ground were the forms of the living and the dead. Men who were worn out from hiking and had to fight in the morning were stretched out in sleep alongside wounded men who had been brought back for treatment and then died. "You just couldn't tell who was dead and who was living," Ervin said.

At 4:30 the next morning the artillery laid down a monstrous barrage. Pershing threw everything he had, plus all the French guns he could get his hands on, into the attack. All told, 386 guns and mortars, throwing high explosives and gas, were used. Ervin stood on the crest of a hill on that hazy morning as the guns were firing. He could see the little village of Cantigny "practically melt down." An hour and fifteen minutes later, Ervin went over the top behind a rolling barrage and smoke screen.

His orders were to carry, with about twenty other men, wire and ammunition to a post in the cemetery to the left of the town. The cemetery was ploughed up with shells, and he jumped into a large shell hole with five engineers who were to supervise the construction of barbed wire entanglements.

Ervin risked his life many times during the war to help the injured. On this day he saved his own life by following that instinct. He left the shell hole to go to the aid of an injured soldier just a few feet away. Seconds later another shell made a direct hit on the hole, killing all five occupants.

He started back with a small group to bring ammunition up, wading through a field of high green grass or wheat. Something moved and he realized it was a German soldier with a broken arm.

"And so I got down and took a pasteboard box or something he had there and a stick and tried to tie his arm up." Ervin had studied German, but could not understand what the man was saying, although he could tell he was in great pain. The German, according to one of Ervin's companions who spoke the language, asked if they were British. He refused to believe they were Americans because, he said, German submarines would not permit them to get across the Atlantic.

A German machine gun opened fire, and Ervin, who had been kneeling down to help the wounded man, was shot clean through his left foot. "Wir sind verdammte Schweine," the German cursed apologetically (We are damned swine). Ervin repeated the German's words as though they had just been spoken.

Ervin walked back to the aid station on his heel, and was sent to a hospital for two or three weeks. The wound was not serious but it became infected because he had been wearing dirty socks. The Americans took Cantigny and held it against several enemy counterattacks but at the cost of ninety-four lives, all from Company 1. Ervin received a citation and later a Silver Star for gallantry in action.

When he returned to the front there were rumors that his unit would be sent to Orléans, south of Paris, for a short rest. But first, the Americans who had received citations marched in the Bastille Day parade in Paris. The Americans led the parade and Ervin, being tall, marched in the first squad. It was quite a celebration. Parisians by the thousands cheered for "Les américains" and strewed flowers in their path.

While Ervin was in Paris the Germans began a new drive toward the city. Big Bertha, the biggest cannon then in existence, was brought within range. No one knew exactly where it was, but Ervin could hear its monstrous roar and see the fearsome shell holes it made in the streets of Paris.

The men got a day's leave in Paris on the 15th, then climbed aboard the railway boxcars referred to by the French as "quarante hommes–huit chevaux"—forty men–eight horses— about 9 o'clock that evening. They expected to wake up the next morning in Orléans.

"I waked up at some ungodly hour of the morning and I could hear the tramp of feet marching by. So I looked out the door of the boxcar and saw these French soldiers marching up. I knew we weren't down at Orléans."

They were at Soissons and about to go into battle. Ervin learned later that it was one of the fiercest and most decisive battles of the war—the Second Battle of the Marne. Marshal Foch, who was, in Ervin's words, "a great man for the attack," wanted this one to be a complete surprise. Just before daybreak the men who had marched gaily two days before in Paris went into hiding in the forests near Soissons.

The next night they marched up to the front, but before they set out on what was to be an all-night trek, a Catholic chaplain stood before the battalion and spoke to the men in words Ervin never forgot:

` "I see before me a cross-section of America. I see before me Protestants and Catholics, Gentiles and Jews. You stand on the eve of one of the great battles of history and before tomorrow's sun goes down many of you will have paid the supreme sacrifice for our country. But I have a conviction that any man who's willing to die for his country will be saved." Ervin believed it. And so did Sergeant Hall, a tough career man and the best poker player and crap shooter in the regiment. "Ervin," he told the young private, "I don't know what your religion is, but I'm a chicken eatin' Methodist and that doctrine he's preachin' sounds pretty good to me."

That night, Ervin said, was the "doggondest night I ever saw." It rained with tropical fury, and the only visibility in the inky blackness was provided by blinding sheets of lightning. The thunder and lightning were "like a prelude to the great tragedy upon which the curtain would rise at dawn," an official record of the First Division said.

The road to the front was choked with every imaginable form of man, beast, and vehicle. Trucks, animal-drawn guns and caissons, cavalry, and tanks were wending up the narrow road as

ambulances carrying the wounded passed in the opposite direction. All this traffic forced the marching soldiers to the side of the
road.

"About the time you got used to the darkness the lightning
would flash and blind you," Ervin said. "And you had to see
your way by holding the shoulder strap of the man in front of you
and the man behind you held your shoulder strap. They were
always sliding into some hole and four or five falling down on top
of each other." The battalion arrived just before the attack,
which began at 4:35 on the morning of July 18, as the Allies
unleashed a rolling barrage of gunfire. It was not strong enough
to knock out the enemy, but gave the advancing troops some
protection.

Ervin was nervous, but then so were just about all the men in
his company. Just before they started the attack a man named
LaTour from Louisiana was killed by enemy shell fire in the
presence of his younger brother. It was unnerving. But Ervin
said, "After you get over the top you sort of get lifted out of
yourself and you're comparatively free from emotions."

The advancing troops had French tanks in front of them,
crushing enemy machine gun nests, and moved with relative
ease. They had to wade knee-deep through a large swamp, and
Ervin lost both his leggings in the process.

"In the meantime my platoon leader was killed. It was sort of
a horrible death. He had a bunch of signal rockets in his
knapsack on his back and some shell or something exploded
behind him and ignited them and they spewed in every
direction." Ervin, though still a private, was given charge of the
platoon. His first duties included taking a number of prisoners,
many of whom were throwing up their hands and shouting,
"Comrade! Comrade!"

As the platoon advanced the men ran right into the sights of
a machine gun crew that began raking them with heavy fire. It
was picking off men in Ervin's and neighboring platoons, and the
only thing to do was to go after it. Ervin, who believed to a

certain extent that you go when your time comes, called for volunteers to go with him to silence that gun. Ervin and four others began their deadly one hundred-yard dash through a murderous hail of bullets, firing their unreliable French automatic rifles as they ran. Ervin was pretty sure he killed one of the crew members as he rushed forward, the only man he has ever killed. Two of his volunteers died in that charge, and he was stopped short of the embankment.

"Right before I got to the gun pit I felt a blow like a sledge hammer on my left thigh. It just knocked me down flat. It didn't hurt. I didn't know what it was. I had an automatic clip bag slung over my shoulder with several clips or cartridges and whatever hit me just cut through the clip bag and cut through the cartridges like it was a sharp instrument." It was a shell fragment that ripped into the marrow of his bone. Had he not had the clip bag there to slow it down, the fragment probably would have gone through the bone to the large artery, and nothing could have stopped him from bleeding to death.

He raised up on his elbows and knees and saw the two survivors, Corporal Arlie Openheim and Private Dewey Price, reach the machine gun nest and shoot down the gunners. The men returned to Ervin, bandaged his wound, and offered to carry him back to a very deep trench they had crossed a short distance before.

"No, if you carry me, all three of us will make a good target," Ervin told them. "I'll crawl back there the best I can. Y'all go and get back to the line."

He crawled back to the trench, which was "about six feet deep, not one for fighting. It was what they called a communicating trench—for getting from one point to another." Just as he got into the trench, a French tank rolled over it right above him. The tank was hit by a German shell and was knocked over on its side. The French crewmen crawled out just before it was demolished by more shelling.

Ervin crawled to a rock quarry at the end of the trench,

where he saw several American and French soldiers. Among them was Samuel I. Parker of Concord, North Carolina, a classmate of his at Chapel Hill, who had just led another party in the capture of several machine guns at the rock quarry.

Parker said he had seen the machine gun nest Ervin's crew had attacked. He had expected trouble from it and wondered why it had suddenly fallen silent. When he saw Ervin he understood.

"The first thing I knew I saw Sam Ervin standing down there and he was leaning on his rifle and he was bent over," Parker said in an interview. "Blood was all over him. I just saw it was Sam and I told him he ought to go to the rear. He said, 'No, I want to stay with you. I'll help you organize for a counterattack.' I said, 'Okay, you lay here and organize this point.' So he did and he stayed with me until we had the strong point reorganized."

In testimony that later helped Ervin win the Distinguished Service Cross, Parker said he noticed that Ervin "was growing paler and weaker from the loss of blood and I ordered him to the rear. Private Ervin refused to be carried because he said two rifles could not be spared from the firing line. He crawled down through the trench and over the hill, dragging his wounded leg." That was the last Parker saw of Ervin until after the war.

Ervin didn't get very far. "I was so tired from loss of sleep," he said, "I just lay down and nodded off. Sometime later somebody shook me and waked me. I looked up and it was a very small Frenchman. He said, 'Pas une place pour coucher.'" Translation, with a little southern flavor, by Ervin: "That's a mighty poor place for sleepin'."

To prove his point the Frenchman pointed around the corner of the trench Ervin had been sleeping in. There was a German who had been killed days before. It was a gruesome sight. "The weather'd been awful hot. When people lie out in the open like that their bodies just swell up from gas just like an animal does."

The little Frenchman assisted Ervin through the trenches

until they came to his home. He took him into his basement, where two or three wounded French soldiers were being cared for. The wine in the Frenchman's basement, unsweetened vin rouge, helped ease the pain which by then had begun to throb in his thigh. He stayed there until daybreak of the next day. In the late afternoon an American medical corpsman came and gave him a shot of antitetanus serum. He was carried on a stretcher to a large cave hollowed out of the hills around Soissons.

He was in great pain by then but managed to find something amusing, at least for a southern boy. All the others in the cave were Frenchmen except one, "the blackest man I ever saw in my life." The black man turned to Ervin and in a very pronounced Irish brogue asked if he had a cigarette. Ervin asked him how he learned to speak English like that and the man replied, as Ervin retold it with a southern brogue, "Oh, I was reared in Cork, Ireland."

He lay that night in the cave and then, again just before daybreak, was taken by ambulance to "a great big ole chateau" several miles behind the lines. He was greeted by a French doctor with long whiskers, who insisted on giving Ervin another shot of antitetanus serum. "I tried to tell him I'd already had one. And he thought I was asking for a double dose, I reckon. He couldn't understand me and I couldn't understand him. And so he gave me another shot of antitetanus. I got the worst case of hives."

Ervin spent another agonizing night, having had no more treatment than an overdose of antitetanus serum. The following morning he and the Frenchmen were taken by ambulance to an American Red Cross hospital in Beauvais. "Lord, my leg was sore then," he said. "They didn't take X-rays. They used a fluoroscope and moved you so they could see the fragments in your leg from different angles and it sure was painful."

Ervin was then stretched out on an operating table, a piece of gauze placed over his mouth, and raw ether splashed on it. He felt momentarily as though he would gag, and then something seemed to hit him on the back of the head. He was out cold when the surgeon removed the small piece of shell fragment from his bone marrow. He hadn't slept since he'd been wounded, and the ether put him into a sound sleep. When he woke up he asked for a cigarette, and felt a wave of nausea as he took a drag. For Lieutenant-turned-Private Sam Ervin the war was over. But Soissons was a nightmare that would never quite go away.

In *The War to End All Wars*, Edward M. Coffman described the battle in these words, "All that remains of the exhilaration, the exhaustion, the fear—the complex emotions which Soissons provoked—are the memories of men now grown old. For those who were not there, there are only the words . . . the flies on the corpses . . . the incessant din. The wounded, thirsty and in pain, lying in the sun—Soissons."

A Jesuit priest and stretcher bearer who lived through that battle and became a distinguished scientist and philosopher, Corporal Pierre Teilhard de Chardin, marveled at the courage of the American forces. "The only complaint one would make about them is that they don't take sufficient care; they're too apt to get themselves killed. When they're wounded, they make their way holding themselves upright, almost stiff, impassive, and uncomplaining. I think I've never seen such pride and dignity in suffering."

Ervin spent the rest of the war in a series of hospitals. Every time his wound seemed to be healing it would get reinfected and start draining pus. He went back to the lines briefly, but the wound acted up and he had to return to the hospital.

His memories of these places are of spirited people like the French minister in Beauvais, whose surplice was so ragged and torn the nurses kept taking up a collection to buy him a new one. Every time they did, he would take the money and spend it for the benefit of the poor.

For some reason mail from home was not reaching him, and his father was furious. As Ervin's mother wrote to his brother Joseph at Chapel Hill on October 3:

> I wish you would return the letter of Samuel's about his not getting his mail while in hospital. Your father wants it right away to write to the War

Department & urge them to try and fix a way for wounded soldiers in Hospital to get mail from home, at a time when it would do them so much good.

Ervin was in a convalescent hospital for Americans in Brittany on November 11, when the armistice was signed. "I remember Armistice Day very well because the doctor who was in charge had a celebration and the French mayor came up on the platform—and the French are very emotional and a French man will kiss another man—and so he threw his arms around the doctor who was baldheaded as he could be. He kissed him on both cheeks and you could see him turning red clear to the back of his head."

While he was in one of the many hospitals during that year in France—he spent his twenty-second birthday in one—Ervin bedded down next to a French ambulance corpsman who had served with Robert W. Service. Ervin became intrigued with the Canadian poet who tinkered with his rhymes beside the dying and the dead, and began sending books of his poetry to Margaret. Forty years later, Service denounced war as "the devil's madness," but during the war he sang of the inevitability of savagery.

In *Rhymes of a Red Cross Man*, published in 1916, he wrote about "Faith." It was the same sort of faith that lifted Ervin out of himself as he charged the enemy:

> Since all that is was ever bound to be;
> Since grim, eternal laws our Being bind;
> And both the riddle and the answer find,
> And both the carnage and the calm decree;
> Since plain within the Book of Destiny
> Is written all the journey of mankind
> Inexorably to the end; since blind
> And moral puppets playing parts are we:
>
> Then let's have faith; good cometh out of ill;
> The power that shaped the strife shall end the strife;
> Then let's bow down before the Unknown Will;

> Fight on, believing all is well with life;
> Seeing within the worst of War's red rage
> The gleam, the glory of the Golden age.

After several frantic months of not knowing where their son was, the Ervins finally received a letter on February 18, 1919, saying he was at Base Hospital 85 awaiting evacuation to the States. "He is not bedfast but is able to be up and around, and is as well as could be expected under the conditions," said Lieutenant Colonel Royal Reynolds.

Ervin sailed from Nazaire, France on April 12, 1919, bearing scars and pain that would never quite leave him. His war records were lost until 1932, when he received the Distinguished Service Cross for extraordinary heroism in action. "Pvt. Ervin's conduct in this action exemplified exceptional courage and leadership and was an inspiration to his comrades," his citation read.

World War I was a shattering experience for Sam Ervin, but he never once doubted America's reasons for entering it, nor his own obligation to bare his breast to the enemy. "That was what you were expected to do," he said, simply, "and so that's what you naturally did." If America had not gone to war, he said, Europe would have been crushed. "I think the lights of liberty in Europe would have been extinguished."

He has always felt a strong sense of duty, to do what he felt history had called upon him to do; to strive, like Ulysses, and not to yield. His country seemed so right in 1917; but even in later years, when it seemed so wrong, he stood behind men like Lyndon Johnson and Richard Nixon. He considered Vietnam a great fiasco, but he would not take away a president's power to keep it going or end it. He supported nearly every request for military appropriations. "America," he said in the Senate on May 27, 1967, borrowing some phrases from Kipling, "must keep her heart in courage and patience and lift up her hand in strength."

"I have seen war, and I hate war," he said in another speech.

"But sometimes war is the only road to peace and safety," he added. He put himself in the same league with John J. Crittenden, who said during the Mexican War, "I hope to find my country in the right; however, I will stand by her, right or wrong."

Amnesty for those who would not participate in the Vietnam War was out of the question. "I think the ones that fled the country or the ones that dodged the draft ought to come and take their medicine, whatever it is. I think it's important for people to do their duty. I think everybody owes certain obligations to the country such as the obligation to serve in time of war if their country needs them, and also the obligation to pay taxes." He believed those obligations held whether they were wise or foolish; that's for the country, not the individual, to decide. This point with him was absolute. It rested on as tough and unyielding a principle as that which says this is a country of laws, not of men.

"Oh, War's a rousing game!" said a wounded-but-still-fighting soldier in one of Service's poems. And perhaps it was to "Burke's Boys," to Ervin, and to the men of the class of '17.

It was still, to some extent, when Sam J. Ervin III, his son, became subject to the draft during World War II. He made his father proud when he answered the draft questionnaire by saying, "When the government needs me, I'm ready." Luckily, it didn't need him until the war was over.

It took Ervin years to overcome the shocks of war. "For a while he was terribly nervous," his wife said. "He smoked excessively. You could just tell he'd been through a ravaging sort of thing. He gradually seemed to get over it. You could certainly tell it was nothing you'd want anybody to have to go through if you could help it."

For years he told his wife, whenever anything went wrong, not to worry. "It won't make any difference fifty years from now." And gradually he began to take his own advice.

5. Cambridge
and Raleigh

> Let us not in our anxiety to protect our-
> selves from foreign tyrants imitate some
> of their worst acts, and sacrifice in the
> process of national defense the very lib-
> erties which we are defending.
>
> ZECHARIAH CHAFEE, JR.

WHEN SAM ERVIN RETURNED from France in the spring of 1919, civil liberties in America had all but ceased to exist. Like all wars, World War I provided a handy excuse for depriving people of their constitutional rights, especially the right to criticize their country and its leaders. The tragedy was that once the war was over, there was no great rush to restore these rights. In fact, things got worse instead of better.

The Espionage Act of 1917 was supposed to ensure that people who were out of sympathy with the war did not interfere with the draft or help the enemy. These were perfectly reason-able goals. But the act was enthusiastically distorted by prosecu-tors, judges, and the states to apply to all forms of dissent. Thousands were prosecuted for criticizing the war, and many more—untold numbers of Americans—were too scared to speak out about anything.

The war that took more than 50,000 American lives brought victory, but not peace, to Europe and this country. The lights of liberty still burned in Europe, but in many ways they were snuffed out at home. The Red Scare of 1920 frightened the government itself into making massive arrests and holding kangaroo deportation trials.

The war also resulted in an orgy of religious intolerance that reached its zenith in the South. Newfangled notions that man came from any place other than the Garden of Eden were denounced and those who believed them were said to be in league with the devil.

There was plenty of tolerance for returned war heroes, however, and Sam Ervin found no obstacles in his path toward a career in the law. He took a refresher course at the University of North Carolina in the summer of 1919. After completing half the course he looked forward to becoming his father's law partner. He wrote to him in July, "I will certainly be glad to try my legal ignorance out in practice." But after he passed the bar, he decided the practice would wait; he would first get the best legal education he could find by enrolling at Harvard Law School. Then, as if to prove that there was nothing so special about Harvard—and that he would just as soon swim against the tide as with it—he took his courses in reverse order and literally went through backwards.

He said the reason he took the third year of law school first, then the second, and finally the first was that he was afraid Miss Margaret would not wait another three years for him. He had some serious competition for the pretty, dark-haired girl, but from the way she told it, that was a mere formality. Sam could have gone and gotten all the law schooling he wanted, front-wards or backwards, and she would have waited. In any event, Ervin met all the other students at Harvard going in the opposite direction.

Harvard was a national law school, where he could absorb general legal principles instead of narrow cases. It also gave the country boy from North Carolina a sophisticated view of worldly issues and broad constitutional principles. He studied under some of the country's best teachers. "Unlike the Harvard of later years," Ervin remarked, "they didn't teach politics." During the Watergate hearings, when witnesses professed to see strange new meanings in the Constitution, Ervin could not resist saying that he was just a country lawyer who read the English language the way it was written. Vice-chairman Howard Baker took that opportunity to accuse him of having graduated from Harvard Law School—with honors. In his defense Ervin retorted: "I had a friend introduce me to a North Carolina audience. He said he understood I was a graduate of Harvard Law School, but thank God no one would ever suspect it."

But in the 1920's Harvard was the place to go, even for young men from the South. In fact, there was a large southern delegation at the law school, including many of Ervin's Chapel Hill brothers like Albert Coates, Floyd Crouse, and Thomas Wolfe.

Ervin gained much of his respect for the law from Harvard Law Dean Roscoe Pound, who advised his students that "A lawyer should know his law like a sailor his ship—drunk or sober." Ervin marveled at the ability of men like Pound, who could lecture for an hour without looking at a book and, like his father, rattle off cases by name and page. But this man could do it for most of the states of the union and sometimes, with a little extra flourish, for other countries as well.

Pound was a tiger on individual liberties and warned of the consequences when, by democratic means, we surrender those liberties. In *The Development of Constitutional Guarantees of Liberty*, he wrote, "Democracy does not require that its agents have absolute power and be, like the Eastern Roman Emperor, free from the laws. A generation which is willing to give up the legal inheritance of Americans and set up a regime of absolute rule of a majority may find in the event it is under the absolute rule of a leader of the majority."

One of the reasons Ervin became a stickler for preparation might have been his luck in drawing teachers at Harvard. One of them, Edward H. Warren, had such a caustic tongue that he "frightened the students to death." Ervin said he saw a number of students, grown men who had fought bravely during the war, get down on their knees and crawl under their seats and out the back door of the classroom to keep from being confronted with one of Warren's questions.

"I remember a typical remark he made. He'd give a student a hypothetical state of facts and say, 'Now on those facts the court decided so-and-so. What do you think of that?' And the student said, 'Well, Mr. Warren, I can conceive of the court reaching that decision on those facts.' And then he gave him another hypothetical state of facts and said, 'Well, on that the court decided so-and-so. What do you think of that decision?' And the student said, 'Well, I can conceive of the court reaching that decision on those facts.' Then he gave a third hypothetical state of facts and said the court ruled so-and-so on that. 'What do you think of that decision?' And the student said, 'Well, I can conceive of the court reaching that conclusion on those facts.' And Mr. Warren said, 'Well, Mr. So-and-so, you have conceived three times and haven't given birth to a single thought.' The result was that you were afraid not to be prepared."

Except for Felix Frankfurter, who, according to Ervin, taught everything but public utilities in his course on public utilities, Zechariah Chafee, Jr., was the only one who came close to being a controversial figure at Harvard. Chafee, a traditionalist, was in Ervin's estimation "a great champion" of libertarian principles.

While Ervin was at Harvard, Chafee produced one of the classic books on free speech. It was written in response to the climate of fear that gripped the country after the war. "Never in the history of our country, since the Alien and Sedition Laws of 1798, has the meaning of free speech been the subject of such controversy as today," Chafee began in *Freedom of Speech*.

There were over nineteen hundred prosecutions involving speeches, newspaper articles, pamphlets, and books during the war, followed by widespread attempts by state legislatures and Congress to pass laws punishing radicals. Between 1919 and 1920 seventy such sedition bills were introduced in Congress. The House Judiciary Committee recommended the death penalty for sedition.

"On one occasion they prosecuted some people for showing a film entitled 'The Spirit of '76' on the ground that they violated the espionage law, because it made reflections upon King George and the English people who were our allies," Ervin recalled.

The courts were floundering. Even the Supreme Court, with Oliver Wendell Holmes writing for the majority, failed to live up to its own "clear and present danger" test when it upheld the conviction of Eugene V. Debs for deploring the brutality of war.

Chafee made Ervin aware of men like Judge Learned Hand, who said during the war that political agitation, no matter how effectively it arouses others to violate the law, is not the same thing as a direct incitement to violent resistance. "The distinction is not a scholastic subterfuge, but a hard-bought acquisition in the fight for freedom," Hand said.

Chafee wove Thomas Jefferson's tough, radical words into his lectures and speeches. "If there be any among us who wish to dissolve this union, or to change its republican form, let them stand undisturbed, as monuments of the safety with which error of opinion may be tolerated where reason is left free to combat it," the great Virginian said in his First Inaugural.

Echoing Jefferson in countless speeches on First Amendment freedoms, Ervin said in later years he had no fear of the truth "as long as truth is left free to combat error." Once again, truth. Without it, democracy did not stand a chance.

In 1920 Chafee came to this conclusion: "There should be no legislation against sedition and anarchy. We must legislate and enforce the laws against the use of force, but protect ourselves against bad thinking and speaking by the strength of argument and a confidence in American common sense and American institutions, including that most characteristic of all, which stands at the head of the Bill of Rights, freedom of thought."

Twenty-one years later, in the midst of another war, Chafee

updated his book, calling it *Free Speech in the United States*. It ends with a prelude to the seventies: "You make men love their government and their country by giving them the kind of government and the kind of country that inspire respect and love: a country that is free and unafraid, that lets the discontented talk in order to learn the cause for their discontent and end those causes, that refuses to impel men to spy on their neighbors, that protects its citizens vigorously from harmful acts while it leaves the remedies for objectionable ideas to counter-argument and time."

Ervin watched the witch hunts of 1920 from his perch at Harvard with growing alarm. President Wilson's attorney general, A. Mitchell Palmer, let the country see Red by staging a massive nationwide raid on private homes and labor headquarters on a single night in January, 1920, arresting over four thousand supposed Communists in thirty-three cities. Although most unproductive in finding revolutionaries, the raids made Palmer, a practicing Quaker, a national hero. On May 1, the National Guard was called out because of Palmer's repeated warnings of a plot to overthrow the government. Ervin felt that the attorney general "grossly abused" the law.

"There was a lot more of this sort of thing around," historian Samuel Eliot Morison said, "more hate literature, more nasty, sour, and angry groups promoting 'hundred percent Americanism' than at any earlier period in our history, or any later one prior to the 1950's."

The one consolation Ervin found in all these horrors was that North Carolina was having no part of them. The state, falling back on its libertarian traditions, declined to enact the kinds of repressive laws that many states were embracing.

The same hysteria that spawned the "Red Menace" produced one of the greatest miscarriages of justice in American history—the Sacco-Vanzetti trial. The trial took place in the vicinity of Harvard, and many of the school's faculty, particularly Felix Frankfurter, were outraged by the outcome. Ervin did not study directly under him, but learned a great deal about criminal justice from him as Frankfurter fought to reverse the convictions.

Nicola Sacco and Bartolomeo Vanzetti were accused of killing two men in a payroll holdup in South Braintree, Massachusetts, on April 15, 1920, and were convicted the following year. The prosecution made little of the evidence and much of the radical views of the defendants and their foreign backgrounds. In an analysis of the case, Frankfurter said, "By systematic exploitation of the defendants' alien blood, their imperfect knowledge of English, their unpopular social views, and their opposition to the war, the District Attorney invoked against them a riot of political passion and patriotic sentiment." The judge, he added, "connived at" the process. Nevertheless, all appeals were rejected and Sacco and Vanzetti were executed on August 22, 1927.

Ervin's finest moments at Harvard were times of hard work and of inspiration from great teachers. But he also remembered with great fondness the comic relief that shared the stage in Cambridge.

Among his fellow students was George Smucker from Dallas, quick with the one-liners and southern to the core. "This bunch of us were at the same table in Harvard Memorial Hall, a dining hall which was a memorial to the Union war dead of Harvard College. And we had this boy from Braintree, Massachusetts, who brought one of his friends in to have lunch with us one day. And his friend asked him, 'What is this hall?' And he explained that it was a memorial to the Harvard College war dead who served in the Civil War. And George spoke up and said, 'You're all wrong about that. This is not anything in memory of the Union. This is a monument to the accuracy of southern marksmanship.' "

One of Ervin's all-time favorite stories involved the fattest girl and the biggest cigar in Boston. It began during his last year, when he went to his old friend Floyd Crouse to borrow his notebooks for first-year courses. Crouse was on the phone talking with a Wellesley girl whom he was dating.

"And I could tell by listening to his part of the phone conversation that she was suggesting to him that he get one of his friends to go out with one of her friends." Ervin agreed to the blind date. Southern students at Harvard had a club that held a dance once a month at the Copley Plaza Hotel in Boston. "So we met them there in Boston and this girl I had the blind date with was about the fattest girl I ever saw. I used to say facetiously that every time she took a step on the dance floor that the whole Copley Plaza Hotel shook and trembled. That wasn't quite accurate but it sort of illustrated her weight. She weighed two hundred and seventy-five if she weighed a pound.

"So none of my friends would break [cut in] on me and I danced with her about half the night. But then Floyd's conscience got to smitin' him for gettin' me into that predicament. He came over and whispered to me that he'd dance with her the next time. I told him I'd appreciate it cause I'm going to go out and smoke.

"He said, 'Well, I want you to give me your solemn assurance that you'll only have one smoke and that you'll come right back in.'

"So I assured him I would and I went out in the lobby of the hotel and asked to see the biggest cigar they had in the house. And so they gave me a great big cigar for fifty cents. That was a lot of money in those days.

"So I sat down in an easy chair in the hotel lobby and I smoked that cigar very slowly, smoked it down to about half a inch. Then I went back in and Floyd was dancin' with my girl. And I'd look up at the ceiling and he'd dance almost up against me and I'd look up at the ceiling some more. Finally I went and broke on him.

"The dance ended and they had a little intermission and I went over to Floyd and Floyd said, 'You broke your solemn promise. You told me you weren't going to smoke but once. I said, 'No, I kept my word. I did only smoke once. But I did get the longest cigar there was in Boston.' "

When Ervin told the story fifty years later, he was seated on the edge of a bed in his hotel room in Raleigh. He managed to keep himself from bursting open with laughter by holding himself cross-armed around the tummy and then rocking back on the bed and kicking his heels in opposite directions. Like the poor girl's tread on the dance floor, Ervin's laughter was enough to cause the hotel to shake and tremble.

With all the suffering and tragedy in the world, Ervin has always been able to dig down and find some evidence of human comedy to lift him and those around him over the rough spots. It helped keep things in perspective. "I can't imagine how a person gets through life, takes the rough licks he gets, without a sense of humor," he said, recalling a little rhyme he kept in his mental file: "This old world we live in is mighty hard to beat; you get a thorn with every rose, but ain't the roses sweet."

With the help of Crouse's meticulous notebooks, Ervin raced through his third year at Harvard in about two months. One notation, written in green ink in the wide margin in Crouse's constitutional law notebook, says: "The 14th Amendment applies to state action and not action by individuals—and interference with any right under state government—voting, etc., does not raise a federal question. But interference by individuals with voting for federal officials is an offense that Congress can deal with." It took forty years for Congress and the courts to recognize that voting discrimination does raise a federal question, a development which Ervin, when the time came, diligently sought to postpone.

Ervin held a number of offices he did not seek, which is not to say he didn't want them. His political career began with characteristic self-restraint. While at Harvard studying for final exams he received a telegram from Charles F. Kirksey, chairman of the Burke County Democratic Party, advising him that he had been nominated as a candidate for the state legislature.

Ervin's father is said to have grumbled that he sent his son to Harvard to be a lawyer, not a politician. Years later an Ervin friend commented, "It done look like he's run off at the political end." Politics was the last thing he had in mind but he dutifully accepted the nomination. If he won he could practice law about half the year and legislate the other half. He figured he would not stay in politics long.

Ervin was twenty-five then and still painfully shy, though with friends he could be witty and engaging. His head was full of law and poetry and he needed no prompting to recite either. Then, as now, good law to Ervin *is* poetry, or at least soaring prose.

He returned to Morganton and went into business with his father, adding a room to S. J. Ervin's little office building on the square. He won the election to represent the traditionally Republican county in Raleigh. In preparation for the opening session of the legislature, he went through the state mental hospital and the school for the deaf, both in Morganton, to see what special needs they had. As a result, he developed a lasting interest in the well-being as well as the legal rights of the mentally ill.

Ervin was also making frequent trips by train down to Concord to see Miss Margaret Bell, carrying under his arm a five-pound Whitman's Sampler and often a book of poetry. He had a weakness for chocolate candy and sweet verse and indulged in both. He might blush but he recited Elizabeth Barrett Browning anyway: "How do I love thee? Let me count the ways. . . ."

In January, 1923, he went to Raleigh as a legislator, and received the staggering sum of four dollars a day plus travel expenses. The General Assembly took care of the entire legislative needs of the state for two years by March and then adjourned. By today's standards, state government was practically nonexistent. The counties raised and spent all the money for schools and roads, and that was about the only thing government did in those days. "The only financial argument we had was whether the license tax to operate a service station should be raised from $3.50 to $5.00. I think we debated that for several days. That was about the most serious problem we had," Ervin recalled.

Notwithstanding advice from Morganton philosopher Lum Garrison—who told Ervin, "Pass no more laws and repeal half of those we've already got"—one of the first things Ervin did in public life was to sponsor legislation for a bond issue to improve the black school in the Oliver Hill section of Morganton. It had been separate and unequal, and Ervin at least did something about the unequal part. In the 1920's that was the limit of concern for a white politician. Often, when he became defensive about his failure to support civil rights bills, Ervin would mention this 1923 bond issue as evidence of his interest in the welfare of blacks. His interest was genuine, and it puzzled him that blacks failed to appreciate that and would be satisfied with nothing less than full legal and social equality with whites.

There would be more challenging issues later on, but for the most part Ervin's mission to Raleigh was to look after such concerns as the game season in Burke County, the charters of small country towns, and the drainage of Muddy Creek.

* * *

ON JUNE 18, 1924, Ervin married Margaret Bell, his one and only sweetheart. They had a large wedding in Concord, attended by just about everyone except Ervin's father, who didn't care for social affairs.

In the fifty years since then Sam and "Miss Margaret" have been utterly devoted to each other, although for two thirds of that time he held public office and held it so tightly that he seldom had time for anything else.

They met in the summer of 1916, after a major flood in Burke County. The first time he saw her she was riding in a car, and he was immediately "smitten by her . . . first by her looks and then a day or two later, I met her and I've been in love with her ever since." While she was in Morganton at her uncle's, they would borrow his car or go on hayrides with picnic baskets on their arms or go to the silent movies. They played tennis and went square dancing—something Ervin continued doing long after he joined the Senate.

They went places with other couples, although Mrs. Ervin thought her future husband shy and not very interested in mixing with others. It was not that he was afraid of other people but that he was unafraid to move in his own sphere, a small planet in his own private galaxy. Frequently he would go to the homes of friends or relatives and lose himself in books.

"I felt like he was different from anybody I had ever met," Mrs. Ervin reminisced. "He certainly was of the intellectual type. Most of the boys in our crowd didn't have any special ambition. I could tell Sam was different in that respect." By ambition, she did not mean yearning for personal success, but that "everything he undertook to do he would do well."

She thought she was marrying a more worldly person than he turned out to be. "He went to a lot of concerts in those days at Harvard and I thought he was going to be someone to enjoy cultural things. But I never have gotten him back on that track," she chuckled softly. "He always took every job he had so seriously." When they married they went off to Yellowstone Park with tickets given to them by Southern Railway, a longtime client of his father's. "I thought we'd take a fine trip every year on June 18," she said, somewhat wistfully, "but trips have been few and far between since then, usually only where the business of the Senate takes him."

Ervin's father gave the young couple a small lot next to the family home, right on the spot where Sam and his pals used to play baseball on those carefree days before the world asked him suddenly to become a man. They set out to build a modest, one-story home while renting a room at Mrs. Ervin's uncle's place. That was the year the town decided to pave Lenoir Street.

The road builders dug down and leveled it off, and then it rained and rained and rained until the street became an enduring sea of red mud.

Ervin idolized and protected Miss Margaret in true southern fashion. The gods had given her to him as "wife and ministering angel," as he once told the graduates of Converse College, her alma mater. She gladly accepted the role. Walter Malone, an obscure Memphis poet and one of Ervin's favorites, gives us this ethereal picture of the way all good southern brides should be:

> I see thee coming robed in spotless white,
>   My stately swan, my pure and peerless dove,
> My star of morning, diademed with light,
>   Bringing me lilies from the land of love.

The same sentiments that made young maidens swoon in 1924 would make their counterparts fifty years later shake their undiademed heads with disbelief. To which Ervin only chuckled and found something—which to him was gallant and to them chauvinistic— to say.

Ervin, in fact, was always dominated by women and happily so. Women ordered him around and women protected him like mother hens—the way his mother did. But there was one area where they did not dare tread: his career. That was beyond their reach, just as it often seemed to be beyond his. He said he would leave the decision about whether he should retire from the Senate and go back to Morganton to "the family dictator," his wife. But she knew the decision was really governed by his sense of duty and she would never insist that he give up his career, even if she never got to go home to her garden and her grandchildren.

"Love me? She must," Ervin declared to the *New York Times*. "She's put up with me so long, I would think there are some rough corners in my personality that require a good deal of forbearance from a wife. If I've done anything that's worthwhile, it's due to the fact that she stood beside me in shadow as well as in sunshine."

Some women are professionals and some are ministering angels. When the Ervins were married Mrs. Ervin made the decision—and it was easy for a woman of her era—never to stand in his way. "I felt he had much more to contribute to the country than I had," she said. "I decided that whatever he wanted to do was what I wanted."

* * *

THE 1923 LEGISLATIVE SESSION had barely ended when the prelude to the 1925 session took place at the city auditorium in Raleigh. William Jennings Bryan, the populist who twice lost bids for the presidency, was leading the prairie fire crusade against the infidels who taught that mankind contained the blood of the brute apes rather than the breath of the Almighty.

Bryan was traveling from state to state, fanning the sparks of fundamentalism, which were ready to consume all who taught the evolutionary heresy. On April 28, 1923 he cried out to a tumultuous crowd in Raleigh that the teaching of evolution was "the only menace to religion that has appeared in the past nineteen hundred years." He challenged "any son of an ape" to match cards with him. And then he urged Christian taxpayers to drive the infidels from the public schools.

Bryan and Billy Sunday and a host of others were stumping the South, urging state legislatures to pass laws prohibiting the schools from teaching the theory that man descended from apes or any other lower form of creature. They succeeded in Florida and Oklahoma and almost in North Carolina. The governor of North Carolina, Cameron Morrison, ordered a book picturing a man and a monkey on the same page banished from the schools.

The antievolutionists found fertile soil in North Carolina, where frontier traditions of piety ran thicker than moonshine likker. Most folks, if they didn't quite buy everything about that old-time religion, had just enough of it in their blood that a little revivalism stoked by a riproaring public debate would tug hard at their souls. The prevailing winds of conformity that swept the

South after the war added to the traditional attitudes created the perfect setting for the overthrow of religious tolerance.

It was inevitable that someone like David Scott Poole, a pious member of the legislature from rural Hoke County, would introduce a measure at the beginning of the 1925 session which expressed disapproval of the teaching of "any evolutionary hypothesis whereby man is linked in blood relationship with any lower form of life."

The uproar was deafening. Crowds packed the hearings and debates and preachers took to their pulp'ts as they had not done since pre-Prohibition days. Politicians said Christianity itself would collapse. Poole warmed things up during the public hearings, contending that "the religion of the Lord Jesus Christ is at stake." But men of some courage led the opposition to the bill. University of North Carolina President Harry W. Chase called the legislation "tyranny over the mind." William Louis Poteat, a Baptist minister, biologist, and president of Wake Forest College, was almost expelled for having taught evolution, but he continued to urge students to search for truth beyond the Bible.

The public debate was no less heated. In a letter to *The Charlotte Observer*, John W. Kurfees of Winston-Salem maintained that "a majority of the people of North Carolina believe in the God of the Bible, as the creator of all things, and that His Son, Jesus Christ, the Savior of the World, was miraculously conceived and born of the Virgin Mary, and that a like belief is held for every other miracle in that sacred volume."

A mysterious letter, signed "Anonymous," appeared in the *Raleigh Times*. But those familiar with the style and the frequency of his letter-writing knew that it came from S. J. Ervin of Morganton. He said that "we" desire to oppose the bill, without saying whether he was speaking for himself or a group of people. Chances are it was just the old man himself, then seventy years old, tromping back and forth on his porch, gesturing at one of his daughters as he dictated.

"How absurd the whole thing is and what a spectacle it

makes of our state before the assembled world!" he wrote in the letter. "How feeble our faith in the word of God when it has to be propped with statutory enactments and enforced by pains and penalties in order to uphold it!

"How contrary to the spirit of protestantism, to the genius of a free people, to the light of civilization, and to the spirit of Christ, this unwholesome proposal is!"

On February 12, 1925 the House Education Committee disapproved of the bill by a one-vote margin, but Poole introduced it on the floor anyway. Debate was scheduled for an extraordinary evening session on the 17th.

This is how the AP, in bloated prose, led its story for the next morning's papers: "Unwilling to proceed in the face of the throngs of humanity that stampeded the hall tonight and refused to move, even at the earnest solicitation of the sergeant-at-arms, and after the speaker had indicated that orderly procedure would be impossible in the face of such congestion, the House of Representatives which met tonight at 8 o'clock to consider the Poole anti-evolution bill as a special order, adjourned until 11 o'clock tomorrow morning."

The old state capitol had been the scene of bedlam, as a seething mass of unyielding humanity jammed its rotunda. Women begged to be allowed inside the chamber, red-capped students from the state university came to see the show, along with hundreds of local citizens. The main participants in the debate, the state representatives, fought vainly to get through them. The blind doorkeeper made a futile attempt to close the doors. The show could not go on.

The next day a motion to table the bill failed 49–52, and suddenly it looked as though it would pass. The legislators were, as the expression went, silent in seven languages. Sam Ervin, nervous and untrained as a public speaker, but urged by his father to oppose the bill, got to his feet and made the strongest speech of his twenty-eight-year-old life. The next morning's papers said he was "vigorous" in his opposition.

"I know nothing about evolution," Ervin began, "neither do I care anything about it. To be very frank with you, gentlemen of this House, I don't see but one good feature in this thing, and that is that it will gratify the monkeys to know they are absolved from all responsibility for the conduct of the human race."

There must have been general laughter or applause at this point, and Ervin fought for control. "This is a serious matter," he said. "It is an attempt to limit freedom of speech and thought and for that reason I am opposed to it." The cause of civil liberty had at that point been handed down from father to son.

"If this measure is consistent, then let's pass laws against witches," he said, unable to surpress another bit of humor. "Why, according to the proponents of this bill, Columbus ought to have been told, when he started away from Spain: 'No; you can't go, because the earth is flat and you might fall off.' "

Then, in the crescendo style that became the pattern for his later speeches, Ervin shouted, "The passage of this resolution would be an insult to the Bible. It would be an insult to the people of North Carolina. I don't believe the Christian religion's endurance depends upon the passage of some weak-kneed resolution of the General Assembly of North Carolina. It is too big, too strong for that."

Judge Carlyle Higgins of the North Carolina Supreme Court, then a colleague of Ervin's in the legislature, said Ervin's speech was by no means the best during those two days of debate. It was typically Ervin: stumbling and nervous, but effective. "His mind works faster than his tongue does," said Higgins. Then, summing up the man with whom he had been friends for half a century, he said, "Sam's true blue. Nobody will bluff him."

Ervin declined to accept credit for rallying the opposition to the bill. But his speech was the first, and there is no doubt he gave many others the backbone to stand up against it. It was defeated on February 19 by a vote of 46–64. Despite attempts to revive it in later years, it never again came close to becoming law.

Five months later, the raucous, carnival-like Scopes trial took place in the sleepy little town of Dayton, Tennessee, with William Jennings Bryan prosecuting and Clarence Darrow defending a hapless high school teacher. An antievolution bill had passed into law practically without opposition in Tennessee, and the trial that followed marked that state for years to come as a crossroads of intolerance. The same sort of trial could have taken place that year or the next in North Carolina and ended the state's right to claim the progressive leadership of the South.

It was noted sometime later that most of the legislators who voted against the Poole bill were graduates of the University of North Carolina and Wake Forest, places where the gospel that was taught was religious liberty.

A history professor at Chapel Hill who later became the symbol of liberalism at the university—and briefly a U.S. senator—observed shortly after the defeat of the bill that North Carolinians once declared that they would have "a place where there is always a breath of freedom in the air . . . and where finally truth shining patient like a star bids us advance and we will not be turned aside."

The young professor, Frank Porter Graham, said in a letter to *The Raleigh News and Observer*: "To preserve this spiritual possession of the people for the inheritance of their children, North Carolinians will fight against the false fear of truth and foes of freedom whatever be the power."

Ervin had no interest in making a career out of being a state legislator and went to Raleigh for only three sessions, 1923, 1925, and 1931, long enough to become acquainted with just about every state law there was, and to gain many friends across the state. He served on the Judiciary Committee, where he sponsored changes in judicial procedure and legislation to allow juries to recommend mercy in capital cases. At that time anyone convicted of a capital offense was automatically sentenced to death, and Ervin, who had seen enough death in his young life, felt the law was too harsh. His bill did not quite make it but one very similar to it did a few years later.

He pushed for bigger spending for education, and sponsored legislation to take care of the special employment needs of the deaf. In 1931 he joined the bitter opposition to a state sales tax. The country was in the depths of the depression, and, although the state desperately needed new ways to raise money, Ervin felt the sales tax would be extremely unpopular. However, it passed during the following session, with his friend Floyd Crouse leading the fight for it.

Ervin's favorite legislative story involved no great issue, but was instead the detailed account of a comic interlude involving one Bascom Lamar Lunsford, Ervin's candidate for House reading clerk. He told it with flourishes of detail, all in a great rush, sentences running together, chanting with a singsong cadence, almost out of breath.

The problem with the reading clerk, chosen at Ervin's insistence over a couple of smooth-tongued radio announcers, was that he, like Ervin, frequently stumbled over difficult words. Words like "chiropractor" were reduced to "cheropiter," which Ervin thought was not all that terrible. But the principal reading clerk, Thad Eure, most recently North Carolina's secretary of state, said Lunsford "couldn't read worth a damn." A lot of others in the House thought so too.

"Some members of the legislature should have been more patient and shouldn't have been troubled by such pronunciations," Ervin said. "They seemed to get very troubled with it, including the Speaker of the House, Willis Smith (later U.S. senator). They came to me and they charged that he couldn't read, which wasn't right because he could read and write, except he couldn't pronounce a few of the words correct. Neither can I. And they said I was responsible for him being elected and they wanted me to get him to resign and they said they'd give him another job in the legislature and pay him just as much or even more.

"So I said I'd take it up with him; so I took it up with him and he said he was elected reading clerk and he was going to do that readin'.

"Well, it finally got to the point—there was a small group that was so irritated by his lack of correct pronunciation of a few somewhat difficult words—they decided that since they couldn't get rid of him by some amicable means of persuasion, they would get rid of him by a very drastic legislative operation. So they introduced a resolution that declared that the office of reading clerk was vacant and that the House would proceed to the election of a reading clerk to fill the vacancy.

"Well, as I say, the speaker was very much interested in vacating the office of reading clerk on his theory that the reading clerk couldn't read. They had this all very well planned out and the speaker wouldn't recognize anybody except the people he knew were going to speak in favor of the resolution.

"So one of the speakers for the resolution was a man of whom I was very fond, Union L. Spence of Moore County. He was chairman of the Finance Committee of the House which he always called the '*Finn*ance Committee.'

"Well, finally they ran out of speakers and had to recognize some of the rest of us who were opposed to the resolution and the first one they recognized was me. And I said that among other things I was opposed to the resolution because if they expelled people from legislative office because they mispronounced words they'd have to expel all of the members of the House except my good friend, the gentleman from Moore. Because he was the only man out of 120 representatives who knew that the word 'f-i-n-a-n-c-e' spells '*finn*ance' and not '*fi*nance' like the rest of us thought.

"And I said, 'Now I'm a great admirer of the gentleman from Moore. He's got very broad shoulders and great capabilities, but I don't want to put all the burdens of this House on the shoulders of my good friend from Moore.' So I asked them to vote down this resolution.

"Then there was an old fellow, J. L. Gwaltney from Alexander County, who took the whole thing seriously. He'd been educated before the public schools were very far advanced and he got up and took it so seriously the tears just streamed down his face. He said he just didn't have the educational opportunities like so many members of the legislature and perhaps he mispronounced many words.

"Then Jack Morefield from Graham County got up and said he thought it was a bad precedent to expel a man from an office. He said, 'Now this office is not vacant. There's not a word of truth in that statement that it's vacant. There's the reading clerk sitting right up there. In fact he insisted on reading this resolution when it was presented. It would be very bad to expel any man from office just because he's incompetent to fill it.' He said, 'There's President Hoover; everybody admits he's incompetent to be president.' Said, 'There's Max Gardner, the governor of North Carolina. Many people think he's not competent to be governor.' And said, 'If they're going to adopt this kind of principle, I can see myself being expelled from this body and, of course, leading a great multitude of others out of this hall.'

"Well, that's how it went. We had a few more speeches and we had the vote. And we overwhelmingly defeated the motion and we kept the reading clerk who allegedly couldn't read."

In spite of all the fun he had at it, Ervin was not all that interested in a political career. It kept him away from his first love: practicing law, both in the courtroom and in the office and down at the jail cell. In spite of his education, which was considerable for his time, he was basically a country lawyer.

During the voting rights hearings in 1965 he told a story about legislators that smacked of Will Rogers. He had picked it up somewhere on his travels around the legal circuit.

"One time they called a character witness to the stand down in the North Carolina court presided over by a friend of mine,

Judge Harlin Johnson. The lawyer asked his witness, 'Are you a member of the State Legislature?'

"Judge Johnson said, 'What are you trying to do, impeach your own witness?'"

6. Country Lawyer

The government of the United States
has been emphatically termed a
government of laws, and not of men.

JOHN MARSHALL

PINK MITCHELL called everybody "Honey." It didn't matter who they were, how old they were, or what their sex happened to be. They suffered the common fate.

Mitchell came from a rough section of Burke County known as the Laurel, but he was a God-fearing man who made sure his next of kin got a proper Christian upbringing. He had a healthy respect for the law, which he proved by naming his twin boys after the past two county sheriffs, Manny McDowell and Forest Berry. But even with this precaution he got into a little trouble with the law one day and figured he'd best get himself a lawyer.

"Honey," he said to Sam Ervin, "Ah've got a case in the big cou't and I want you to look after it."

Ervin grimaced but inquired, "Well, Pink, what kind of case is it?"

"They got me falsely accused of makin' moonshine likker," Mitchell said earnestly. "I found me a bee tree down in the woods and I got to thinkin' how the old lady and Forry Berry and Manny McDowell would like some of that honey. So I went down in the woods with mah axe and I'se cuttin' down that bee tree and somebody came behind me, tapped me on the shoulder and said 'Pink, you're under arrest.' I looked around and there was a officer. And I says, 'What for?' And he says, 'For bein' at that still.' And I looked over there and, sure enough, there was a still."

The jury did not believe Pink Mitchell's story, and his lawyer wasn't able to do very much for him. He got four months in jail and would have stayed there if Mrs. Hughson, the widow of the former Presbyterian minister who brought the word of God down to their home Sunday afternoons, hadn't vouched for him and persuaded the judge to let him out.

A lawyer in a small country town really gets to know the people—their hopes, their fears, their passions, their hates. All their problems and desires blend with the law and give a man with an ear for life's poetry and a love for its drama a certain sense of satisfaction.

Sam Ervin was a lawyer for fifteen years before being appointed to a state judgeship. Seven years later he went back to his law practice and stayed with it until 1948, when he reluctantly accepted an appointment to the North Carolina Supreme Court. He often said that if he ever retired from the Senate, he would like nothing better than to return to the courtroom as a lawyer. It was always his first love.

In June, 1922 Ervin built a small addition to his father's two-room law building across the square from the courthouse, installed a telephone over his father's objections—he still distrusted the contraptions—and a flattop desk and went to work.

The most depressing thing that can happen to a young lawyer is to lose his first case. But that is exactly what befell Sam Ervin in the summer of 1922. He defended a man against having a lien placed on stacks of fodder in his corn field. His client was too poor even to pay the court costs, and so Ervin paid them for him.

Ervin had a lot of learning to do, but he had an experienced teacher. His father told him that when he was preparing a case, "Salt down the facts; the law will keep." In other words, learn everything there was to know about the case before worrying about the law. It would be there when he needed it. He also taught his son that cases were never won in the courtroom but in the work and study that went into them beforehand.

What father and son had lacked in their retationship as man and child they made up for as partners in the practice of law. Their medium of communication was the law. It was said that Ervin's father loved Southern Railroad first, "Little Sam" second, and all the rest of the children third. He was protective about some things, reminding his son to take his umbrella at the slightest sign of rain. But he did not shield him from the dangers of the courtroom.

S. J. Ervin told his son that it was not advisable for a young lawyer to practice with his father because the senior member of the partnership tends to regard the junior member as still a child and to turn him into a mere brief toter. "I'm going to give you a chance to make a lawyer out of yourself if I lose every client I've got," he told Sam. He lived up to that promise, giving him more and more responsibility, and soon let him go into court alone.

When they disagreed about the law of a case, Ervin and his father had a standing policy that the one who believed the law to be on the side of their client would handle the case in court. Once, when Ervin was sure they would lose in a bankruptcy suit, he told his father, "I have no faith in the cause of our clients." "Well," said his father, "I have complete faith in them, so you don't have anything to do with this case." They won.

As complementary as father and son were professionally they were as different from each other personally as the eras in which they grew up. The elder Ervin's struggle for survival had robbed him of warmth. As he once told one of his daughters, "I have the respect of people; my son has their love."

The Burke County Bar consisted of only about twelve lawyers. Among them were Izaak Avery, a fine storyteller and colorful lawyer, who once got up and shouted in the courtroom, "I deny the allegation and defy the allegator"; Cousin Will Ervin, with his handlebar mustache; Joseph Spainhour, a very dangerous man before a jury; and of course S. J. Ervin himself, fearsome-looking with his full beard and swallowtail coat. The lawyers stood up and battled out their cases, neither asking nor giving quarter. Cases were not often settled out of court for the simple reason that there were fewer automobiles around and therefore fewer lawsuits arising out of accidents. The lawyers always went armed for legal combat, and that was excellent training for the newest member of the bar.

The courtroom itself was a dismal place heated only by a stove in the center. "One extremely cold day," Ervin said, "the lawyers had gotten over there and crowded around the potbelly stove and this poor juror who'd come twenty-eight miles in the cold and was almost frozen to death, he couldn't get in close to the stove for the lawyers, and he finally said he'd had a funny dream the night before; he'd dreamed that he'd gone to hell. And the lawyers said, 'Well, how is it there?' And he said, 'It's just like the Burke County courthouse: you can't get to the fire for the lawyers.' "

The courtroom was a source of endless amusement. On one of his first days in the courthouse Ervin watched Avery defend a group of black youths who had got into a fight one Sunday afternoon at their church. One of them, Wiltz Collett, was six-foot-three and had about the biggest feet Ervin had ever seen. "And he was sitting on the witness stand he could raise up his foot and his foot was so big it almost obscured the the view of him from the courtroom." Avery was cross-examining him, and most of his answers were rather favorable to the defendants. But Avery dared one question too many and the answer was devastating. "Mr. Avery was taken aback and so he sat there in silence for a couple of minutes and there was Wiltz sitting on the witness stand with his foot going up and down. And Wiltz said, 'Come on witcher conversation, Mr. Avery. Come on witcher conversation.' "

The Ervins, father and son, defended a great many black people. In fact, most blacks in Morganton considered the Ervins their lawyers. When times were hard, payment was not often demanded. It was not surprising, therefore, that Ervin had about as many stories about black clients—and stories they told him about other blacks—as he had about whites. He used to tell the stories without giving much thought to whether the characters were white or black. He told them with affection and love, but the stories about blacks did not go over very well in Washington. Coming from a white southerner who opposed civil rights laws, they sounded bigoted or at least insensitive. Ervin reluctantly dropped them after a few years.

One of the first cases Ervin got under his own steam had to do with the will of Aunt Clara Fleming, an old black woman who had accumulated a house and some insurance and died leaving a will and a lot of dissatisfied relatives. Ervin was trying to prove she was of sound mind when she made the will, and he chose the strongest witness he could find to testify on her behalf—Betty Powell, his family's former cook. She was a very positive individual who would be hard to shake on cross-examination. In will cases, he had learned, it was best to put the strongest witness on first because most of the testimony is repetitious. He called her to the witness stand and asked, "Will you please tell his honor and the jury what your name is?" What followed was a lawyer's nightmare.

Betty Powell looked disgustedly down at Ervin and said, "Look here, Mr. Sam, don't be axin' me no fool questions like that. You know my name as well as you do your own."

He dove into the law and the law books, and relished it, especially the hardest part, the tedium of the books. He could devour great quantities at one sitting and commit much of what he read to memory. He was not born with a photographic memory, but almost. One afternoon, when handling a complicated patent case, he took down four immense volumes on patent law, and, as he put it—in a manner that left no doubt as to whether he stuck to it—"sa'down" and read them.

In 1928 he got himself a Model T Ford and began traveling

the backroads through Burke and the neighboring mountain counties, chugging up and down the hills, singing as he went, the engine purring softly. "When it's springtime in the Rockies . . . ," he would chortle as he drove through the beautiful North Carolina mountains.

Ervin gained a reputation as a lawyer who was not afraid to work. He became, literally, a lawyer's lawyer. Other law firms brought him in to help with their important cases. It was a good thing for Ervin's family that they did because those were the only times he made big money. He did not seem to be very interested in collecting money from his own clients.

Ervin, in fact, had a disdain for money. He paid his bills ahead of time, without regard for the interest his money could be earning if he kept it a little longer. He never invested in any of the smart deals lawyers always seem to know about. About the only thing he invested in was books, hundreds and hundreds of books, driving his wife to distraction.

He was an aggressive courtroom lawyer and highly inventive. Earl Franklin, recently chairman of the county board of elections, was a justice of the peace when Ervin was practicing law. "I remember one time I got pretty aggravated with him," Franklin chuckled. "We had a speeding case where a patrolman had to chase down this man. Sam didn't have any defense at all, so he reached up in thin air and pulled one down. He said if the defendant was speeding, the patrolman was speeding too and ought to be guilty."

Ervin was also given to flights of courtroom oratory that caught the imagination of some but must have caused others to think him somewhat "quair."

His sister Jean had never seen her older brother in court until one day when her school civics class visited the courthouse and jail. "Father used to say the courthouse was no place for young ladies," she said. "The class went into the courtroom and sat in the back. Sam had a client who must have been guilty—a murderer probably. We had been reading Shakespeare, and there stood Sam making a plea for mercy in Shakespeare's words . . .

> The quality of mercy is not strain'd,
> It droppeth as the gentle rain from heaven
> Upon the place beneath: it is twice bless'd;
> It blesseth him that gives and him that takes:

There is oftentimes a big distinction between justice and mercy. The last thing a guilty client wants is justice. And whether in the words of *The Merchant of Venice* or in plain country talk, Ervin could plead for mercy with feeling. His mother had taught him to love sinners while hating sin.

Ervin got his first taste of corrupt politics in 1926 when he ran for district solicitor, the equivalent in most states of prosecutor. It was the first time he had sought elective office on his own, and the only time he was ever beaten. It was apparent to Ervin's supporters that he lost the election to L. S. Sperling of nearby Lenoir because the ballot boxes in Caldwell County had been tampered with.

His father was outraged and set out to find the guilty ones. "He said he wanted to go and shoot a couple of people over there," said Harry L. Riddle, Sr., a Morganton banker and old friend of Ervin's. "He wanted to sue them all, take them to court. His father was a very high-tempered man. But Sam—there's no venom in Sam—Sam went and got him back." He told his father, according to other accounts, that if his opponent wanted the election that badly, he could have it.

He and his father were very active in Democratic Party politics. He managed the primary campaigns in Burke County of three governors, and one year acted as chairman of the local party. His father made rip-roaring speeches for a number of candidates but, except for the judgeship race in 1900, never sought office himself.

Political blood ran thick in many of those mountain counties.

Ervin told a Young Democratic Club banquet in 1967 the story of Uncle Billy Hallyburton, a local magistrate, and his lifelong friend, Calton Chiles, who had a falling out over politics.

Uncle Billy joined the Populists in 1896, and Chiles caught wind of it. When confronted by his friend with this "foul slander," Uncle Billy said, "That is no slander; that is the truth."

Chiles replied, "You remember when we were boys and we joined the church together and promised to get down on our knees and pray for each other every night for as long as we lived? Well, Brother Billy, I have kept that promise. Every night before I got into bed I have gotten down on my knees and in my supplication to the Almighty I have prayed for you. But, Brother Billy, from now on you can do your own goddam praying!"

If joining the Populists in 1896 was a transgression, joining the Republicans at any time was mortal sin. There was quite a bit of Union sentiment in Burke County during the Civil War, which resulted in bitter rivalries that exist to this day. It was not just rhetoric for a man like Ervin to denounce the Republican Party, but more a part of his soul. He would stick with Democratic candidates, up to and including presidential candidates, through thick and thin—and in recent years it was mighty thin.

Ervin's father got very exercised in 1928 over the attacks on Democratic candidate Al Smith's Catholicism, and fired off a letter to *The Asheville Citizen* on the subject of religious liberty. "This provision is embodied in the constitution of the nation and in that of every state of the union and he who would lay unhallowed hands upon or nullify this safeguard of the rights of free men, whether he knows it or not, is a dangerous enemy of free government among mankind."

Throughout his long career, Ervin came by many of his opinions because of things that touched him in a personal way. The converse—that he held fast to other views because things did not personally touch him—is also true. He worked to secure legal rights for mental patients because he represented many of them, and charged many juries as to the legal meaning of insanity.

He became interested in bail reform because of his many legal contacts with moonshiners. "Their only vice was makin' moonshine likker and they felt that they were doin' no harm, that they had a prescriptive right to do that. They were honorable, paid their debts, told the truth." A prison official told him they made very well-behaved inmates. Many of these upstanding citizens, unable to pay bail while awaiting trial, languished in jails where, as a former client once wrote to him, there were many bad and disreputable men and he didn't want to associate with them.

So North Carolina moonshiners contributed to one of the most advanced reforms in American criminal justice. Sam Ervin's 1966 Bail Reform Act permits defendants of good character to be released on their own recognizance pending trial. It applies, of course, to many other categories of persons accused of crime besides those in the honorable profession of making illegal whiskey.

"There was a time up in Burke County it wasn't necessary for cups to be empty because they had a lot of fruit jars and a lot of what they call moonshine likker. And we had a fella named Joshua Hawkins who was charged with manufacturing moonshine likker down in the federal court before Judge James E. Boyd. And Judge Boyd was one of these judges who loved to kid everybody—the jurors, the lawyers, the parties to the case. And Joshua Hawkins was sittin' back in the back of the courtroom and they called the case against him and Joshua Hawkins answered 'here' and got up and started down the center aisle agoin' to the bar to be tried. And Judge Boyd said, 'Mr. Hawkins, I noticed your Christian name is Joshua. Are you the Joshua that the Bible tells us about who made the sun stand still at Jericho?' And Mr. Hawkins said, 'No, your honor. I'm the Joshua what's accused of makin' the moon shine in Burke.' "

Soon after Ervin began practicing law, his minister, Carey Gregory, asked if he would teach a men's Bible class on Sundays. With the same dread he had felt about praying in public, the young lawyer begged off, saying he was not spiritually equipped for that sort of thing. Gregory replied, "If people waited until they were fit to do the Lord's work, none of the Lord's work would ever be done. I've observed your life and I don't think you've ever been guilty of as much bad conduct as the apostle Peter was. He denied the Lord; he didn't even know Him when the Lord was in trouble."

So Ervin took up the Lord's work on Sunday mornings and stuck with it for several years. It was a discipline which caused him to soak up a fair amount of theology and commit to memory much of the great poetry and most of the dictates of the King James version of the Bible. He did not consciously memorize them, but, like most things he read and reread, they became part of him; they blossomed in his writing and his speaking, and he believed their stern, simple formulas: be strong and of good courage; a good name is better than precious ointment; men love darkness rather than light because their deeds are evil; whatsoever a man soweth. . . .

He did not take everything he read literally. "The story of the creation, for example: I think it's entirely immaterial whether you think that God created the world in six days or whether you think the earth was created by an evolutionary process that required eons of time. The fact is that human beings are here and it's not so important how they got here as what they're going to do while they are here." But the Bible taught fundamental principles of morality to guide one's uncertain footsteps.

He also joined the local lodge of the Scottish Rite Masons, an ancient fraternal order that teaches, with the help of elaborate symbolic ceremonies, simple precepts of morality, charity, and obedience to the law of the land. The only political interest of Masonry or Freemasonry is to maintain strict separation of church and state. Its traditions stretch back long before the

Founding Fathers, many of whom, including Washington and Franklin, were members.

Ervin believed in God as the force that took blind atoms and shaped them into man and the universe. He had to look no further than the majestic mountains around him to find all the evidence he needed to confirm the existence of a supreme being. And from that conclusion, it was only a step further to belief in life after death. "After all," he said in a speech at a Masonic banquet in 1967, "there is nothing more miraculous or mysterious in immortality than there is in our life on earth or the existence of the universe."

"Another thing about immortality," he said, sitting in his library one afternoon six years later, "is that God has put something here—at least nature affords something—that satisfies almost every desire of mankind. If there is no afterlife, that's about the only hunger the human heart has for which there's no satisfaction."

He could think of no better description of life in the hereafter than the imagery of Kipling's "L'Envoi." He recited the entire poem, lyrically and flawlessly:

> When Earth's last picture is painted,
>   and the tubes are twisted and dried,
> When the oldest colors have faded,
>   and the youngest critics have died,
> We shall rest, and, faith, we shall need it—
>   lie down for an eon or two,
> Till the Master of All Good Workmen
>   shall put us to work anew.
>
> And those that were good shall be happy:
>   they shall sit in a golden chair,
> They shall splash at a ten-league canvas
>   with brushes of comets' hair;
> They shall find real saints to draw from—
>   Magdalene, Peter and Paul;
> They shall work for an age at a sitting,
>   and never be tired at all!

And only the Master shall praise us,
  and only the Master shall blame;
And no one shall work for money,
  and no one shall work for fame;
But each for the joy of the working,
  and each in his separate star,
Shall draw the Thing as he sees It
  for the God of Things as They Are!

It had become unfashionable in the cynical postwar years to express emotions; it was a "so-what" era marked by caution and disillusionment. That is why Ervin made such an impression on those attending his class reunion at Chapel Hill in 1929. Oliver Ransom, a friend and classmate of Ervin's, had been killed in the war, leaving his new bride and a son he had never met. When his son, by then ten years old, was introduced, Ervin moistened several eyes. He stood and spoke of duty and heroism and, in the words of Rupert Brooke, of those who:

. . . poured out the red, sweet wine of youth,
Gave up the years of work and joy,
And that unhoped serene that men call age;
And these that would have been their sons,
- They gave their immortality.

"I was transfixed to hear this person," said Gladys Coates, the wife of Ervin's former schoolmate. He was tall, erect, and slender, with an eagle nose and sparkling blue eyes; she thought he resembled a Sargent portrait. "I knew he traveled in his own orbit and he wasn't afraid to express his feelings."

* * *

ERVIN HAD BUILT up a successful law practice by the late 1920's, earning somewhere around $9,000 a year. When the stock market crashed and the depression set in it seemed like the Reconstruction era all over again. The South, already depressed, sank to the bottom of the economic curve. Ervin's income fell to about $2,000, and for the only time in his life he was in debt. But many people were far worse off, and he gave whenever he could to those who stopped him in the street for money to buy a cup of coffee.

The impact of the depression so affected Ervin that, in spite of his fear of the tyranny of the federal bureaucracy, he revered Franklin Delano Roosevelt. He listened avidly to FDR's fireside broadcasts and applauded when he heard the President say on March 4, 1933, "The only thing we have to fear is fear itself—nameless, unreasoning, unjustified terror which paralyzes needed efforts to convert retreat into advance."

But Ervin's father, nearly eighty at this time, seemed to fear Roosevelt more than the depression. He got so irritated at the New Deal that he was almost ready to renounce his lifelong allegiance to the Democratic Party. Imagine the government meddling in the affairs of business and agriculture, regulating hours and wages paid in factories, acres that could be cultivated, and extravagantly spending money it did not have. It was just too much.

He considered it a sure way to turn the Democratic Party, "with which we, our fathers and grandfathers before us have been affiliated, [into] a socialist, agrarian party and we are to come under the rule of a dictator and bureaucrats with power centered in Washington." States would be deprived of their constitutional rights to "regulate their own internal domestic affairs," he wrote to the *Greensboro Daily News* in December, 1935.

"Unless the administration and the new dealers, the Wallaces, Tugwells, Frankfurters and others of that ilk who surround the throne are checked in their mad career and we return to the ways of our fathers and again have some respect for the constitution, I fear private, industrial and national bankruptcy followed by inflation and repudiation and above all I fear that the miners and sappers who are steadily at work will finally undermine and overthrow our form and system of government, establishing in its stead a socialist government ruled by a dictator or bring about a revolution in the attempt." His son never shared that disillusionment with Roosevelt: "I didn't agree with him on all his policies but I thought that on the whole he saved the country from a very serious situation."

However, Ervin felt that Roosevelt should not have run for a fourth term, and that those around him who urged him to do so did him and the country a grave disservice. "I felt his ill health affected his mental capacity to deal with Stalin. When Roosevelt at his fourth inaugural had to take his oath of office in the White House and couldn't make a public appearance, I began to suspect that he was in a very much deteriorated state and that it would have been better for his reputation if those around him had kept him from running a fourth time."

* * *

HE HAD OFTEN ENCOUNTERED death during war, but death at the hands of the state was something Ervin could not stand to play a part in. He favored capital punishment in the abstract but he could not bear to see his clients or those over whom he later sat in judgment go to the gas chamber.

One of them did, a black man who had broken into the infirmary at the North Carolina School for the Deaf and raped a sick twelve-year-old girl. Curiously, the suspect was found asleep in the infirmary. The judge assigned the Ervins and another lawyer to defend the man, and they did the best they could under the circumstances. But there was an ugly mood in Morganton over the crime. "We had one fellow on the jury who had a very peculiar sense of humor and other jurors told me that when they went out to make up the verdict that somebody facetiously asked whether it would be a hung jury. And this fella said, 'If we go out there and say not guilty, we'll be a hung jury.' "

It was, as Ervin said, an atrocious offense, and the man was sentenced to die. It was an almost unwritten law in the South that black men who have carnal knowledge of white women against their wishes must die. Such rape is considered by many, including Ervin, worse than murder, because in their minds it forever shames and damages the victim.

The fidelity with which this unwritten law was carried out is attested to by the number of blacks who were executed for the offense. It may be true, as Ervin believed, that the reason so many blacks were sentenced to death was that so many blacks succumbed to the urge to rape white women. But one would think from a look at the executioner's roll that whites never had the inclination to rape black women.

Ervin was severely criticized for appealing the case to the State Supreme Court. The appeal was based on very technical grounds. The judge, he said, should not have been holding court in Burke County since the regular judge was available. The higher court rejected his argument. Ervin received $12.50 from the court for his services in defending the man, and spent $80 of his own to appeal the case.

One of the really sensational murder-rape cases in the county's history involved poor Gladys Kincaid. The sheriff followed her killer up into the hills and shot him dead, and the story was all over the papers. Soon afterward, Ervin was asked to defend a black man accused of chasing a young white girl with intent to rape her. Ervin suspected that she might have the Kincaid case on her mind, and under cross-examination got her to admit that the assault had taken place in her imagination. "As a matter of fact, this man never did get anywhere near you, did he?" Ervin asked the girl. "No," she confessed.

Crime was a daily preoccupation with the young lawyer. Crime, lust, and death. He could not begin to estimate the number of murder cases he appeared in, either as a lawyer or judge. It was a painful experience for a sensitive person who tried to find good in the most vicious individuals.

One of the most intriguing murder cases Ervin had involved the corpse of Bud McKinney. McKinney lived in the mountainous section of the county known as Jonas Ridge. One day he disappeared. The sheriff searched for days and finally found the body buried in a shallow grave in a laurel thicket near his home. A number of clues turned up in McKinney's home: drops of blood on the staircase, bloodstains on a tarpaulin upstairs, a small box that had been pried open with bloody hands. The theory was that Bud McKinney had been murdered in the upstairs part of his house, carried down the steps, and buried in the laurel thicket.

Who killed Bud McKinney? One man was tried for the murder but there wasn't enough evidence to convict him. Almost a year went by before Mabel Percy, who lived up in that part of the county, came forward. Beau Franklin and Charlie Franklin, no relation to Beau, had done it, she said. Beau Franklin claimed he was innocent, but he had a bad reputation going for him and was regarded as a dangerous character. He had been convicted years before of killing his son-in-law and had served several years in the penitentiary for manslaughter. The man who had served as special prosecutor and put him away was Sam Ervin. But he and Ervin had wiped the slate clean since then.

"One day I was drivin' through Jonas Ridge from bein' in court over in Avery County and Beau, who had served a term for murderin' his son-in-law, was back home. I was goin' down the road, sort of the lonesome road, and Beau flagged me down. I didn't know what he might do to me, having prosecuted him. But he greeted me like a long lost brother and he said, 'I found some fox cubs; I want you to stop in and look at my fox cubs.' So he was very cordial to me."

Nevertheless, Ervin was somewhat surprised and apprehensive when Franklin called him down to the jail and said to him, "You sent me to prison last time; I want you to keep me out this time." It was the beginning of one of the most interesting murder cases Ervin ever handled as a lawyer.

"Beau protested he was absolutely innocent. But they had this preliminary hearing and Mabel Percy identified him as the man that she saw kill Bud McKinney at his (Beau's) house in the presence of his lady friend named Pansy Townsend. She testified that the killing occurred about 3 o'clock in the afternoon and they hid his body up at the barn and took it down and disposed of it at night."

Another man, Lons Henson, was questioned as a witness to the murder. He refused to give the state any information and was put in jail as a material witness. The first person he talked to was Sam Ervin; he called him down to the jail and said he wanted to make a statement. Ervin got him to sign a sworn statement in the presence of witnesses that he knew nothing about the murder, and that the last time he had seen Bud McKinney was when McKinney stopped by his home to pay him for some flour.

The grand jury indicted Beau Franklin, Charlie Franklin, and Pansy Townsend for the murder.

It happened forty years ago, but as Ervin told it he was back in the small, hushed courtroom, with its rows of spectators seated at an incline as though in a theater. The drawn, hard, distant faces of witnesses and defendants who came down out of the mountains to stand before the only government they would ever know all came back to life.

In picking the jury, Ervin had chosen a man he figured to be "driftwood," that is, he didn't have a mind of his own and would follow whatever the others decided.

"It was a queer case. I don't know why the state did what it did. But anyway, first they put on Lons Henson and he testified that he was present with Mabel Percy and Pansy Townsend and Charlie Franklin and Beau Franklin and that Beau Franklin killed Bud McKinney by hittin' him on the head with a stick and it happened about midnight in Beau Franklin's house."

The state's case seemed so full of holes that Ervin could have driven his Model T Ford through it. And he did: "I pulled out my statement that Lons had signed and asked if he didn't give me that statement. And he said, yes, he did. And I said, 'You told me that was the truth in the presence of these witnesses.' And he said yes. And I said, 'Why don't you stick to your story that you told me?' And he said, 'Well, I've been kind of threatened.' He never did tell who threatened him.

"Well, then they put Mabel Percy on and I cross-examined her. And she couldn't even describe Bud McKinney. I was satisfied she never saw Bud McKinney in her life because he was a man who had a mouthful of gold teeth and was baldheaded. And she couldn't tell whether he had long hair or red hair or black hair or gold teeth or no teeth or pure white teeth.

"Well, she had been having relations with Charlie Franklin and got mad at Charlie because she wanted Charlie to leave his wife and run off with her—so Charlie told me. Well, anyway, she said the killin' occurred about 3 o'clock in the afternoon and that Lons Henson was not even there when it occurred. See: he had said it was midnight and that she was there with him."

That, in substance, was the state's case.

Ervin took part in many murder cases and always had more luck defending his clients on the grounds of self-defense, for psychological reasons. "If a man denies that he committed the murder, he's always in danger if they've got any circumstantial evidence against him of any kind. Because the instinct of the sleuth lurks in every man and he tries to figure out who the guilty party is. But if the man goes on the stand, admits the killin' and claims he was fightin' in self-defense, he stands a whole lot better chance of getting clear."

But Beau Franklin was an unusual witness. He was "one of the coolest and calmest witnesses I ever saw on a witness stand and he had a tremendous native intelligence. He went up, made a fine witness, denied he had any knowledge, denied he'd done anything."

Ervin then introduced evidence to show that the murder had taken place at Bud McKinney's (the murdered man's) house, instead of at Beau Franklin's: the blood stains on the stairs and the tarpaulin and the bloody fingerprints on the box. But the judge said, "You can't do that; that's circumstantial evidence."

He got out a case he had tried as a lawyer in which it was ruled that at a murder trial the defense cannot show by circumstances that someone else committed the crime. "Judge," Ervin protested, "that can't be the law."

"So I went out and looked up the law and I found plenty of cases that entitled it. But the judge would't recede from his ruling, wouldn't let me put that in evidence, which I thought was very strange." So Ervin told him:

" 'I don't know what you can do in a case like this where the only thing I have to argue is that Bud McKinney committed suicide and then went out and buried himself.' But the judge was very patient with me and ruled against me still. I think I'd have gotten a new trial."

But that wasn't necessary. The jury went out, and returned saying it couldn't agree. The juror Ervin had spotted as "driftwood" had tied it up. The other eleven were for acquittal.

The case was never retried and was eventually dismissed. "Years after that, Beau Franklin died. And I've been told that on his death bed he admitted that he was the man that killed Bud McKinney."

Sam Ervin as a child

Samuel J. Ervin, Sr.

Family Snapshots, 1916

Sam's sister Laura, left,
and Margaret Bell.

Laura, far left; Margaret Bell, leaning on shoulder;
Sam's sister Catharine, sitting; Sam, in bow tie.

Laura Powe Ervin

Margaret Bell, on rear wheel; Catharine, steering;
Laura, behind hood; Sam, lying on ground.

Catharine, left;
Sam, in hat, behind net.

Senior picture, University of North Carolina, 1917.

Miss Margaret Bell, later Mrs. Sam Ervin, at 17.

Ervin during World War I.

Ervin in 1923 at the state legislature.

Ervin in his hometown law office.
© *New York Daily News.*

Ervin arriving at Union Station in Washington, 1954. From left, his daughters Laura Powe and Leslie, the senator, Mrs. Ervin, Betty (wife of Sam III), and Sam J. Ervin III. *World Wide Photos, Inc.*

Senator Sam Ervin reenacts his oath-taking with then Vice President Richard Nixon, June 11, 1954. *World Wide Photos, Inc.*

Senator Ervin presiding at the Watergate hearings, 1973.
World Wide Photos, Inc.

The Watergate committee in action.
Washington Post photo.

'NOW, MISTAH PREZDINT, YEW KNOW AH'M JUS' A SIMPLE COUNTRY LAWYA, AN' US NAWTH CALINA FOLKS DON' PLAY NOTHIN' CEP'N OCCASIONAL GAME A DOMINOES — NONE A THIS HAH CLASS INTEELECTUAL CHESS — CHECK ...'

7. Itinerant Judge

Dost thou not tremble to assume thy seat,
And judge thy fellow travelers to the tomb?
Dost thou not falter as thy lips repeat
Thy Comrade's downfall, thy Companion's doom?

WALTER MALONE

MOST GOOD LAWYERS want to be judges, even those who suspect they would be happier and wealthier if they stayed right where they are. Sam Ervin wanted to be a judge.

He got his first chance in 1935, serving part-time as county judge, sitting up in the old gray courtroom disposing of petty cases while continuing to work as a lawyer. But what really interested him was a Superior Court judgeship, a job which beckoned toward the end of 1936. He discreetly asked friends to mention his name to Governor Clyde Hoey. Hoey got the message and appointed him in January, 1937 to be a special Superior Court judge.

The appointment was well thought of. "The new judge," said the *Winston-Salem Journal*, "has one of the keenest legal minds in North Carolina, a high conception of the ethical and equitable in law, and possesses a genial and disarming personality." The *Journal* said Ervin's father was one of the state's outstanding lawyers, "and the keen intellectual qualities of the sire are mingled with intuitive understanding and a tolerant sense of humor."

Ervin sat on the bench for seven years, long enough to become sick at heart—and hurting in his stomach—at the endless stream of human beings over whom he had to pass judgment.

Unlike the regular judges who operate within the few counties which constituted their districts, Ervin was a rover. The special judges were moved all about the state, plugging holes in the judicial system and relieving crowded court dockets. He was on the road forty weeks of the year. He did his judging mostly in urban areas like Charlotte, Winston-Salem, and Durham, but he also traveled the circuit all over the western mountains and down to the eastern coast. He held court five and sometimes six days a week, trying as many as thirty-five cases, including guilty pleas, each day.

At night, when he wasn't poring over the law books, he would hold court among the local lawyers and the other judges. Ervin spent many an evening smoothing the benches and rockers on the porches of hotels and rooming houses, exchanging that most precious and enduring commodity, the courtroom story. On summer evenings the laughter of those men rang robustly as they celebrated the humor, the pathos, and the absurdities of the human condition.

Ervin collected these stories, not in any systematic way, but he remembered them, told them, and retold them until they were part of him. Many years later, the stubborn, cantankerous, wise mountain folk came to life again in the pages of the *Congressional Record* and the records of committee hearings. The stories would disarm earnest witnesses, disrupt serious debates, and infuriate the sponsors of legislation. They would also help destroy a demagogue. But on the court circuit they were told for their own sake.

"That reminds me of the time I was presiding over a first degree murder trial," Ervin would say. "They had a special venire [jury panel] summoned in from another county, and I asked one of these jurors if he could give the defendant a fair trial. He said, 'I think he is guilty of murder in the first degree and he ought to be sent to the gas chamber. But I can give him a fair trial.' "

The word *epithets* recalled an incident concerning a good old-time lawyer, Mose Harshaw. "Mose used to be a lawyer in Caldwell County, which adjoins my county. Sometimes his words became mixed up. Mose had a client who was convicted of assault and battery upon another man who had applied epithets to him. In begging the court to extend mercy to his client, Mose said: 'I hope that in passing sentence on my client upon his conviction for assault and battery, your honor will bear in mind that he was provoked to do so by the epitaphs hurled at him by the witness.' "

An old justice of the peace was exasperated by the tactics of a young lawyer trying his first case. "The young lawyer kept rising and exclaiming: 'I object. You are not proceeding according to law.' Finally the old magistrate could stand it no longer. He shouted: 'Young man, quit jumping up and saying, "I object. You are not proceeding according to law." I'll have you to understand I am running this court. The law hasn't got a damn thing to do with it.' "

It now takes about an hour to drive from Morganton to Newland, the county seat of Avery County. It is only forty miles away, up and over the Blue Ridge. But when Ervin went there to hold court, the trip took twenty-four hours. The only way to go was by train: he had to leave Sunday morning, stop in the town of Marion for lunch, get back on board for the trip to Johnson City, Tennessee, spend the night, and the next morning catch a ride on the "Tweetsie Railroad" for the last leg of the journey to Newland. Once there he did not want to leave, and held court the whole week, until it was time to reverse the process and go home.

In all seven years as a judge Ervin missed going home for the weekend only once, when he was icebound in the far western corner of the state. Later, cars and highways simplified the traveling but took away that special institution created by the lonesomeness of judges and lawyers who found storytelling a tolerable way of passing the time.

Ervin received $8,500 a year as a judge, much less than he could have been making at that time as a lawyer, and out of that he paid all his expenses, including car, railroad fare, hotels, and meals. Living on the road was fairly cheap. A decent hotel room cost four dollars a night and a good meal could be had for a dollar. But since Ervin was gone virtually all the time, he did not have much money left over.

His father, eighty-two when his son went on the court, was still holding forth occasionally in the courtroom as a lawyer. He advised Sam, Jr., never to forget that he had once been a lawyer himself, and to be patient with the ones who came before him, especially those he thought to be wrong.

"He also said the first quality of a judge should be that he was a gentleman and to treat everybody with consideration, lawyers and parties and witnesses and jurors and everybody else. Try to make them as comfortable as possible."

Ervin took the advice literally on some days. On the first day of a hot spell in Winston-Salem he told the jurors to take off their coats, on the second day the lawyers, and, on the third day, he took his own coat off and held court thereafter in his shirtsleeves. In contrast to the days when judges put on wigs and gowns and were escorted from their quarters to the courthouse by a bailiff with drawn sword, judges in Ervin's day did not wear robes.

Ervin loved the law. It was imperfect in many ways but represented the best efforts of men to govern themselves. He upheld what he believed to be its letter and its spirit with all of his nervous, but seemingly limitless energy. A trial judge, he felt, was entrusted with one of the most important offices in the country. He was the only contact the vast majority of people had with their government, "about the only man who sort of incarnates in their eyes the magistrate of the law."

Ervin considered civil law far more interesting than criminal law. It was more voluminous and full of new things to learn, harder, and therefore more challenging. "You enjoyed the stimulation of finding out some principle of law that you didn't know to start with." He took the cases as they came along: simple cases, difficult cases, boring cases, exciting cases. Some judges, Ervin said, do not like to exercise their "mental muscles" very much. Ervin apparently kept his in top condition. "I had a lawyer over in Rutherford County pay me a tribute one time by saying I could start in a case knowing nothing about it but before I'd been in it very long I'd know more about it than the lawyers on either side. Because I'd go out and study."

He did his studying in lawyers' offices at night, slogging through the books to prepare for the next day's cases, and if he could anticipate what was coming up the next week he would spend his weekends buried in the law books in his library at home.

There was some companionship when he was on the road, mostly from lawyers and other judges. They went out to dinner together, told stories, and talked endlessly about law. But more often than not Ervin was left to himself. He carried a small library of books, including detective stories (especially Sherlock Holmes), in the back of his car. They were his hotel companions, his mistresses of the night.

There was not very much passion in civil law; that was another reason he preferred it to criminal law. Ervin was full of emotions himself, and managed to keep them just below the surface. But that was harder to do when he was face-to-face with a pleading human being.

About the only criminal cases he really enjoyed were the ones in which he could show compassion toward the defendants. His sentences were generally less severe than those handed down by other judges. He tried, as he said, "to temper the winds to shorn lambs." When defendants appeared to be innocent or on the side of the law, Ervin became their advocate on the bench.

A poor black man was indicted for drunk driving one Sunday in Pineville, a small town in the shadow of Charlotte. A policeman saw him coming down the street, zigzagging from one side to the other with a carload of people. Furthermore, the man seemed to have the smell of rubbing alcohol on his breath. When he took the stand in Judge Ervin's court, he claimed he had been cold sober.

"The black man took the stand and said he was on his way home from church that day when he was arrested. And he said—now it was during the Second World War when they had tires rationed—he said, 'I'm a poor man. I have a hard time getting tires. So all I could do, I got two tires for my front wheels and one was a big tire and the other was a little one. The little tire was on the left hand side and it would pull me to the left of the road and I jerked it back to the right. That's the reason I was going somewhat zigzagged.'

"Well, the prosecuting attorney conducted a very vigorous examination of this man, but he didn't shake his testimony much and finally at the end he asked one question too many. He said, 'You say you were on your way home from church. Well, then suppose you tell his honor and the jury the text the preacher preached on.'

"And just as quick as a flash this black said he preached on the writings of the prophet Nahum where it says that God is slow to anger and is great in power and will not at all acquit the wicked." Someone handed Ervin a copy of the Bible and he noted with approval that the defendant had quoted the passage perfectly. Ervin had decided by that time that the man was innocent and, after adjourning court for the night, went up to his hotel room and found the short book of Nahum in the Gideon Bible. When he saw that it described "jumping chariots" rushing to and fro through the streets of Nineveh, he decided he would have some fun with the jury.

"Gentlemen of the jury," he said the next morning, "in order that my charge might harmonize with the writings of the Prophet Nahum, I will use the word chariot to mean automobile." Then he went on to say that the defendant was charged with driving a jumping chariot through the town of Nineveh on the Sabbath day while under the influence of intoxicating liquor. But he contends that "he has not even emulated the example of St. Timothy and taken a little wine for his stomach's sake and he also contends that if he ever drinks again he's not going to start out with rubbing alcohol."

Then Ervin instructed the jury: "If the state has satisfied you beyond a reasonable doubt that the defendant drove a jumping chariot on a public street in the town of Nineveh while under the influence of intoxicating liquor, you will return a verdict of guilty. But if you find that at that time the defendant was sober enough to remember the text that the preacher preached on, then you will return a verdict of not guilty."

The jury went out and filed right back in with an acquittal.

It helps to have a sympathetic judge, especially if you've known him all your life. Such was the case with Aunt Elsie, who had bought a large piece of property near Morganton with her inheritance. But the deed was mistakenly made out to her husband because he had purchased the land with her money. Her stepchildren by her second marriage tried to take the land away since it was not technically hers.

Aunt Elsie's case would have been a lot easier if she had not retained Mr. C. C. Lisenbee, whom Ervin described as "not the most profound lawyer." She took heart when she saw Ervin come into the courtroom. "Honey," she said, "is you going to hold this here court?" When he said yes, she added, "Honey, I'm expectin' you to help me win my lawsuit."

Things went badly for Aunt Elsie, however, because Lisenbee, her lawyer, kept asking improper questions and Ervin had to sustain the other side's objections. Aunt Elsie looked at Ervin as if he had sold her down the river. But there was a rule of law that if one party furnishes the purchase price of land for another, then the second party is a "constructive trustee" for the first unless otherwise agreed. The problem was that Lisenbee did not understand the rule, even after Ervin prodded him.

"Mr. Lisenbee, don't you want to amend your complaint?" Ervin asked.

"No, my complaint's áll right."

"I just thought you might want to amend your complaint to allege that your client furnished the purchase money for the land and that the title was taken in the name of her husband, her late husband, and that since she furnished the purchase money and he got the title that he held the land as her trustee, for her benefit."

Lisenbee finally got it. "Since your honor mentions it, I would like to amend."

"Suppose you dictate your amendment to the court reporter," Ervin said helpfully.

"Will your honor mind dictatin' it for me?"

Although Ervin had to dictate the amendment for the hapless attorney, he nevertheless gave the other side what he thought was a completely fair trial. When he stated Aunt Elsie's side to the jury, she sat there and said, "Bless Jesus, that's so. Bless Jesus, that's so." And of course when he stated the other side she looked at him again as if he had sold her down the river.

When the jury came back with a verdict for Aunt Elsie, she said to Ervin, "Thank you, honey, thank you."

"Don't thank me, Aunt Elsie. Thank the jury. The jury's the one that decided the case in your favor."

"Yes," she said, "But honey, they wouldn't a done it without yo' help."

Later on, a lawyer, joking with Ervin and others in a courtroom before the court met, told the other lawyers, "I just want to warn you members of the bar that Judge Ervin has got a reputation of being a fair judge. But if you go up to Burke County and you have a case against Aunt Elsie McKesson, don't you let him try it."

While on the court, Ervin had the privilege of having one of the cases he presided over appealed to the Supreme Court and upheld. The majority opinion was written by one of his guiding lights in law school, Felix Frankfurter. It was a divided, controversial decision that showed that in at least one respect, marriage, Ervin was no libertarian. "At best, marriage is for keeps," he said years later. "The greatest relationship to be found between two people is an enduring marriage."

The case involved a man and a woman who had left their respective spouses and gone to Nevada for quickie divorces. They then married each other and returned as husband and wife to North Carolina. But according to North Carolina law, they were still married to their old spouses. They were taken to Judge Ervin's court on charges of bigamous cohabitation. Ervin instructed the jury that the divorces were not valid if the two went to Nevada "simply and solely for the purpose of obtaining" them and neglected to set up permanent residence there. The jury promptly found them guilty, and they were given prison sentences.

Speaking for the court, Frankfurter said in *Williams* v. *North Carolina* (1944), "Divorce, like marriage, is of concern not merely to the immediate parties. It affects personal rights of the deepest significance. It also touches basic interests of society." To allow the law of one state to wreck the social institutions of another state "would be intolerable." There was nothing to suggest that Ervin had not submitted the issue fairly to the jury, he concluded.

Justice Hugo L. Black, joined by William O. Douglas, wrote a stinging dissent, saying that until that day Anglo-American law had steadfastly maintained that before anyone could be convicted of a crime he must be proven guilty beyond a reasonable doubt. The man and woman had every right to assume that since they were legally divorced and then married in one state, they should not have to face the penitentiary in another. "The fact that two people can be deprived of their constitutional rights impels me to protest as vigorously as I can," Black said. Implicit in the decision, he said, was that "divorces are an unmitigated evil, and that the law can and should force unwilling persons to live with each other."

*   *   *

SAM ERVIN TRIED TO PASS along the same love of truth and integrity that his father had drilled into him not so much by lectures or punishment but by example. That is why Leslie and Laura, his two daughters, were shocked one day to find him hiding in the yard behind some boxwood bushes. Embarrassed, but continuing to maintain his hiding place, he explained that a woman client who had been driving him crazy was there to see him and he did not want her to find him. She would talk to him, and he would listen patiently for hours, about how she wanted to rest in a mausoleum instead of a grave. Both his daughters recalled the incident with fondness and a touch of lingering surprise. It was the first time anyone ever saw Ervin duck something or someone.

Although his children did not see much of him while they were growing up, they regarded him with a mixture of awe and bemused fondness. He communicated with them at great length on some occasions and on others not at all. If he became angry with them he rarely showed it. He left most of the upbringing to his wife and to their cook, Essie Tate.

Sam J. Ervin III was born in 1926, then at four-year intervals, Leslie and Laura Powe. All three of them tried, on numerous occasions, to distract their father from his work or reading but soon realized that he could surround himself with an impenetrable child-noise barrier.

One day, when Leslie was a child, she saw her father walking toward her on a street in Morganton. She stood watching as he sailed past her like a stately ship, the private motors of his mind churning, oblivious to the world and the little girl who was too shy to call out or tug at his sleeve. Her father, the judge, was deeply absorbed in the law or the facts of a case over which he would preside the next day. It wasn't that he would bite her head off if she intercepted him. In fact he always seemed to have time for his children, and could shift gears easily from his world to theirs. Though he was an easy touch for candy or money for toys, they usually left him alone, just in case his thoughts were more important.

Conversations at home were often about the law or individual liberty. The children knew that they themselves were important to their father, and that even though he might disapprove of their goals in life, they were free to have them. Ervin had a ritual at home of bringing up current subjects and getting his children to discuss them, then arguing the case for the opposite side and forcing them to defend their positions. "Consequently, when he went off to Washington, I wasn't sure what his views were," his son said.

He was always dropping little poems or aphorisms. It infuriated Laura to have him come up with a silly little saying to make her laugh when what she really wanted to do was scream and holler. "A merry heart doeth good like a medicine," he would say, with his bemused cherub grin, and she would find it hard to maintain her scowl. They would get quarters for memorizing poems. Lines from Kipling, Alfred Noyes, or Rupert Brooke were the most appreciated.

He was always reciting poems to them, like Kipling's "The Gods of the Copybook Headings." It was one of his favorites because it dealt with eternal truths: without motherhood, the human race has had it; let down your arms and your enemies enslave you; the wages of sin is death; if you don't work you die. The gods of the copybook headings were those who reigned over the aphorisms schoolchildren were required to memorize. The gods of the marketplace were the smooth-tongued wizards who proclaimed that virtue was whatever worked, even if its benefits were temporary.

> And that after this is accomplished, and
>   the brave new world begins
> When all men are paid for existing and
>   no man must pay for his sins,
> As surely as Water will wet us, as surely
>   as Fire will burn,
> The Gods of the Copybook Headings
>   with terror and slaughter return!

Life viewed in those terms was simple and uncomplicated, especially if one happened to be smart and self-reliant. Ervin's children were both. All of them excelled in college, and Sam and Leslie graduated from law school with honors. "I've often thought," Laura said, "that if any of us were incapable of doing well in school, it would have been difficult for him to handle."

Although Leslie became a lawyer as well as a mother, she was not encouraged to follow her father into the traditional man's world of law. She did it on her own, partly out of curiosity about what so preoccupied her father. He did not discourage her, but he did make it rather plain where he thought her true interests should lie. He had a maddening little number that went something like this: "Men were born with big shoulders to carry the weight of the world; women with big hips to bear the children for the next generation." He said it in his usual kidding way, but Leslie always suspected that he was at least partly serious. When his daughters got into an argument with him over the proper role of women, Laura said he would recite "an awful poem" that compared girls to pure little white birds, and "that would defeat us right there. We gave up."

Ervin drove off to some mountain town at the beginning of each week, singing his songs and carrying along his books, and was gone all week. Frequently he brought his tangled legal problems home on weekends. Except for the rare occasions when he took them swimming—and then, it seemed, out of a sense of duty—he didn't do very much fathering in the traditional sense.

Like his father, Sam Ervin planted a victory garden during the war. It was the only time his children ever saw him in bib overalls. He had never been much of a gardener, but he made up in zest what he lacked in precision. To plant his own patch of potatoes, he sliced up some he already had, but neglected to make sure that each one he stuffed into the ground contained an eye.

The few times his family got him off to the beach for a proper vacation, he would wind up enjoying it more than anyone. Then he might decide to stay for several weeks, lolling about by the ocean and splashing in the surf.

On the whole Ervin was not much for discipline. Sometimes he denied the children movies as a punishment and, on at least one occasion when young Sam left the house without saying where he was going and did not return until after mealtime, his father acted swiftly and decisively with a switch.

He believed in self-discipline, however. In fact he regarded it as a great tragedy if parents neglected to teach self-discipline to their children. "If people don't learn in their youth to discipline themselves, they are sooner or later going to be disciplined by life, and life is not going to be a very easy teacher when it goes to imposing discipline on them." But the way to teach discipline was not to order them around like a drill sergeant; it was to practice self-discipline in their presence. "Example's a much greater teacher—sort of like the old expression, 'What you do speaks so loud, I can't hear what you say.'"

On Sundays they were all marched off to church, where their father taught the men's Bible classes. Church was where the moral foundations were laid, where one learned what was right and what was wrong, and one behaved accordingly.

Staying out late was not viewed as one of life's virtues, especially not for young ladies. Their father took a dim view of some of their boyfriends, particularly a painter who was dating Laura. He had long hair, which in the early 1950's was definitely out, and he committed the unpardonable sin of painting a nude female body, which Laura in turn asked her father to take back to Morganton from Chapel Hill one year. "Daddy didn't like that one bit."

Their father was always extremely kind toward blacks, particularly those who worked for them. When Essie Tate, their cook, died, the family drove down from Washington for her funeral. But in spite of the kindness, the children were not very comfortable with some of the old traditions in Morganton, like blacks looking for work or handouts automatically coming to the back door.

All three of Ervin's children disagreed with him about civil rights but they understood that he was a product of his generation as they were of theirs. It was that simple. His son, a judge like his father, said, "I might have voted differently on civil rights, a result of a difference of generation and outlook. He was influenced by his period. I never felt his opposition to civil rights bills was based on lack of affection for any individual."

Whereas Ervin felt strongly that all men should be equal but none should be given special privileges, not even to right a long-standing wrong, his son made the point that "If we feel a particular group is dealt with unfairly, it is natural to compensate by giving them greater rights in the present. But perhaps in the long run that's not a wise thing to do."

The Ervin children all went to segregated public schools and, unlike their father, who played with the children of his family's servants, had no black acquaintances. They grew up totally unaware that there was any other way. But because they came out of another generation they accepted new ideas more easily. They respected what their father did because of the way he did it, without—as far as anyone has been able to detect—a trace of racism.

*   *   *

ERVIN'S FINEST MOMENTS in court were not the sort that would live in history. He was so intrigued by the day-to-day entanglements of civil procedure that he rarely had a chance to propound great legal principles. He undoubtedly advanced the right of speedy trial because he was very quick and could settle courtroom disputes without having to excuse himself to go look up the law.

He became irritated with lawyers who neglected their homework, and on one occasion he told two opposing counsel: "Gentlemen, I don't mean to say anything derogatory to anybody, but I'm bound to say that since you don't have any legal authorities, you are like the comforters of Job: you multiply words without knowledge." Lawyers should spend their spare time in the law library, not on the golf courses, he often declared.

But even Judge Ervin could be wrong on occasion. On a case having to do with employment he was decisively shot down by the state Supreme Court. Arthur Causby, an old friend, hung an enduring adage on Ervin: "Sam's not wrong often, but when he's wrong he's bad wrong."

Ervin probably could have used an occasional walk around the golf course. His Spartan sense of duty would not permit him, however, and he allowed the law to dominate him and damage his health. Whether it was from nervousness, overwork, or both, during his seven years as a judge he developed his famous involuntary twitching of the eyebrows. They would jump up and down of their own accord, without his being aware of them, as if to warn of approaching storms.

The criminal cases upset him. He had to sentence two men to their deaths for first degree murder. One was a field worker who confessed that he tried to rape his employer's wife and, when she tried to run, shot her and then bashed in her skull with a shotgun butt. The other murdered a woman who was said to have been a hundred and three years old. He hit her with a stick and snatched a twenty-dollar bill that was pinned to her underclothes.

In both cases, Ervin appointed the best lawyers he could find to defend the men and gave them an extra fee on condition that they appeal the cases to the Supreme Court. It was an unusual precaution for a judge to take, but Ervin found it unsettling, as one of his poets once said, to judge his fellow travelers to the tomb. "I didn't want a man to be executed under a judgment of death assigned by me until the State Supreme Court had found that I had committed no error of law."

In spite of the anguish it caused him, Ervin staunchly supported capital punishment, and felt it was the height of folly to call it cruel and unusual. What the Founding Fathers had in mind in that regard, he contended, were such nasty customs as cutting out the tongues of perjurers. A death for a death was *usual* punishment. Ervin took the brutally simple position that capital punishment may or may not deter others but it obviously prevents a murderer-rapist-kidnapper-arsonist from repeating his crime. "I think there's some crimes that are so atrocious that if society doesn't execute people that commit them a segment of society is going to turn into a mob and execute the party themselves."

Finally he succumbed to the pressure of sitting in judgment over others by coming down with a bleeding ulcer. Looking back on that experience, Ervin felt it was the best thing that could have happened to him. He resigned from the court on December 31, 1943, and began systematically to overcome his nervous tension, to put people problems, if not out of mind, at least far enough away so he could handle them.

It took some time for Ervin to slow himself down. While his son was in training at Fort Sill, Oklahoma, he worried frequently about his father's health. In a letter to his grandmother on September 8, 1944, he confided, "I agree that Dad is working much too hard. Each letter that I receive tells of some new trip of his. I hope that he will take a rest before the work begins to place him under a strain."

Ervin's father, who had wrestled vigorously with life from the swamps of South Carolina to the courtrooms of North Carolina, died on July 13, 1944, at the age of eighty-nine. He had been forced to give up the law a few years before when his eyes and ears began to fail him. He said he hated that "worse than a mess of salt pork." The *News-Herald* called him a "noble patriarch," who stood for "the finest traditions embraced in the term 'southern gentleman.'" An old friend of the Ervins put it differently: "Sam's father wasn't scared of the devil himself."

* * *

CHRISTMAS, 1945, began as a bright, happy day. The war had ended and Sam Ervin was back home in Morganton, where he most liked to be. He and his family, his mother, and brothers and sisters, were all planning to get together later in the afternoon for Christmas dinner.

But for Joe Wilson Ervin, Sam's younger brother, it was a day of anguish and despair. He was alone in his home in Arlington, across the Potomac from Washington, where just a year before his career as a member of Congress had begun. Joe Ervin was exhausted from overwork and his old leg injury was throbbing.

His life had been a series of operations, beginning when he was six and continuing until just before he was elected to Congress. Most of the time in between was spent on crutches. As a child he missed out on most of the games his brothers and sisters played.

The fall from the family apple tree had resulted in osteomyelitis, a painful inflammation of the bone marrow. As soon as the leg seemed to heal from one operation and give him hope that normal life would return, the pains returned, and another operation was necessary. Much of the bone had to be removed and he was left with a permanent limp.

Before wonder drugs came on the scene, one of the treatments for osteomyelitis was to implant maggots, tiny wormlike insects, near the infected bone, place a small cage over the incision so the maggots could not escape, and leave them there to eat away at the diseased bone tissue. It worked, at least temporarily, but it was a mortifying experience for the patient.

Ervin went to the hospital one day to see his brother and Joe told him, "This is the greatest agony I've ever undergone, feeling a live maggot wandering around inside my body. I don't know how I can stand it much longer." Joe Ervin stood it and recovered, and then, in 1944, he was elected to Congress.

If there ever was a politician in the Ervin family, Joe Ervin was the one. All his moves were calculated, deliberate. He was intense, bright, ambitious, and likable. The regard in which younger members of his family held him bordered on hero worship. He knew how to win people's hearts and their votes. He worked his way through the University of North Carolina and established himself as the leading campus politician, generating the personal magnetism which his older brother never felt the need to display.

He was more of a city lawyer than Sam was. In 1925, he moved to Charlotte, a metropolis compared with Morganton, and set about practicing law, patiently building meanwhile toward the day when his political break would come. He drove himself relentlessly, taking a taxi to work every morning at 5 and spending the early morning hours buried in his law books.

Although he walked with a slight limp, he had always seemed able to overcome his handicap. He was a dapper dresser, who wore straw hats in the springtime. He went obligingly to all the parties, and gamely tried to waltz.

When he went to Washington in January, 1945, at the age of forty-three, he threw himself into the job with typical Ervin abandon, working, working, working, and worrying, perhaps more than he should have, about the problems of the world. Unlike Sam, he worried constantly about what his public positions should be. He worked in his office from dawn to well after dark, skipping meals and recreation, causing his colleagues to worry about his health.

North Carolina Congressman Graham (Hap) Barden took

him aside one day and told him to ease up. "I knew of the nights that he was spending in his office working in addition to the time he spent there during the day," Barden said. "He was not at all regular with his meals. It didn't make any difference to him. He felt that he had to be either in his office, in some department of the government, or in this hall attending to his duties. I told him then, in my opinion, his health would be much more secure if he would take a few days off and rest."

"Hap, I just haven't the time," Joe Ervin said.

Joe sent his wife to her parents' home in Morganton that Christmas, promising to join her a few days later. At noon on Christmas day, Sam Ervin got a call from Lamar Caudle, a North Carolinian who was then head of the Criminal Division of the Justice Department. Caudle told him that Joe had been found dead that morning. He had turned on the gas jets on the stove and died of asphyxiation. As Ervin figured it, "He took the notion that his osteomyelitis was coming back on him and it was just too much for him."

He left his wife a note that did not explain why he took his life. It was instead "a love letter," his widow, Susan Graham Williamson, said. "He thanked me for the happiness I had given him and said that no man ever had a sweeter wife."

Ervin's mother, then eighty, had tried to impart to her children the strength to accept whatever came their way, and now she told them not to find fault with Joe for taking his life. But her remorse was not unmixed with shame. A short time later, when her son Sam was being discussed as a candidate for Congress, she told him, "Well, I wouldn't mind you running for Congress because I'd like for people to find out I got one son that can stand up and face life, regardless of what's in it." Sam admonished his mother gently, "You've got to remember I've never been confronted by the discouragement that Joe's had."

North Carolina congressmen who had known Joe Ervin expressed their sympathy for him during a special session in the House on January 14, 1946. They offered the only explanations they could for what he had done. "During my long service as a member of the House of Representatives, I have never known any man to take his duties more seriously or conscientiously, nor to discharge them with greater earnestness, ability, sincerity and fidelity," said Robert L. Doughton. "In fact, in my opinion, overwork and, if possible, taking his duties too seriously, were the main causes of his untimely death."

Ervin at first rejected all suggestions that he become Joe's substitute in Congress. All seven counties in the congressional district put up candidates at the Democratic convention held in Newton. After countless ballots, the situation was deadlocked. Joe Blythe, who later became treasurer of the Democratic National Committee, called Ervin and asked if he could "help us out of a bad spot."

Ervin accepted, but only on the condition that he would serve out the remainder of Joe's term—one year—and not seek reelection. He would uphold his brother's political trust. "I've never had any desire to go to the House of Representatives," he told Blythe.

The Republicans, meanwhile, did not have the heart to give Ervin much opposition. Two of the leading Republicans in Hickory, a nearby city, were the heads of a corporation Ervin was then defending in a lawsuit. He told them, jokingly, that if they did not put up a candidate against him he would be able to keep his mind on the case. Ernest Whisnant said he and his brother Clarence had already considered that and had gotten county politicians to agree to lay off Ervin.

There was at least one Republican, however, who was opposed to rolling over and playing dead. Bill Barkley, a Republican delegate from Burke County, got up at a meeting and said, "Anybody who was a New Dealer ought to have opposition in every precinct." Then he launched into his favorite speech, calling the Blue Eagle of the NRA the "Blue Buzzard." Bennet Riddle from Burke, an old friend of Ervin's, shot him down with, "Bill, I've heard that speech 40 times and I'm tired of it," and with that stepped out in the hall to wait until Barkley finished. Others at the meeting figured it would be pretty hard to get Republicans out to vote on a cold day in January, and even if they did, they would probably vote for Ervin anyhow, since he and his father had represented so many of them. Ervin was elected later that month without opposition.

He did not make a big splash in Washington during his seven short months in Congress, although he worked hard and got his first dose of national public office. He found it distasteful but habit-forming.

Brooks Hays, an Arkansas congressman who was later rejected by the voters for standing for sanity and moderation during the Little Rock school crisis, said Ervin "struck me as a rather retiring and modest person," still grieving over his brother's death. Hays used to walk with Joe from their offices to the Capitol and he saw in both of the brothers "that Presbyterian solemnity" that rests on the assurance that their destiny is secure. Ervin, he said, "fitted the usual southern standard of conservatism" and did not then distinguish himself as a speechmaker or defender of liberty.

Ervin's first remarks, made on the floor of the House on February 14, 1946, were entirely forgettable: "Does not the gentleman think the appropriation to the REA could be decreased if the REA would abolish its asinine policy of denying contracts to contractors who sometimes do work for private utilities?"

The year was unimpressive, as might have been expected of a lame-duck freshman congressman. He showed some of his conservatism by suggesting that federal housing programs were "based upon the theory that all home owners of America need a guardian," and foreshadowed his opposition to civil rights laws when he declared, in a speech condemning a coal workers' strike and the laws that allowed it to happen: "the government should extend equal rights to all men, but grant special privileges to none." He said the government should seize the mines to avert a national disaster. "There is no natural or constitutional right for any group of men to strike in cases where the public safety and the public health and the public economy are involved."

Ervin played it safe at the very beginning of what became the McCarthy era. He voted an increased authorization for the newly formed House Un-American Activities Committee (HUAC), which he later came to detest, and in favor of a contempt citation against Edward K. Barsky, head of the Joint Anti-Fascist Refugee Committee. Although sanctioned by the government, the committee was alleged to have some Communist leanings. HUAC subpoenaed its records, but Barsky appeared without them, saying his committee had declined to turn them over. When the House voted overwhelmingly to cite him for contempt, few opposed the resolution, not even Ervin.

Sam Ervin had lived through two world wars, once as a participant and once as an anxious observer, and he became convinced that the way to prevent another one was not only to trust in the Lord, but, as Cromwell said, to keep the powder dry. When the House got a chance to amend a hastily considered bill to exempt eighteen- and nineteen-year-olds from the draft, Ervin delivered his only major speech in the House. He got all of four and a half minutes to speak but still managed to tell a story—the first of hundreds he told in Congress—quote some lines of poetry, and make a passionate plea for military strength.

Today the story seems tasteless and flat and somewhat offensive to blacks. He said he and some other members of his church had gathered one day in the churchyard to clean up the weeds and briars. A "colored boy" was pulling up some weeds near a tombstone. "All at once he broke into laughter such as might reasonably be provoked by the act of a solemn body like this passing a draftless draft law. I said, 'George, what are you laughing about?' He says, 'Boss, don't you see that joke that is written on the tombstone?' I said, 'No, George. What is it?' I got down and read it. In addition to the name and the date of death of the deceased, there were these words, 'Not dead, but sleeping.'

I said, 'George, what is funny about that?' He said, 'Boss, he ain't fooling nobody but himself.' "

That, said Ervin, is what the House had done when it exempted eighteen- and nineteen-year-olds, because all the eligible men over nineteen had already been drafted. The bill would mean no one could be drafted at all. It would also mean that soldiers who were then overseas would have to wait longer to return home. Ervin's son was at that time—May 13th—in Japan with the American occupation army.

He spoke for the young men already in the service and the dead who could not speak for themselves. And he again quoted Rupert Brooke's prayer for those who poured out the red, sweet wine of youth. "For God's sake," he shouted, "do not tell those who have poured out their lives on the battlefield that this Congress is unwilling to keep this nation strong."

Ervin went home three months later, satisfied that his obligation had been fulfilled and determined that he would not again darken the doorways of Congress. Just before he left, his mother visited him in Washington and wrote home, "He was glad to come up here but he will be glad to go back home to his law practice. He does not like politics."

* * *

ERVIN WAS MORE determined than ever to stay out of politics and stick to law. He had pretty well licked the nervousness. He stopped smoking and learned, as he liked to say, to live one day at a time. His all-absorbing mind, which had mastered some of history's greatest literature, soaked up a great deal of its junk as well. He turned to many of the how-to-do-it books in his persistent struggle to gain control over himself.

He swore to follow Dale Carnegie's formula in *How to Stop Worrying and Start Living*: "To break the worry habit before it breaks you, Rule 4 is: Cooperate with the inevitable."

8. *The Supreme Court*

There is no virtue in sinning against light
or in persisting in palpable error, for
nothing is settled until it is settled right.

NORTH CAROLINA SUPREME COURT

SAM ERVIN TOOK HIS WIFE for a drive in the country one afternoon in 1949, heading south from their temporary home in Raleigh and hitting the back roads through lonely country towns. In about an hour they came to a small rural community, where Ervin turned onto one of the unmarked farm-to-market roads and drove deeper into the country. His wife was sure they had never been near that desolate spot, but Ervin seemed to know just where he was going.

"That's Jim Palmer's store over there," he said, "and there's his son's home—Foxy Palmer's home."

"You've been here before, haven't you," Margaret Ervin said.

"No I haven't," he replied. Then coming to a bend in the road, he added to the mystery. "Right around the corner is a little church called Tempting Church."

And there it was, a small, weatherworn country church. It had no sign but Ervin stopped and asked a black man standing outside if that was its name. When the stranger said yes, Mrs. Ervin knew her husband had been to this place before.

In a way he had been there. Although no one saw him, he had been there in another—but no less real—sense, and knew the place and its poor, black inhabitants intimately.

Ervin had been appointed to the North Carolina Supreme

Court the year before. It was an assignment he accepted with great reluctance, but he found that he enjoyed the mental discipline required by the job. He would study each case in fine detail, absorbing not only the testimony of the witnesses but also the conduct of the judge sitting on the case. The one difference between that and being a trial judge himself was that he did not have to confront the accused and the accusers in person, but only in the abstract.

He knew them just the same, as one knows the characters in a mystery novel. He knew all the details about the murder of Otis McNeill in the vicinity of Tempting Church: the footprints and the tire tracks near the scene of the crime, the quilt wrapped around the corpse, and the clumsy attempt to hide it in Deep River near the church. He also knew about the clumsy attempt by the state to prove that Jim Palmer had slain McNeill. All it had been able to show was that the footprints and the tire tracks *might* have been Palmer's.

"The State's evidence may beget suspicion in imaginative minds. But when it is laid side by side with law and logic, it does not rise to the dignity of proof," Ervin said in his carefully written opinion for the court. With that he overturned the conviction of Palmer and freed him from death row.

In his terse opinion, Ervin quoted the passionate Delphidius of ancient Rome, who said, "Oh, illustrious Caesar! If it is sufficient to deny, what hereafter will become of the guilty?" To which the Emperor Julian replied, "If it is sufficient to accuse, what will become of the innocent?"

In this case, the innocent, a black man named Jim Palmer, was freed. But his somber reaction to a newspaper reporter was something Ervin never forgot. "Boss," he said, "we never get off death row. We are on death row from the day we be here until the day we die."

Ervin had come back from his year in Congress hoping to return permanently to his law practice. His son was about to go into law school, and Ervin was planning for the day when Sam

Ervin III would join him in his law office—as he had done with his father. He had no desire to become a judge again.

One day in February, 1948, while Ervin was in court, the clerk rushed up to tell him the governor was on the telephone. With some foreboding, Ervin took the call from Governor Greg Cherry. He knew he was being considered for the Supreme Court, but he did not know what his answer would be. "I'd like to think about this and give you a call in the morning," Ervin said. That night he asked his wife for advice, but she told him he would have to decide for himself.

Ervin lay awake most of the night. "I knew I was getting along pretty well in the practice of law and loved my work." The State Supreme Court had been writing opinions longer than had most other state appellate courts, and as far as it was concerned, it had settled most questions of law. There was nothing very dynamic about donning the robes of such a court. The pay was ridiculously low—$7,500 compared with the $30,000 or more Ervin could be making as a lawyer. And—not the least important consideration—he would not be able to see Table Rock Mountain when he woke up in the morning.

He called Governor Cherry the next day and declined. He felt relieved. It was a good thing the subject of duty had not come up in their conversation because he might have withered under that kind of pressure. Shortly afterward, the phone rang again. Fred Hutchins, a friend from Winston-Salem, was calling to say that Ervin had the unanimous endorsement of the Forsyth County Bar for the Supreme Court vacancy. Hutchins said he had just told Cherry about it, only to learn that Ervin had just turned down the job. Cherry, he said, had agreed to let him try to persuade Ervin to change his mind. It did not take much. He told Ervin the road from Raleigh to Morganton was no longer than the one from Morganton to Raleigh, and he could always go back home if he did not like the job.

One night twenty-five years later, a spry little woman with a hint of blue in her gray hair sat in her office at the North

Carolina Supreme Court thumbing through a little notebook she had made of some of the court's most quotable decisions. Most of them were Sam Ervin's.

Justice Suzie Sharp, a tough-minded conservative whom Ervin frequently recommended for the U.S. Supreme Court, stopped at several places in her notebook. "This is Sam," she would say, and then fondly read the little passages as though quoting from Scripture:

"The evidence indicating that certain persons whose names appeared on the registration books of two of the precincts were dead at the time of the trial does not reasonably tend to establish anything except the tragic truth that registered electors are subject to the unhappy mortality which is the inescapable lot of all mankind."

"Truth does not come to all witnesses in naked simplicity. It is likely to come to the biased or interested witnesses as the image of a rod comes to the beholder through the water, bent and distorted by his bias or interest. The law is mindful of this plain psychological principle when it fashions rules of evidence to aid jurors in their search after truth."

"When the writer embarked on the practice of law, his father gave him this admonition: 'Always salt down the facts first; the law will keep.' " That treasured adage of S. J. Ervin's had wound up in a Supreme Court opinion.

When Ervin went to the staid old court he had a chance to salt down the law with a sharp and occasionally eloquent pen. He wanted to write decisions that were so clear they did not need any interpretation, which he felt was not always the case with appellate courts, including the U.S. Supreme Court.

Suzie Sharp, then a lower court judge, was slightly miffed at Ervin when he overturned her for using the phrase "and/or" in one of her judgments. "I was so disgusted because Chief Justice

Stacy had used it in one of his opinions just a few weeks before," she said. But Ervin thought her choice of words "created a fundamental uncertainty." Later he allowed another judge to use that phrase but gave him a verbal lashing. "The presiding judge murdered the king's and the queen's and everybody's English by using the monstrous linguistic abomination 'and/or' in this portion of the order." He admitted, however, that the judge's law was better than his grammar.

Ervin was a strong member of the court, dissenting often from the majority and from the equally sharp and expressive views of Chief Justice Walter P. Stacy. Some of the other justices who had dissented with Stacy were glad to have Ervin on their side.

In one case involving the right of small towns to send their policemen to Chapel Hill for law enforcement training, Ervin and Stacy spent at least five weeks in a legal tug-of-war, each one adding to his opinion to counter the arguments of the other. Finally, Stacy offered a truce: "If you'll quit adding to your opinion, I'll quit adding to mine." The court voted 4–3 to accept Ervin's as the majority view, settling a crucial question for the Institute of Government, which was giving the training. The same afternoon Ervin went to Chapel Hill to preside over a moot court. When Albert Coates, head of the Institute, asked him anxiously about the Supreme Court decision, Ervin said, "Albert, I thought you made a magnificent argument, but there wasn't a single member of the court agreed with me. I just don't believe you're going to win your case." A little later, Coates received a telegram from the clerk of court saying he had won. "You damn rascal," Coates told him, "you knew that opinion was handed down in my favor today."

When Ervin was struggling with his first opinion for the court, Stacy gave him some judicious advice: "Sometimes you ought to take a case and hang it up on a clothes line and let the sun shine on it and the wind blow through it for some days before you take it up again and you'll find a lot of times the things that perplexed you before have simplified themselves and you have no difficulty writing opinions."

Ervin found while he was on the court that if he put something perplexing aside during the day, often he would wake up in the middle of the night to discover that his subconscious had written the whole thing out for him. The sentences and paragraphs would all be arrayed in his mind, and he could write them down as if he were transcribing a tape.

His fussiness about the meaning of words led him to patch up legislation that the General Assembly had botched. When Justice Emory B. Denny did the same thing with a will an old lady had written on her own, Ervin and he kidded each other. "Well, this is a good will that Judge Denny has fixed up for this old lady. Of course, it's not hers," Ervin said. He told Denny he would tack up a sign on his door saying "Postmortem Wills a Specialty!" Denny replied that he would put one on Ervin's door in retaliation saying "Legislative Repair Shop Now Open for Business."

Ervin and his family moved to a furnished home in Raleigh for several years, but he discovered that he could do most of his reading and writing at home in Morganton. His personal library had become almost as extensive as the one at the Supreme Court.

Ervin was the court jester. He did not allow the forbidding atmosphere or the somber responsibilities of the place to dampen his spirits. "He was just the same Sam Ervin," remembered Adrian Newton, the clerk of court. "He enjoyed life to the fullest extent and you couldn't be around him a moment without he'd have you laughing. You could tell he was getting as much pleasure out of his stories as other people. I never saw him that I recall when he seemed to be blue or down and out in the slightest. He could always see the humorous side of things. He was a joy to have around."

Reporters who covered the court would search through the weekly opinions for the blue folders containing Ervin's opinions because they usually found in them a quotable phrase, a touch of humor, or a passionate defense of human liberty.

"During the past 172 years," Ervin said in one of his first opinions after joining the court, "the organic law of this state has contained the solemn warning that 'a frequent recurrence to fundamental principles is absolutely essential to preserve the blessings of liberty.' " He reversed the conviction of Owen Ballance, a photographer who had been fined fifty dollars for failing to allow the state to check his competency, ability, and integrity before going into business. It was a small matter, but Ervin found a major injustice in it. He said the North Carolinians who wrote the state constitution were well aware of the struggle of the English-speaking people for strong protections against threats to dignity and freedom of the individual. "They loved liberty and hated tyranny, and were convinced that government itself must be compelled to respect the inherent rights of the individual if freedom is to be preserved and oppression is to be prevented." They placed in the state constitution a Declaration of Rights "designed chiefly to protect the individual from the state."

As the junior member of the court, Ervin was required by custom to state his views first during the justices' weekly conferences. That was to help him establish his independence from the more experienced members. During his first conference, in 1948, the nervous Ervin told the other six judges, "This is the day I long have sought but wept because I found it not; I vote to overturn." To his surprise, four of them joined him. Chief Justice Walter P. Stacy and one other were opposed. In this instance Ervin's presence on the court gave it a libertarian majority. The pattern was repeated on several other occasions. Justice Maurice V. Barnhill took him aside one day and said, "I'm glad to have another man who will disagree with Judge Stacy occasionally."

Ervin spent six years on the court, passing on the justice that had been dispensed in cases that ranged from the lurid to the trivial, but this time at a safe, comfortable distance. His ulcer was well under control.

He tried to write opinions that could not be misinterpreted by lawyers or judges. But, as he said during Senate hearings in 1966, that was a difficult task, "because, as Oliver Wendell Holmes said, 'a word is not a crystal, transparent and unchanged; it is the skin of a living thought that may vary greatly in color and content according to the circumstances in which it is used.' "

In the fall of 1951, he ordered a new trial in the case of Christine Warren, a maid who had been terrorized into confessing that she stole from her employer. She had been taken to the police station, stripped of her clothes, badgered for five hours, and threatened with the loss of her job. She was convicted after the judge said her confession was made "freely and voluntarily."

"Ministers of the law," Ervin said, "ought not to permit zeal for its enforcement to cause them to transgress its precepts. They should remember that where law ends, tyranny begins."

He sustained the convictions of Edsel Minton and an accomplice, Ben Bullis, for the slaying of another man who would not let them share the company of Thelma and Mabel, two fifteen-year-old prostitutes he was escorting. Minton had attempted to get Thelma to participate in a cover-up by lying on the witness stand. The fact was that he had shot his rival "plumb through," according to the sheriff. "This illustrates anew the unrelenting truth that 'the sin ye do by two and two ye must pay for one by one,' " Judge Ervin said.

He upheld a lower court that had thrown out a decision by the State Board of Elections not to allow Strom Thurmond's States' Rights Democratic Party on the ballot in 1948. In spite of the Dixiecrats' failure to obtain certificates from county boards of elections, they had more than the required ten thousand signatures. He said that participation in a primary election should not disqualify a voter from signing a petition creating a new party. Stacy, as he often did with Ervin opinions, dissented.

Ervin ordered a new trial for Raleigh Speller, a black man convicted of rape, because Speller and his attorneys had not had enough time to prepare their defense. This was the second trial of Speller the court threw out; the first was overturned because he had been tried by an all-white jury. But on the third appeal the court upheld his conviction and he was executed.

Ervin's capacity for indignation over the mangling of the law by the courts was strongly revealed in the murder case against John Bridges. The prosecutor did his job well in presenting the evidence, but the judge flubbed it by forgetting to tell the jury it had the option of acquitting Bridges. "The state's testimony tends to show that the prisoner coveted his neighbor's wife and slew his neighbor with rare atrocity that his physical enjoyment of the wife's person might be exclusive," Ervin said. "The very sordidness of the evidence strongly tempts us to say that justice and law are not always synonymous, and to vote for affirmance of the judgment of death on the theory that justice has triumphed, however much law may have suffered."

Ervin said the ultimate fate of John Bridges was of minor importance in the scheme of things because "his role on life's stage, like ours, soon ends. But what happens to the law in this case is of the gravest moment. The preservation unimpaired of our basic rules of criminal procedure is an end far more desirable than that of hurrying a single sinner to what may be his merited doom."

If not for events in Washington Ervin probably would have stayed on the Supreme Court for many years, despite the fact that it was socially restrictive and usually legally inert. As a former justice, Willis J. Brogden, told him, "They put you in a mausoleum while you're still living and hang you in effigy after you're gone." It was a political tomb from which few escape. Ervin was not very interested in escaping, however, and probably would have eventually become chief justice. He discouraged a movement to run him for governor in 1952, mainly because his old college friend William B. Umstead was considered a certain candidate.

In that quiet mausoleum, late one night in June, 1973, Suzie Sharp looked up from her little notebook containing the sayings of Sam Ervin and said, "One thing about Sam is, he is so obviously in love with the law and he gets such pleasure out of working hard. The law is no chore to him; it's his life."

*   *   *

On May 17, 1954, the U.S. Supreme Court sounded the end of an era and charted the course of Sam Ervin's life for most of the next twenty years.

"We conclude that in the field of education," the court said, "the doctrine of 'separate but equal' has no place. Separate educational facilities are inherently unequal." One of the four cases which were decided by *Brown* v. *Board of Education* came up from Clarendon County, South Carolina, where Ervin's father had struggled to keep his family alive. Now the son, just a few weeks away from his appointment with destiny, was being drawn irresistibly into a starring role in a losing cause.

Another drama, which temporarily upstaged the one set in motion by the court, was being acted out on nationwide television. The Army-McCarthy hearings had all the elements of melodrama and farce. One did not need a program to tell the good guys from the villain. And the downfall, or at least its beginning, took place before the country's very eyes.

Ervin, who dwelt in the isolated upper atmosphere of the law, was only vaguely aware of Joe McCarthy and the "ism" that trailed after him. He naively assumed that McCarthy was performing a worthwhile service, scaring the Communists out from under the bed and all that.

The event that brought Ervin out of seclusion was the death of Clyde R. Hoey. The dapper senator, who as governor had appointed Ervin to the lower-court bench, died on May 12, while sitting at his desk in the Senate Office Building. The resulting scramble among North Carolina politicians to succeed him was enough to shatter the nerves, if not the health, of the gentle, frail William B. Umstead, the governor, who was faced with choosing Hoey's successor. Largely unbeknownst to Ervin, most of the people who offered Umstead advice recommended Ervin as their second or compromise candidate after failing to agree on a first choice.

Soon after the Supreme Court's *Brown* decision was handed down, Judge Ervin was driving over the country roads to Spring Hope, a small rural town to the east of Raleigh, to deliver a high school commencement address. He realized, looking at the close patchwork pattern of black and white living habits, that the school decision would have a profound impact on the South. But in the North, because of neighborhood segregation, it would have almost no effect at all. The South, however, would have plenty of time to begin imitating the North's housing patterns.

Like most southerners, Ervin believed in the separate-but-equal doctrine set forth in the year of his birth, fifty-eight years before. He was convinced that segregation was the natural result of people freely associating with members of their own race. No matter that freedom was severely restricted by compulsion.

North Carolina reluctantly accepted the Court's ruling. Umstead pointed the way when he said, "The Supreme Court of the United States has spoken. . . . This reversal of its former decisions is in my judgment a clear and serious invasion of the rights of the sovereign states. Nevertheless, this is now the latest interpretation of the Fourteenth Amendment."

The decision may have indirectly affected Umstead's choice for the Senate vacancy. One of the leading contenders for the position was Irving Carlyle, a prominent Winston-Salem lawyer. In the opinion of political observers, he blew his chances in a speech before the Democratic State Convention on May 21. From notes that were scribbled on a piece of hotel stationery, he said at the end of his prepared address, "The Supreme Court of the United States has spoken. As good citizens we have no other course except to obey the law as laid down by the Court. To do otherwise is to cost us our respect for law and order. And if we lost that in these critical times, we will have lost the quality which is the source of our strength as a state and as a nation." Carlyle received sporadic applause, but most politicians knew that they had just heard a position that just would not work in North Carolina.

Ervin was at the Supreme Court writing an opinion when Chief Justice Maurice V. Barnhill, who had succeeded Stacy, said he wanted to see him. When he got to Barnhill's office, the judge went around and closed all the doors, as if, Ervin thought, Barnhill was about to involve him in a criminal conspiracy. Then he handed Ervin the phone and told him to call the governor's office.

Umstead said he wanted to talk with Ervin, but not at the Capitol; that would arouse too many suspicions. They agreed to meet at the governor's mansion. "I have asked you over here," the governor told him that afternoon as they sat on the side porch, "to find out if you will accept the appointment if I offer it to you."

Ervin, remembering those seven unhappy months in Washington, was not overjoyed. In fact, he was deeply troubled. "Bill, I certainly hope that you won't appoint me," Ervin told his friend. "I mean that sincerely. I've spent virtually all my life in the law one way or another and I enjoy that and I would like to stay with it." But of course Ervin added, "If you did appoint me, I would take it. I'd feel like it was my duty to take it." Umstead said he would let Ervin know the next morning. "Just remember I haven't said I was going to appoint you to the Senate. I've made no promises. I might appoint you tomorrow and I might never appoint you. I may appoint somebody else." But he called the next morning to say he was signing Ervin's commission that day to fill out Hoey's unexpired term in the Senate.

The press did not know very much about Ervin except that

he wrote precise and often colorful Supreme Court opinions. When contacted by reporters later in the day, Ervin gave them only a hint. "I believe in clinging to the tried and true landmarks of the past, but I am willing to test the soundness of new ideas." They went back to their typewriters and pronounced him a "moderate." *The Greensboro Daily News*, like most newspapers in the state, was delighted with the appointment, calling Ervin "intensely human."

Ervin's sister, Jean, for one, was surprised that he accepted the appointment. He told her, "It's the kind of responsibility you can't turn down." She thought he would be lost in any place but North Carolina. She remembered the day the two of them drove from their oldest sister's home in Virginia to New England, to attend a meeting of the Mayflower Society in Plymouth, Massachusetts. Ervin drove in his usual abominable style, jerking every time he shifted gears, and tailgated Jean all the way from Richmond to her home in Connecticut, weaving back and forth to stay behind her, afraid if she got out of his sights he would be hopelessly lost. "How will he ever manage in Washington?" she thought.

As though they did not want to let him go, friends in Morganton surrounded the Ervins in a cocoon of praise and congratulations, and thirty or more of them went along to Washington. The train left Morganton on the afternoon of June 10, 1954, hauling two special Pullman cars that had been put on at Asheville, one of them draped with a red, white, and blue banner announcing: "Sam J. Ervin, Jr., U.S. Senator, Burke County."

Ervin did not sleep much that night as the train took him irrevocably away from home. But he remembered his mother's advice that he could get plenty of rest by lying still and relaxing, even if his mind was racing too fast to let him sleep. He was almost fifty-eight years old. He never wanted to be a politician but, as with most things in his life, history had thrust the job upon him.

The train arrived at Union Station early the next morning. Naturally, there was a big reception at Ervin's new office, and while it was going on, Mrs. Ervin slipped out to watch part of the Army-McCarthy hearings. At a luncheon that afternoon, someone commented to Ervin, "I'm glad to see so many of your friends have stoked and banked their stills to come see you sworn in." Jean was impressed with her brother at the luncheon. "I thought 'how poised he is.' It was as if he'd always been a senator."

That was the day that Sam Ervin was sworn in by Richard M. Nixon, Vice President of the United States.

Ervin felt somewhat cool toward the Vice President because of what he had heard about his political tactics. Nixon's first victim had been Jerry Voorhis, a congressman from California whom Ervin had gotten to know well during his previous, brief stay in Washington. Ervin and Voorhis did not think alike, but, because they enjoyed philosophizing with each other, they became good friends.

"I thought Jerry Voorhis was a very fine person with somewhat visionary ideas about how government should be operated, but I never had any doubt about the fact that he was a very loyal and true American, and, I thought, an exceedingly fine human being," Ervin said.

Nixon accused Voorhis of being in league with the Communists and beat him in the election of 1946, at the end of Ervin's year in the House. It was shocking to Ervin. "I'm sure he was just as patriotic an American as anybody else."

Nixon conducted the same kind of campaign in defeating Helen Gahagan Douglas for the Senate in 1950. Two years later, after salvaging himself with his famous Checkers speech, he became Vice President. Ervin was wary of him from the start.

9. The Senate: First Years

The first duty of man is that of
subduing fear.

THOMAS CARLYLE

"I CAME HERE," SAM ERVIN SAID during the Watergate
hearings, "during the days when Joe McCarthy saw a Communist hiding under every bush." And then, condensing twenty
years of history with a surge of his eyebrows, he added, "And I
have been here fighting the no-knock and preventive detention
laws and indiscriminate bugging by people who've found subver-
sives under every bed." It was only a matter of time before the
ghost of Joe McCarthy, who had venomously lashed out at his
accusers in the same ornate Caucus Room, would appear to
haunt the present hearings. To Ervin there was a clear parallel
between the one-man campaign to scare people out of their wits
over Communism and the full-scale effort by the White House—
and, from all appearances, by the President—to scare Americans
into accepting harsh methods for dealing with demonstrators and
political enemies. The senator from Wisconsin had been dis-
graced; now the President of the United States was apparently so
badly crippled that he would be unable to perform his duties
effectively during the second four years he fought so hard to gain.

When Ervin arrived in 1954 Washington was in chaos. There
was not a member of the Senate who did not stand in danger of
being branded an unwitting agent of the Communist conspiracy
if he but looked cross-eyed at McCarthy. The man had become
the symbol of the holy crusade to root out the godless Commu-

nists—even though he never successfully exposed one of them. But McCarthy finally pushed the Senate too far, by smearing the reputations of prominent citizens, insulting witnesses, trying to bully the press, disrupting committees, showing contempt for the Senate by refusing to answer questions, distorting testimony, grandstanding, running roughshod over federal agencies, and, most unbecoming of all for a member of the Senate, ridiculing and defaming with vulgar and base language his own colleagues.

Mrs. Ervin pleaded with her husband when he accepted the appointment to the Senate never to tangle with Joe McCarthy. But soon after he arrived in the Senate, a reporter called him and asked him what he thought about being under consideration for one of the six positions on the select committee to study the censure of McCarthy. Ervin said someone with more experience and stature should be picked. "I don't think it would be the duty of a country boy who just came up from North Carolina." But the "country boy," as some of his friends in the Senate began calling him, could never resist pressure. Lyndon Johnson, then the minority leader, was looking for men with judicial experience, and Ervin and John Stennis of Mississippi, the only ones in the Senate with such credentials, were both prime candidates. Ervin was formally chosen by Richard Nixon, who, as Vice President, was presiding over the Senate.

Ervin went into the hearings of the special committee with as much objectivity as a man in public office could be expected to have. He would judge McCarthy on the facts; and the more facts he learned about the junior senator from Wisconsin the more he disliked him. Ervin was always slow to judge others, but once he had looked them in the eye, studied the evidence, formed his impressions, and weighed everything against his knowledge of the law and the prophets, he could be pretty unshakable in his verdict of innocence or guilt, right or wrong.

He sat with Republicans Arthur Watkins of Utah, Edwin Johnson of Colorado, and Frank Carlson of Kansas, and Democrats Stennis of Mississippi and Francis Case of South

Dakota. Not a very formidable team, it seemed to many at the time. McCarthy, flanked by his attorney, Edward Bennett Williams, was the first witness, as the hearings began on August 3, 1954.

During the lengthy interrogation of McCarthy, Ervin was unusually quiet. No Bible quoting or storytelling. One of the few lengthy exchanges with the star witness concerned his abrasive questioning of General Ralph Zwicker, one of McCarthy's favorite targets at the Pentagon. McCarthy had snapped at him, "Don't be coy with me, general." This rebuke struck the straightlaced Ervin as a queer way to speak to an officer, and he decided to try out a little gentle mockery. As "an old cross-examiner myself," he said, he was very interested in McCarthy's approach to witnesses. The exchange, which appears in the official record of the hearings, was as follows:

> Ervin: Now, I rather admired that in a way. Personally, I would never have been bold enough to have made that observation on a cross-examination of anybody in the military service, unless perhaps it were a wave or a wac, and then I would have been bold enough to do it only under romantic circumstances, where I was surrounded with soft music, moonlight and roses; and I am satisfied I never would have been bold enough to give that admonition to either a general or to a sergeant. But I merely want to ask the senator whether he considered that a proper method of cross-examining a general—that is, General Zwicker.
>
> McCarthy: I did, because he had been trying to be coy—coy and evasive. That was my system of cross-examining. You might have used different language, Senator Ervin, when you have an evasive answer. That is my system of trying to pull teeth. I finally pulled some of them and got some of the information.

The committee issued a mild resolution, condemning McCarthy's failure to appear before a subcommittee looking into his financial dealings and his ungentlemanly badgering of General Zwicker. But McCarthy proceeded to write a much stronger censure resolution for himself by viciously attacking the committee members.

He appeared on "Meet the Press" on October 3 and accused Watkins, Johnson, and Ervin of "deliberate deception" and "fraud" for failing to disqualify themselves. They had, he said, previously said some unkind words about him, and he specifically cited a remark Ervin had made that he tended to be somewhat "rough on witnesses." Then he really got Ervin's goat by issuing a statement calling the three senators "unwitting handmaidens" of the Communists.

Then, as if that were not enough, McCarthy released copies of an undelivered speech he had inserted in the *Congressional Record* on November 10. He took on the full committee this time, fantasizing that the Communist Party "has now extended its tentacles to that most respected of American bodies, the United States Senate," turning members of the committee into its involuntary agents and "attorneys-in-fact." "In the course of the Senate debate I shall demonstrate that the Watkins committee has done the work of the Communist Party, that it not only cooperated in the achievement of Communist goals but that in writing its report it imitated Communist methods—that it distorted, misrepresented, and omitted in its effort to manufacture a plausible rationalization for advising the Senate to accede to the clamor for my scalp."

On November 14, it was Ervin's turn on "Meet the Press," and he showed a toughness that many had not expected to see in that jolly, scholarly man from the South. He said it looked as though McCarthy intended to damage the reputation of any senator who opposed him or disapproved of his "disorderly behavior" in the Senate.

"If Senator McCarthy did not believe those things when he said them about the Senate Committee, then there is a pretty solid ground to say that he ought to be expelled from the Senate for moral incapacity. On the contrary, if he put those things in there honestly believing them to be true, then he has evidently suffered gigantic mental delusions, and it may be argued with much force that he should be expelled from the Senate for mental difficulty."

Although the Constitution provides that Congress may discipline its members, the Senate had never expressed its official disapproval of anyone. There was powerful pressure, by both Republican leaders and McCarthy's fanatical followers, against taking such a step. As Senator Everett Dirksen of Illinois put it, "If this can be done to one member of the Senate, who is next on the list?" No seat in the Senate, particularly the seat of a conservative, would be safe, he said in a Senate speech.

There was little leadership in the anti-McCarthy forces. Most members of the Senate wanted to see him sharply upbraided, if not expelled, but few had the stomach for pushing the resolution through the Senate. Arthur Watkins, the chairman of the censure committee, ducked when it came time for him to make his speech on the Senate floor. Ervin was scribbling some notes on scraps of paper for a speech he was to give the next day when Watkins sent word that he was tied up, and would Ervin mind speaking in his stead.

At 2 P.M. on November 15, five months after coming to Washington, clutching his scraps of paper, Sam Ervin took the floor for about an hour, and in the process made his own reputation and demolished Joe McCarthy.

Since the Senate was in special session with nothing to consider but the censure motion, it was probably the best-attended Ervin speech of his whole career in the Senate. There was nothing else for the others to do but sit and listen. The galleries were packed with tourists and busloads of McCarthy's defenders, who had come down on special excursions to watch the show and protest what was about to happen to their champion.

Ervin began by explaining that his cloistered life on the North Carolina Supreme Court had prevented him from keeping up with what was going on in the outside world. "I had a vague impression that a great storm was raging in the country around the activities of Senator McCarthy. I came to the Senate, however, with the vague impression that, by and large, Senator McCarthy was doing a good job in his self-proclaimed role as the symbol of resistance to Communist subversion." But, he added, since sitting on the committee and observing McCarthy in action, he had changed his opinion completely.

And then came his first story, one which he has repeated many times but never with as much effectiveness: "The following story is told in North Carolina: A young lawyer went to an old lawyer for advice as to how to try a lawsuit. The old lawyer said, 'If the evidence is against you, talk about the law. If the law is against you, talk about the evidence.' The young lawyer said, 'But what do you do when both the evidence and the law are against you?' 'In that event,' said the old lawyer, 'give somebody hell. That will distract the attention of the judge and the jury from the weakness of your case.' "

And that, Ervin said, was what McCarthy was doing in response to the committee's report. He said the claim that McCarthy was being tried because he had fought Communism "has no more substance than a shadow of a dream." Among those who, he said, were fighting Communism "with as much devotion and far more wisdom" than McCarthy was Vice President Nixon.

Ervin mocked McCarthy's charge that he and the other two committee members should have disqualified themselves. Senators did not have to possess vacant minds, "totally devoid of any opinion" about McCarthy to judge him fairly. Had that been the case, everyone in the Senate would have to disqualify himself. "It is doubtful, indeed, that six mental adults could have been found anywhere in the United States who did not entertain some opinion concerning Senator McCarthy and his activities."

Next he ridiculed the McCarthy habit of lifting things out of context and used it as an excuse for his second story: "I now know that the lifting of statements out of context is a typical McCarthy technique. The writer of Ecclesiastes assures us that 'there is no new thing under the sun.' The McCarthy technique of lifting statements out of context was practiced by a preacher in North Carolina about seventy-five years ago. At that time the women had a habit of wearing their hair in topknots. This preacher deplored that habit. As a consequence he preached a rip-snorting sermon one Sunday on the text Top Not Come Down. At the conclusion of his sermon an irate woman, wearing a very pronounced topknot, told the preacher that no such text could be found in the Bible. The preacher thereupon opened the Scriptures to the 17th verse of the 24th chapter of Matthew and pointed to the words: 'Let him which is on the housetop not come down to take anything out of his house.' " (There is a parenthetical observation in the record here that the Senate and the galleries exploded with laughter.)

Ervin said any practitioner of the out-of-context technique could readily find the "top not come down" in that verse. Ervin by this time had the Senate eating out of his hands.

He bore down on McCarthy's accusations against committee members and repeated the suggestion that McCarthy should be expelled for either moral or mental incapacity to perform his duties. He admonished McCarthy that if he wanted to appear innocent of financial misdeeds, he should have appeared on his own behalf. (Here, time seems to leap ahead, to Watergate and to Nixon's refusal to testify or turn over tapes of crucial conversations with aides who had implicated him in illegal activities against his Democratic opponents.)

Ervin said that in his long study of the law, "One rule, based on decision after decision, is that if a charge is made against a person which he would naturally answer or explain, and such person fails to answer that charge or offer an explanation, the finders of the facts may assume he has thereby impliedly admitted the truth of the charge."

Ervin, who frequently talked about understanding "plain human psychology," gently psychoanalyzed McCarthy when he said, "He seems to have an incapacity to distinguish between what he thinks in his head and external facts. I do not say this in unkindness. But this characteristic makes it very difficult to meet him on the same mental plane."

He claimed McCarthy baited, badgered, and browbeat General Zwicker. With droll humor he took apart one of McCarthy's slurs at the General in which McCarthy said, "Anyone with the brains of a 5-year-old child can understand that question." Said Ervin, "Mr. President, I think perhaps I understand it now; but I read it 4 or 5 times before I understood it." He told the Senate it had better wake up to the tragic truth that McCarthy "besmirches throughout the length and breadth of this land" any senator who dared oppose him. And before winding up with his famous plea to the Senate, Ervin told what is perhaps his most classic story. He has not told it often, but whenever writers mention Ervin's storytelling ability, they recall the one about Uncle Ephraim.

"Mr. President, many years ago there was a custom in a section of my country, known as the South Mountains, to hold religious meetings at which the oldest members of the congregation were called upon to stand up and publicly testify to their religious experiences. On one occasion they were holding such a meeting in one of the churches; and old Uncle Ephraim Swink, a South Mountaineer whose body was all bent and distorted with arthritis, was present. All the older members of the congregation except Uncle Ephraim arose and gave testimony to their religious experiences. Uncle Ephraim kept his seat. Thereupon, the moderator said, 'Brother Ephraim, suppose you tell us what has the Lord done for you.'

"Uncle Ephraim arose, with his bent and distorted body, and said, 'Brother, he has mighty nigh ruint me.' "

"Mr. President," Ervin said, "that is about what Senator McCarthy has done to the Senate." Because of his activities and the Senate's failure to do anything about them, the public was left with the "monstrous" impression that the Senate was intimidated by his threats of libel and slander and was too paralyzed to act.

Many of his colleagues may have gotten the nerve and the will to vote against McCarthy from his concluding words: "The Senate is trying this issue: Was Senator McCarthy guilty of disorderly behavior in his senatorial office? The American people are trying another issue. The issue before the American people transcends in importance the issue before the Senate. The issue before the American people is simply this: Does the Senate of the United States have enough manhood to stand up to Senator McCarthy?

"Mr. President, the honor of the Senate is in our keeping. I pray that senators will not soil it by permitting Senator McCarthy to go unwhipped of senatorial justice."

Lyndon Johnson respectfully told Ervin after his speech, "You showed you don't scare easily." Two days later, *The Asheville Citizen* exclaimed, "Somebody had to say it right out and plain. The judge did. Bully for him!"

On December 2, 1954 the Senate voted 67–22 to censure McCarthy, not only for the mishandling of witnesses and contempt for the subcommittee investigating him, but for smearing the committee and the Senate itself.

McCarthy never scared anyone again. In the Senate he became a pathetic figure, for whom Ervin felt great sympathy. He often befriended him during meetings of the Government Operations Committee. When McCarthy died three years later, Bobby Baker called Ervin to say that McCarthy's wife had asked if Ervin would be one of the three Democrats from the Senate to appear at his funeral, but he was in bed with the flu and could not attend.

The brush with McCarthy reinforced Ervin's great contempt for any person who attempts to suppress individuals in the exercise of their constitutional, nay, sacred rights to publish and speak openly and protest against government policies. It also convinced him, as he said in a speech at Duke University on April 28, 1967, "about the most important thing a man has is his right to privacy and individual dignity. During that unfortunate era of fear and whispering those two concepts found themselves, like the whooping crane, near extinction."

After three years in the Senate, Sam Ervin was given one of his most challenging assignments, one that gave the small-town lawyer a close look at big-time corruption personified by some of the shadiest characters ever to appear on Capitol Hill. He was appointed to the Select Committee on Improper Activities in Labor or Management, better known during its three-year life as the Rackets Committee. The televised hearings did for the Fifth Amendment—"I respectfully decline to answer because I honestly believe that my answer might tend to incriminate me"— what the McCarthy hearings had done for "point of order."

During the years 1957 to 1959, Ervin got to know both John F. Kennedy, the young, ambitious senator from Massachusetts, and Robert F. Kennedy, the committee's aggressive chief counsel. The three of them were among the most tenacious questioners, discovering that organized crime and organized labor were in many cases closely intertwined. When the hearings ended, John Kennedy and Ervin proposed major labor reform legislation which became, after being paired with a similar measure in the House, the Landrum-Griffin Act, a major step toward cleaning up corruption in the unions and providing basic rights for the union rank and file.

Kennedy, knowing that Ervin would be effective in gaining southern support for the bill, asked him in mid-1959 if he would co-sponsor it. Ervin said he would be glad to, as long as the unrelated amendments to the Taft-Hartley Act were left out. The amendments would have raised the possibility of revising the open-shop laws, which exempt workers in unionized plants from joining the union, and which are dear to the South. Kennedy promised, Ervin said, but no sooner was the Kennedy-Ervin bill introduced than Ervin discovered, to his great embarrassment, that the Taft-Hartley amendments were still in. Frantically, he tried to get the Labor and Public Works Committee to take them out, but failed. He could get only 29 votes in the Senate for his amendment to strike that part of the bill. But to his relief, the Taft-Hartley provisions were deleted in conference between the House and Senate.

During the long hearings, Ervin subjected witness after witness to his stories and his righteous indignation. He told them they had "good forgetteries." As a judge well exposed to the ways of criminals, he was nevertheless shocked at what the committee learned.

On June 26, 1959, Ervin tangled with Teamster President Jimmy Hoffa. Ervin could not understand why union officials who had been convicted of crimes and sent to jail had not been removed from office, and why they were still collecting salaries when the union constitution said they were supposed to be kicked out.

"What is there to find out beyond the fact that a man has entered a plea of guilty and was sent to jail?" Ervin asked Hoffa.

"I will tell you what it is," Hoffa replied. "I will have to bring the executive board of that union down to the international or go to New York to talk to them. I recognize that under the constitution I don't have to do that. I recognize that.

"But rather than to destroy this union, this is the procedure I would follow. Then, if there, I would go to their membership, if necessary, to have carried out in orderly fashion the constitution, rather than destroy the union."

"In other words," Ervin said, "You are telling us that if you follow the constitution and carry out the powers the constitution gives you to remove from membership or from office convicted criminals, that would destroy your union?"

"I didn't say that, Senator," answered Hoffa.

"If you said anything else, I am unable to understand the English language," said Ervin.

Hoffa kept trying to tell Ervin that the reason for the delay in getting the convicted officials out of office was that he always tried to obtain consent from the local union before taking action. That took a little longer. Like maybe a couple of years.

"I would think it was the duty of the president of the international, when the man abuses his union office and practices extortion, and is sentenced to prison, and his conviction becomes final, and he is actually serving a prison term, I would draw the conclusion that your constitution contemplated that the president of the union, in the event the local fails to act, will then remove him from membership and from his union office. Otherwise, I don't see what they have with such a constitution."

"I don't quarrel with your statement, Senator," Hoffa said.

"Except you don't practice it," Ervin shot back.

A year and a half later, Robert Kennedy became attorney general and went after Hoffa, finally obtaining his conviction for jury tampering and fraud. He had served nearly five years of a thirteen-year sentence when President Nixon commuted his sentence on December 23, 1971.

In his book on labor racketeering, *The Enemy Within*, Robert Kennedy spoke respectfully of Ervin's ability to disarm the toughest witnesses. "I heard Senator Ervin on several occasions destroy a witness by telling an appropriate story which made the point better than an hour-long speech or a day of questioning. He could be particularly devastating when a witness was pompous or overbearing."

One such occasion concerned a Cleveland Teamsters Union official who refused to provide any information besides his name and address. "Mr. Chairman," Ervin said, "it is evident here that you have a union official who professes to help build up the union, and to take salaries and expense allowances for so doing and while he is ostensibly building up the union he is also taking remuneration from trucking companies in which he has an interest which refuse to be unionized.

"So about the most charitable construction to place on this witness' conduct is to say that he is like the man that put vitamins in his liquor so he could build himself up while he was tearing himself down."

10. *Civil Rights*

IN JULY, 1963, ROBERT F. KENNEDY, then attorney general in his brother's administration, sat across the witness table during hearings of the Senate Judiciary Committee and gently but effectively probed Sam Ervin's conscience until he hit a nerve.

Kennedy had gone to Capitol Hill day after day, week after week, to argue in favor of civil rights legislation, and there stood Ervin, with his thin copy of the Constitution and monstrous stacks of law books, ready to argue to the last breath if need be against every sentence of the bill.

Examples of discrimination against blacks were everywhere to be found; and yet Ervin, who spoke so passionately for human liberty, seemed unconcerned. Unable to pierce Ervin's thick legalistic hide, Kennedy went after his emotions.

"How are we to bring up our children, Senator, if there is not going to be some leadership and assistance from somebody such as yourself," Kennedy needled him. "I think you have a responsibility. But you are against every part of this section of the bill." And again: "Senator, with the kind of prestige you have in the United States, you could make a major difference in ending these kinds of practices as well as bringing this country through a very difficult period of transition. That is all I ask of you, Senator."

Ervin was agitated. "The only thing you have a right to ask of me is that I stand and fight for the Constitution and for the basic rights of Americans. That is what I'm doing now.

"You are not correct in saying I have never spoken out against discrimination. All of my life I have fought against it. As a member of the North Carolina legislature many years ago, one of my first acts was to introduce a bill to authorize the issuance of bonds to defray the cost of construction of an adequate school for the Negro children of my hometown. As a member of the school board in my hometown, I fought for equal compensation for all teachers regardless of their respective races. As a member of the legislature of North Carolina, I have always fought for liberal appropriations for the adequate education of all of North Carolina's school children.

"As a citizen, lawyer, and judge in North Carolina, I have always stood for the right of all men to stand equal before the law.

"As a citizen and a public official, I have always stood for the right of every qualified voter to register and vote.

"So you are not very just to me in saying I have not fought discrimination."

As often as Ervin had repeated that defense—although never quite as fervently as in that exchange with Robert Kennedy—he was never able to convince his critics that he was not just another southern segregationist, a political opportunist, and, deep down, a racist.

How could he be a champion of human freedoms when he turned his back on attempts to end the great injustices that were suffered by black people throughout most of his lifetime? How could he righteously condemn the moral shortcomings of others when, by delaying the passage of badly needed legislation, he helped perpetuate one of the most immoral conditions in the history of the nation? How could anyone have such a monumental blind spot?

Ervin winced at questions like those. They were evidence that many people had not understood his patient attempts to educate them about the true meanings of the Constitution and the grave dangers to which it was subjected by civil rights legislation. And how he tried. The records of floor debates and hearings are stuffed thick with Sam Ervin, with his stories, which one critic termed "interminable and intolerable," with stirring poems and the near-poems of the great libertarian justices of the Supreme Court, and with the sage prescriptions of his personal gods, the Founding Fathers.

To those who waited for almost a century for their rights, Ervin's arguments seemed perverse and antiquated, stubbornly contrary to humanitarian principles, and to the Constitution itself. He appeared to be hopelessly trapped in the ideology of his ancestors.

Instead of seeing the civil rights bills as a cure for a persistent evil, Ervin viewed them as the first steps on a forbidden journey to the destruction of fundamental liberties for all men, white and black. The proposed laws were incompatible with liberty. They took away the power of the states, the rights of individuals to hire and fire their employees, and the rights of children to attend the schools of their choice. These rights were being turned over to an increasingly cumbersome, insensitive, and mindlessly powerful federal government. In the hands of a tyrant or fool, these powers could be used to destroy the finest system of government ever conceived by the mind of man.

Ervin fought civil rights legislation, in part, because he had to. It may not have been for political reasons—he was not one to respond to outside pressures, trends, fads, or, in this case, the surge of history—but he could not have been totally ignorant of the consequences of his actions.

He saw the need for correcting the injustice of job discrimination, ghetto housing, and segregated schools. But passing federal legislation, setting up a federal bureaucracy to administer it, and aiming it—especially aiming it—at the South put Ervin in a corner. Like Robert E. Lee, who did not agree with everything that was going on in the South, Ervin felt it was his duty to fight. Like Lee, Ervin believed that "duty" was the most sublime word in the language.

During the early morning hours of March 2, 1960, while most of his colleagues and the rest of the nation slept, Ervin was on his feet on the floor of the Senate, wearily filibustering against the Eisenhower Administration's civil rights proposals. In between the cracker-barrel mountain stories and the legalistic razzle-dazzle, Ervin made a revealing confession about his reasons for fighting so hard. He had seen, as many others in the South had, that integration wasn't so bad after all, and that as long as it could be achieved through voluntary means the South could make tremendous progress and, in fact, solve its age-old racial problems long before the North. But the federal legislation was beginning to drive a wedge between him and his conscience.

"A person who is interested in public service," he said, "is compelled to take a stand for or against compulsory integration of the races whether he is for it or against it. So he can no longer stand on a middle ground and try to do something for the welfare of the community. He is driven to an extreme, one way or the other."

Ervin was driven from the middle ground as early as 1954, when the Supreme Court, with the stroke of a pen, precipitated one of the greatest social revolutions in history. Segregation was not just a theory but part of the texture and fabric of southern life, a seemingly lasting bond of law and custom. For those who grew up in the system it was not something to be questioned. To Ervin, interviewed by *Look* magazine in the spring of 1956, segregation was "not the offspring of racial bigotry or racial prejudice," but instead the result of the exercise of "a fundamental American freedom—the freedom of selecting one's associates."

Ervin's fears that the decision would substantially alter the southern way of life were soon dispelled by the brother of S. I. Parker, the man with whom he fought on the battlefields of France. Chief Judge John J. Parker of the Fourth Circuit Court of Appeals, interpreting the meaning of the ruling, said the Court "has not decided that the states must mix persons of different races in the schools . . . . What it had decided, and all it has decided, is that a state may not deny to any person on account of race the right to attend any school that it maintains."

Ervin and the South were eager to believe that. He fervently believed that Parker's reading of the *Brown* decision was the correct one. He did not realize, as he put it, how much force there was from men for compulsory integration.

He resisted the trend with considerable dignity, always standing on constitutional grounds, never falling in with the racists, never counseling defiance. Ervin had little use for men like James Eastland of Mississippi, who, speaking on the floor of the Senate, said the 1954 decision was "crap," and told the people back home, "You are not required to obey any court which passes out such a ruling. In fact, you are obliged to defy it."

Defiance was very much in the air when Ervin first went to the Senate. James J. Kilpatrick of the *Richmond News Leader* cried "interposition," claiming that the power of the state could be placed between its residents and the federal government. "By every lawful means that can be devised, this tyranny must be resisted, step by step and inch by inch, if the vitality of Southern civilization is to be preserved, and all that is best and finest in our culture is not to be lost in the indolence and degradation of a mixed society."

Southerners in the Senate responded to the pressure. They adopted a "Declaration of Constitutional Principles" on March 12, 1956, encouraging states to resist the law of the land. The Declaration, which quickly became known as the "Southern Manifesto," was written by a committee of three: Richard

Russell of Georgia, John Stennis of Mississippi, and Sam Ervin. Although Ervin went along with it, he said Russell did most of the writing. In truth, it did not read much like Ervin.

"We commend the motives of those states which have declared the intention to resist forced integration by any lawful means," the manifesto said. "We pledge ourselves to use every lawful means to bring about a reversal of this decision which is contrary to the Constitution and to prevent the use of force in its implementation." At the same time it appealed to southerners "to scrupulously refrain from disorder and lawless acts."

The manifesto was not meant to be a blood oath, but that was what it amounted to. Two North Carolina congressmen, Charles Dean and Thurmond Chatham, refused to sign it and were soundly defeated for reelection that year. Governor J. P. Coleman of Mississippi rubbed it in by saying it was a warning to all other southern politicians "not to insult the South's convictions."

Ervin, who had to run for reelection two years after being appointed, had already cemented his political base. Mayor Marshall Kurfees of Winston-Salem, who had said Ervin "could have put his talent to better use by helping us with the problem of how to comply with the law of the land," lost all one hundred counties to him in the Democratic primary in 1956.

It was also a presidential election year. Ervin, chosen to sit on the Democratic platform committee, walked into a major fight with liberals who wanted to adopt a plank endorsing the Supreme Court's ruling. Believing the South would bolt from the party, Ervin made some emotional appeals during committee meetings. "I love the South," he declared. "Many persons whose blood runs in my veins died for a cause they believed to be right. I honestly believe that if usurption by the court continues, the Constitution of the United States will be destroyed."

In January, 1957, Eisenhower began his second term, saying the country had made progress in the field of equal rights, but "unhappily, much remains to be done." He asked Congress for a full range of civil rights bills, including one which would give the attorney general the power to obtain court orders against civil rights violators.

The introduction of the bills coincided, however, with a highly important moment in the career of Sam Ervin—his assignment to the Judiciary Subcommittee on Constitutional Rights. The subcommittee was then the conduit through which all civil rights bills in the Senate had to pass. Here they underwent the stubborn scrutiny of a man defending the South against an invasion of laws no less real to him than Sherman's march to the sea.

Ervin fought with all of his considerable energy and tenacity against every civil rights bill that came down the road between 1957 and 1968, succeeding in some cases in killing or watering them down, but most often only in delaying them. There was too much steam behind the civil rights movement for twenty-two senators from eleven southern states to stop it for long.

During the hearings on the Eisenhower program, Ervin got into a confrontation with Attorney General Herbert Brownell which he never forgot. Brownell had singled out three small North Carolina counties as evidence that blacks were being denied the right to vote, and Ervin, naturally, wanted proof. Brownell said the information came from FBI reports but would not let Ervin see them. Ervin found out that the problems in those counties had been corrected before the May, 1956 primary —when the blacks were supposed to have been denied the vote. He demanded an explanation from Brownell and the Justice Department but he did not get one until long after the hearing records were closed. He never forgave Brownell for that.

During the 1957 summer recess, Ervin stayed in town and painstakingly wrote a thirty-one-page minority report, which he and Olin Johnston of South Carolina submitted in opposition to the committee's favorable report on the bill. It contains some of the best explanations of Ervin's civil rights positions.

He began by saying that the raging debate over the issue was impairing the country's sanity and diminishing its ability "to see the United States steady and to see it whole." Here are three of the key paragraphs:

> S.83 [the bill] is based on the strange thesis that the best way to promote the civil rights of some Americans is to rob other Americans of civil rights equally as precious and to reduce the supposedly sovereign states to meaningless zeros on the Nation's map.
>
> The only reason advanced by the proponents of S.83 for urging its enactment is, in essence, an insulting and insupportable indictment of a whole people. They say that southern officials and southern people are generally faithless to their oaths as public officers and jurors, and for that reason can be justifiably denied the right to invoke for their protection in courts of justice constitutional and legal safeguards erected in times past by the Founding Fathers and the Congress to protect all Americans from governmental tyranny.
>
> Congress could do well to pause and ponder this indisputable fact: The provisions of S.83 are far broader than the reason assigned for urging its enactment. If these provisions can be used today to make legal pariahs and second-class litigants out of southerners involved in civil rights cases, they can be used with equal facility tomorrow to reduce other Americans involved in countless other cases to the like status.

He added that the bill ignored the primary lesson taught in history: "That no man is fit to be trusted with unlimited governmental power."

When the bill reached the Senate floor, the Democratic and Republican leaders, Lyndon Johnson and Everett Dirksen, agreed to allow all-night sessions to break the southern filibuster. But it didn't work. The Southern Caucus, under the generalship of Richard Russell, decided to show the leadership no more mercy than it had shown them. It divided into three teams, each with responsibility for a twenty-four-hour period, and ran the Senate ragged. Each three-man team—Ervin was with Lister Hill of Alabama and Allen Ellender of Louisiana—would hold the floor while the other teams slept. Meanwhile, the leadership had to produce forty-eight senators to answer roll calls.

Russell's instructions were to hold the floor until the worst possible hour for those who were enjoying their meals and their beds—dinner time, 2 A.M., or just before daybreak—and then demand a roll call. "We did that to perfection," Ervin chuckled. "Mike Monroney (from Oklahoma) said after being roused from sleep at 2 o'clock in the morning that we looked fresh as newly bloomed crocuses." Both the South and the rest of the Senate finally pooped out, passing a voting rights bill watered down by an Ervin amendment that provided for jury trials for persons charged with preventing blacks from voting.

The "Ervin school," as it was referred to, had won out. Writing in *The New York Times* on March 25, 1957, William S. White said the southerners, "who in the past spoke in terms of harsh racism have been largely quiescent and overshadowed." The "soft southern approach," inspired by Ervin, adhered carefully to legal arguments and helped to win concessions from the North.

Was Ervin wrapping himself in a cloak of constitutional garments to conceal deep-down racial prejudice? Was he subtly passing the word back to North Carolina voters that he was a redneck at heart, who would deliver them from the civil rights agitators and their do-good friends on the Supreme Court? Or was he really convinced that the civil rights laws made legal and constitutional angels weep? Was he putting up, as a lawyer, the best legal defense he could for a guilty client? Those questions can only be answered by studying the man, his background, and his record.

However lofty his intentions, he practically assured himself of a lifetime job in the Senate by lying down in front of the civil rights steamroller. He could survive the slings and arrows of the northern liberal press; it was the voters back home who mattered, and whether he acted deliberately or not, they loved him for it.

He won three six-year terms in the Senate with hardly any opposition and without any political organization worthy of the name. Coincidentally, it was this unbeatable political strength that allowed him to perform a number of courageous libertarian acts while both liberals and conservatives played it safe.

Ervin soon became the intellectual darling of the segregationists, the legal crutch upon whom those less informed about constitutional principles and more interested in racist politics leaned for support. He gave their cause a veneer of legal class.

Some of Ervin's admirers felt he never would have come into the power and prestige he enjoyed among his colleagues in the Senate if he had not played out his role as defender of the South. He certainly would not have lasted very long with North Carolina voters if he had looked the slightest bit liberal on southern gut issues. This is the classic rationalization for politicians who have to do certain things in order to stay in office to serve noble causes. But politics is full of rationalizations, and it is unquestionably true that if Ervin had tried to play hero, he would have been beaten and replaced by someone far worse. (That happened, shortly before Ervin's appointment, to Frank Porter Graham. One of the most liberal voices in the state, Graham was smeared with racist epithets and defeated for reelection to the Senate.)

In the fall of 1957, three North Carolina cities, Charlotte, Greensboro, and Winston-Salem, began voluntarily integrating their schools. At the same time, mobs were threatening black students attempting to enter Central High School in Little Rock, Arkansas. President Eisenhower responded by sending federal troops, and Ervin, thus provoked, called it "a tragic day for constitutional government in America."

Tragic day or not, it must have given Ervin a strong jolt of pride that, by contrast, North Carolinians were responding to the new requirements of the law in peace. Throughout the era of civil rights reform, he fiercely guarded his state's moderate racial image. While there may have been some deplorable goings on in the rest of the South, he chose to ignore them. But let an attorney general or a civil rights spokesman say a word about the most backward North Carolina county, and Ervin would pounce like a great grizzly defending his part of the forest. It was an emotional, motherly protectiveness. "I have never heard an attack made on North Carolina without coming to its defense," he said during one civil rights hearing.

The fact is that North Carolina did have some serious problems with discrimination, but by the time Congress started to move into the field the state was way out ahead, and Ervin was not going to allow it to be "condemned" along with the rest of the South.

One story he told a couple of times suggests that he might have preferred it if the rest of the South had been left to defend itself. "I am like the man who went to the circus and the circus attendant tapped him with a stick and he raised an awful howl. The circus owner went around and said, 'I saw that man hit you. He just barely tapped you. He didn't hurt you.' The fellow said, 'No, but what makes me mad, he tapped me with a stick with which he stirs the monkey's wheel.' "

Many of the civil rights laws were not as urgently needed in North Carolina, and Ervin wanted to make sure that everyone knew it.

By 1960 the pressure to do something about racial discrimination in the South had grown apace. The first lunch counter sit-in demonstration, which Ervin denounced as a lawless trespass on private property, was held in his own state. And yet he apparently failed to see that a great movement had begun, which cried out for official accommodation. He helped filibuster Eisenhower's 1960 civil rights legislation almost to death. All that survived was a weak, unenforceable voting rights bill.

At the 1960 Democratic National Convention in Los Angeles, in a repeat performance of his 1956 role, Ervin led the fight against a civil rights plank in the platform. He went committed to Lyndon Johnson and wound up trying to save the South for John F. Kennedy.

Ervin did not cover himself with glory at the convention. In delivering the South's minority report on the civil rights plank, he put on one of his worst performances, ranting and stumbling before national television about how doing away with literacy tests would create a government "by the idiots and the ignorant for the idiots and the ignorant." He warned that the South's traditional loyalty to the Democratic Party was wearing thin and would vanish if the "studied vilification" continued.

The next morning, Gladys Tillet, one of the delegates and a friend of Ervin's since their days as children in Morganton, found him sitting alone in the hotel restaurant and sat down to breakfast with him. The spunky little woman who had marched for the right to vote in the early 1900's was angry with Ervin and could not refrain from scolding him.

"Sam," she said, "what you did last night did not help you and it did not help the South, and I just wish you hadn't made that speech. I really suffered sitting there listening to you. I know the plank ought to be in there, and I believe there must be something in you that can tell you it ought to be in there from the standpoint of human rights. I just can't sit down here without saying that."

"Gladys, I had to do that," said Ervin. "They were all threatening to walk out and Kennedy would never have been nominated."

Among Kennedy's early supporters at the convention was Terry Sanford, one of the most promising politicians in the South. He had been elected governor of North Carolina in 1960, and was trying to lead his state out of the dark ages of human rights, inventively seeking solutions to poverty and discrimination at the same time that Ervin was pulling up the drawbridge. He and Ervin were natural political rivals.

"I think Sam didn't have clear in his mind either the conditions of the South or his own position," Sanford told me. "The South needed more creative leadership and his was a position that was definitely no longer valid. The time had come for the liberation of the black man."

Before coming to the Senate, Ervin had been considered a moderate on the subject of race, and if he had been given a chance to demonstrate his theory that racial problems can best be handled by states and communities, he might have responded differently to the challenges of the era. He might have become one of the South's progressive leaders if he had been a governor instead of a senator.

But in the Senate, Ervin saw nothing but treachery in the civil rights laws, which he believed would forever rob the states of their ability to respond. He fought against them with such stubbornness and orneriness that many of the impressive things he did in other areas were greatly overshadowed. For Ervin's reputation, they were wasted years. He seemed to be, as one observer once said, "a great man whose mind is in chains."

Civil rights laws were only a small part of the rough beast Ervin was fighting: the central government with its programs and studies and data banks and personality profiles; its power, whether benevolent or malignant. Every time another program was established in Washington, whether it was child care or care of the elderly, the federal system—that "indestructible union of indestructible states"—died a little.

These seemed alarmist fears during the days of the Great Society, but when President Nixon established a "super cabinet" within the White House, set up one man as his "domestic czar," and gave budget examiners a strangle hold on funds for the poor, the hungry, and the ill-housed, the fears seemed more like prophecies.

Thus, Ervin, in an article in the fall, 1963, *North Carolina Law Review*, said with conviction, "The proponents of current civil rights legislation, many of them undoubted men of good will, would, in an attempt to meet a genuine problem concerning the inflamed nature between the races in this country, trounce upon an even more pressing need—the need to preserve limited, constitutional government in an age of mass bureaucracy and centralization."

Ervin tuned out the urgent voices and listened instead to his private warnings that said over and over again: government is destroyed by good intentions; the states are the only breakwater against oceans of federal tyranny.

He probably didn't even hear—or didn't want to hear—Robert Kennedy, who pleaded during the 1963 hearings: "I think it would have been much better if it had been done at the state level rather than having the federal government become involved." But the states had failed miserably at providing equal justice under their laws, and Congress had a right to see that constitutional rights were not denied.

Kennedy was arguing the merits of his brother's 1963 civil rights bill. "Being quite frank about it," he said to Ervin, "I don't think we can wait any longer. If we didn't have this problem, Senator, I wouldn't advocate this legislation. But I think it is essential in view of the situation in our country today. The injustices have existed for a long period of time, and it does not appear that they will be remedied internally by a local community or state in a number of areas of the country."

Ervin was fond of Kennedy. They had worked together on the McClellan Committee, and he had supported him when John Kennedy sent his name up for attorney general. But he must have thought the young man a little too eager to grasp at easy solutions without weighing what they would do to the Constitution—or at least to Ervin's Constitution.

"Do you think that all Americans of all races ought to be robbed by the federal legislation of the right to use their own property according to their own wishes, and the right to determine whom they shall serve in order to confer a supposed equality by the coercive power of law for the benefit of one segment of our population?" Ervin asked.

Kennedy confirmed Ervin's worst suspicions by answering that he did not think any property right was absolute; he added that most of the things the civil rights bill sought to correct were already covered by federal law. What was needed was a short cut.

Ervin did not do much Bible quoting during the civil rights era, probably realizing that his opponents needed only to turn to the New Testament to refute him. Though some may find in his position a serious blindness to reality as well as justice, the fact is he was not opposed to civil rights *per se,* but only to the methods and the nature of the solution of those who pushed for change. He frequently said he would support any civil rights bill that left the rights of the states and individuals alone. Impossible? Maybe not.

He told many stories during the civil rights debates, but often they were not very funny and served only as cues for deep-bellied laughs from his fellow southerners, which unnerved the liberals. "Mr. President," New York's Jacob Javits said once after listening to one of Ervin's moonshiner tales, "I would like to say this is an illustration of why our problem is made more difficult. Those who oppose the bill, with very deep conviction, are very charming people and know such good stories."

A civil rights lobbyist recalled seeing Missouri's Thomas Hennings, then chairman of the Constitutional Rights Subcommittee, emerge from a closed meeting with a look of disgust on his face. "I just told Alex Wiley [committee member from Wisconsin] if he'd stop laughing at Senator Ervin's jokes, we might be able to get this bill out of the subcommittee," Hennings said.

Some of the stories were just wacky enough to throw a witness off stride. When he was interrogating Attorney General Brownell, Ervin said there were some state election officials who had "the virtue that enemies call obstinacy and friends call firmness" and who would defy an order from the attorney general just to defy him. "We had a man down in my state that did not agree with anybody about anything. He found that cabbage didn't agree with him, and thereafter he wouldn't eat anything but cabbage."

When Ervin defended the South against charges that it tied up the Senate with filibusters, he told his favorite shaggy-dog story: "We are charged with tying things up under present Rule 22. I regret to have to admit we are like the Kazook Society that Jiggs joined. We haven't got enough members to do that.

"Jiggs went over to Spain with Maggie, and he found out there was a mutual protection society of husbands over there and he joined it because each member of the society was sworn to come to the rescue of any husband member who got into a controversy of any kind with his wife.

"In this cartoon, Jiggs and Maggie were walking along the streets of Madrid, and Maggie took umbrage at something Jiggs had said, so she began to beat him. Jiggs hollered 'Kazook!' About a thousand members of the Kazook Society came running to Jiggs's rescue. Maggie took an umbrella and laid them all out in the street. And the last picture in the cartoon showed Jiggs in the hospital all swathed in bandages. He observed, 'The idea behind the Kazook Society is pretty good, but it hasn't got enough members.' "

When Robert Kennedy tried seriously, using statistics, to show the depth of black educational deprivation, Ervin rattled him with the following: "This story has no application to the Attorney General. Down in my country an old storekeeper had been selling groceries to a mountaineer on credit. The mountaineer came in to pay his grocery bill. The storekeeper told him the amount of the grocery bill, which exceeded considerably what the old mountaineer thought it would be. The old mountaineer complained that the bill was too large. The storekeeper got out his account books and laid them on the counter and said: 'Here are the figures; you know figures don't lie.'

"The old mountaineer said: 'I know figures don't lie, but liars sure do figure.'

"Honest men also figure.

"I have lived in North Carolina all my life, and know some of the inferences you have drawn from your figures are not very accurate. In saying this, I do not challenge your good faith."

Kennedy replied, "Senator, I am just giving the figures."

"That is what the storekeeper was giving the old mountaineers," Ervin countered.

"That is why it is so difficult even to proceed," Kennedy said, "because if we are not going to recognize that there is a problem, if we are going to state that figures do not mean anything, that everything is fine, that we are making satisfactory progress, then we are not going to get any place. If we cannot recognize the fact that there is a problem, Senator, we are not going to get very far."

Ervin came back with a characteristic answer: "Mr. Attorney General, I will maintain at any time, and in any place, under any conditions, that North Carolina is more like heaven than any other place on earth. Despite this, I will admit that we have many unsolved problems down there. But I think we could solve them much better if we did not get so much interference from up here on the banks of the Potomac."

Ervin was quite aroused at this point. Even though his story was meant to blunt Kennedy's remarks about his state, it made him own blood run hot. Chairman Eastland had to call for order.

There was no sham in Ervin's performance. The civil rights laws offended several of his fundamental convictions. "Like Voltaire said about the laws of France, they forbade the rich and the poor alike to steal bread and sleep in parks," he said during an interview. "They are passed solely for one segment of our population."

Ervin believed there are certain things that ought to be decided among individuals and not regulated by government at all. As much government should be kept at home as possible, "because a local government can't practice tyrannies on people like a distant government." Another of Ervin's convictions was that a man who invests his talent and money in a business has the inherent right to hire, promote, and fire without governmental interference.

He thought the Interstate Commerce Clause was a silly peg on which to hang the Public Accommodations Act. For example, he said, "the federal government could require murder to assure the flow of caskets in interstate commerce. It could regulate sexual intercourse because children are created by that method and that's responsible for the increased flow of diapers and diaper pins."

He accepted the public accommodations principle, however. When a man opens a motel or restaurant to the general public he does not have the right to make restrictions. But private property was something else. "I don't think there's anything illegal for me to prefer to rent a room in my house or sell a piece of my land to a man of my own race or my own religion or my own national origin."

He introduced into the record of one of his hearings an article entitled "The Right to Be Nasty," by Laurence H. Eldredge, formerly professor of law at the University of Pennsylvania. In it Eldredge said, "It has always been a fundamental part of the Anglo-Saxon tradition of law that private citizens have a right to lead their own lives as they see fit, to make utter fools of themselves and incur community condemnation, and to be eccentric, unreasonable, bigoted and nasty, if they choose to lead that kind of life."

Ervin was upset with governors like Ross Barnett of Mississippi and George Wallace of Alabama, who had staged their defiance of the law—and thus encouraged the same from others—by standing in the schoolhouse door. "I do not believe I would change the whole system of constitutional government in America on account of illegal actions of Ross Barnett or unwise actions of George Wallace." Their antics were making it harder for Ervin to fight the legislation on its merits. On September 3, 1963, he said, "I do not approve of the recent actions of Governor

Wallace as reported in the press. These actions make him a chief aider and abetter of the efforts of those who advocate the passage of this particular bill." Five days later, a black church in Birmingham blew up, and there was no longer any doubt that the bills would pass.

Time had run out for Ervin and the South by 1964. The revolution was at hand, and all the southerners could do was tie up the Senate until public opinion turned harshly against them and moderate Republicans joined the efforts to end the debate. It was a low point in the national image of southern senators.

Eunice Ervin recalled that she was working in New York when her brother was leading the opposition to the 1964 bill. She was keenly aware at the time of the resentment toward "the southerner of Caucasian descent." She, like her brother, felt pangs of guilt about the southern treatment of blacks, and yet the back-bristling idea that the northern liberals would ignore their own racial problems and continue to punish the South for the Civil War, to continue to extract, as southerners would say, the last ounce of blood from their unrepentent hides, was too much.

She remembered attending the Madison Avenue Presbyterian Church when its parishioners were eagerly signing a petition supporting the very Civil Rights Act her brother was trying to defeat. And yet, she recalled, with the bemused inner smile of the Ervins, "The congregation was relatively indifferent to Harlem." Her neighborhood was "the most segregated community in which I ever lived." She had grown up with blacks and had known them intimately, and for that reason suffered in New York because she never came into contact with black people. "It seems to me that Sam was trying to stay the day when the South would be coerced. He was trying to delay a fundamental social revolution."

Discrimination against black voters in the South was indefensible, and Ervin knew it. He felt that those found guilty of depriving others of the right to vote on racial grounds "ought not only be stuck in jail but they ought to have the jail mashed down on them." The point was, he wanted—fervently wanted—the states, or at least local federal courts, to do the mashing, not the Justice Department; he wanted the accused given the right of trial by jury, instead of being enjoined by a court at the whim of the attorney general. No bad attorney general should have that kind of power; no good attorney general should want it.

But the bloody spectacle of Selma, Alabama, changed all the rules and made passage of the Voting Rights Act inevitable. Ervin thought George Wallace should have gone down to Selma and talked to Martin Luther King and his marchers to find out what their grievances were, instead of letting brutality take its course. On the other hand, civil rights leaders like Clarence Mitchell, head of the Washington office of the NAACP, felt that Ervin himself had to share part of the blame for Selma. He based that harsh judgment on the fact that the southerners blocked an effective voting rights act in 1960 and kept the lid on dangerously tight. "Those who opposed in 1960 the type of law we were trying to get really laid the groundwork for the confrontation that took place in 1965."

The 1965 law was aimed almost exclusively at the South; it clearly did away with the right of the states to set the qualifications for its voters; it was a discriminatory act designed to end discrimination. And it worked.

Hundreds of thousands of blacks throughout the South, men and women whose fathers and grandfathers had been robbed of their right to vote by such measures as North Carolina's literacy test amendment—enacted when Ervin was four years old—suddenly had the power of the ballot.

Ervin thought the purpose of the act was good, but the means evil. "It's pretty bad when a court gets so outraged by misconduct that it perverts the Constitution. I think the perversion of the Constitution is worse than any kind of conduct."

"I would support any proposed legislation which is consistent with the 15th Amendment itself and with other provisions of the Constitution, and which operates fairly against all states alike," he said in a Senate speech in 1965. "But S.1564 is not such legislation. It is patently unconstitutional in its utter disregard of the fundamental principle that the states have the sole right to prescribe voter qualifications."

But the Supreme Court ruled differently. It said states are insulated from federal overview when they act within their own interest. "But such insulation is not carried over when state power is used as an instrument for circumventing a federally protected right."

Harvard Law School Professor Archibald Cox also disagreed with Ervin. During hearings in 1970 to extend the act, he said, "I would suggest, Senator Ervin, that when Congress exercises many of its powers under the Constitution, it may supersede state laws that stand in the way of the exercise of the powers." And later: "Congress has very wide discretion to determine what is necessary to enforce the guarantee of equal protection of the laws."

Ervin, who had studied at Harvard fifty years before—when constitutional law was taught a little differently—did not rise up and smite Cox with one of his 18th-century alarums. The two had a friendly, scholarly debate, agreeing on nothing, and then Cox had to rush to the airport so he could get back to Cambridge for his 3 P.M. lecture.

"I hope that when you teach that class that you will teach them sound law," said Ervin, perhaps a little wistfully.

"I will begin by telling them the advice I have received," Cox replied.

Ervin reacted to every attack on the South as though it were an attack on North Carolina. His own state was the least at fault in denying voting rights, but he stretched that point considerably when he said there was no discrimination at all. That may have been, as Earl Franklin, the chairman of the board of elections in Ervin's own Burke County, figured it, "a little too broad." But the problem, Franklin contended, was more one of custom than discrimination when blacks did not register to vote. "They just never presented themselves. They didn't want to be embarrassed."

Perhaps North Carolina wasn't so bad; only thirty-nine counties were included under the act. But the South in general had been flagrantly violating the constitutional guarantee that no citizen of the United States could be denied the right to vote on account of race, color, or previous condition of servitude. Congress had the right to enforce it with appropriate legislation.

During the 1970 hearings, Joseph Tydings of Maryland asked Ervin incredulously, "Does the chairman deny that thousands of Americans have been denied the right to vote?"

"I have lived in North Carolina all my life," Ervin said, "and so far as I know, I have never known a single man to be denied the right to register to vote on account of his race." There was plenty of testimony, in fact, about discrimination in his state, including the charge that a registrar in one rural county locked the courthouse doors to keep blacks out, but Ervin dismissed that as being unsupported.

Exasperated, Tydings pressed on. "All right, let's eliminate the state of North Carolina. You don't deny that hundreds of thousands of Americans have been denied the right to vote, do you?"

"I don't know about voting . . . ," Ervin began, but before he could finish, Tydings exploded, "Mr. Chairman, are you going to sit there and tell me you don't know what's been happening?"

It is hard to believe that Ervin imagined the rest of his homeland to be no worse than the South Mountains of North Carolina. Either he really did not know—he once said the only time he had ever been to Mississippi was when he passed through asleep on a Pullman car on the way to Memphis; and, no thanks, he did not want to go there again with his eyes open—or he chose to ignore what he knew. He obfuscated the issue by drawing a parallel between civil rights laws and the bills of attainder convicting British subjects of bygone years without trial.

"I fail to see any significance—any connection whatsoever," Tydings said.

"Well, I can't help what the senator from Maryland can't see," said Ervin who saw it, as he liked to say, as clear as the noonday sun in a cloudless sky—in historical perspective.

The fact that Ervin may have been right in the long run overlooks the very human problems of the present, and they represent much more than just a footnote to history.

Ervin was perfectly consistent in 1967 when he adamantly opposed Lyndon Johnson's nomination of Thurgood Marshall to the Supreme Court. Marshall, for many years one of the chief spokesmen for civil rights causes, did not exactly fit Alexander Hamilton's prescription of judicial restraint. He was an activist— or so Ervin thought. But it was not easy for Ervin to avoid the suspicion that he opposed Marshall primarily because he was black.

During the Senate Judiciary Committee hearings on Marshall's confirmation, Ervin subjected the former solicitor general to a grueling examination about his convictions concerning voluntary confessions. It was a year after the Court's 5–4 *Miranda* ruling, which voided convictions based on confessions made by defendants before they were advised of their right to remain silent. As so often happened with Ervin, the judge part of him bubbled to the surface. He was outraged at the *Miranda* decision. Marshall, however, refused to comment about the case because several others like it were on their way to the Court.

"If you have no opinions on what the Constitution means at this time, you ought not to be confirmed," Ervin told him. "Anybody that has been at the bar as long as you have, and has as distinguished a legal career as you have, certainly ought to have some very firm opinions about the meaning of the Constitution."

But Marshall, as many nominees have done, respectfully declined to comment because of the possibility that he would have to excuse himself from sitting on such cases after joining the Court. Ervin thought President Johnson had instructed Marshall to remain silent until he was confirmed, and he let his anger show. "I do not know what is the use of holding hearings on your nomination, because it would be absolutely worthless," he told Marshall.

His speech to the Senate on August 30 opposing Marshall showed none of that intemperance, and was even eloquent in places. Ervin admitted that in opposing Marshall, "I lay myself open to the easy, but false charge that I am a racist." He added, "I have no prejudice in my mind or heart against any man because of his race. I love men of all races. After all, they are my fellow travelers to the tomb."

After diligently studying Marshall's record as an appeals court judge, Ervin said he found him to be "by practice and philosophy a legal and judicial activist." Then, after stuffing the record with articles, opinions, and studies on the Court—most of which would never be read—Ervin said:

"I love the Constitution. I love the Constitution with all my mind and all my heart. I love the Constitution with all my mind and all my heart because I know it was fashioned to secure to all Americans of all generations the right to be ruled by a government of laws rather than government of men."

Ervin apparently convinced no one. Marshall was confirmed by a vote of 69–11, with all of his opposition coming from the southern and border states.

Ervin's fears were largely unfounded because Marshall turned out to be a fairly conservative member of the court, "a classic middle class black conservative," as one of Ervin's staff lawyers described him. Except for civil rights, he agreed with Ervin on most issues.

And then came the paradox: Ervin approved, in fact fell over backward, when Nixon nominated to the Court one of the most vigorous judicial activists of all time, William Rehnquist, a right-wing activist at that, who, as legal brief toter for the Justice Department, had opposed many of Ervin's civil liberties positions. Yet Ervin was convinced of his "professional competence," and said during his confirmation hearings, "I'm not going to ask you any questions because I do not want to be shaken in my conviction." There were raised eyebrows on the part of some who had seen his performance with Marshall.

Lyndon Johnson, whom Ervin had supported in 1960, was a great disappointment to Ervin during his presidency, primarily because of the great mass of social legislation he threw at the country's problems. He kept Ervin so busy fighting his programs that Ervin had little time for relaxation. One weekend Johnson called Ervin at his office to invite him and Mrs. Ervin to spend the afternoon on his yacht. Ervin declined. "If he wouldn't send these fool bills down here, maybe I'd have time to go," he told an aide.

Ervin considered Johnson "a man of great strength and great weakness. My greatest criticism would be, I don't think he was ever anchored to any fundamental principles. He did whatever was expedient." As a result, Ervin felt "he made awful mistakes."

During the Johnson years, Ervin once summed up Johnson's major shortcoming: "He never reads a book unless it's written about himself."

Ervin was dissected in April, 1967, by James K. Batten of *The Charlotte Observer*, who described the Ervin "paradox" like this: "An immensely successful politician who is not really a politician at all. . . . A man who seems to battle the Negro revolution for one reason, but whose battle wins popularity for another reason. . . . A sensitive man who recoils from wrongs against individuals, but who is curiously obtuse about an injustice that many admirers regard as one of the greatest moral questions of our time."

Ervin responded to the article by sending a letter to Congressman Basil L. Whitener. The letter and the article were placed alongside each other in the *Congressional Record*.

> For the record—and I do not think Mr. Batten has indicated otherwise—I have never said an unkind word about any man because of his race. My stand is unequivocal: No man should be denied the right to vote on account of race; no man should be denied the right to seek and hold any job, the right to live by the sweat of his own brow; no man should be denied the right to have a fair and impartial trial by a jury of his peers; no man should be denied the right to a decent education or to enjoy any other basic human right. I have publicly and privately deplored violence or threats of violence against any man because of his creed or color; and, where necessary, I have supported federal remedies for such violence.
>
> But we will not fool history as we fool ourselves when we steal freedom from one man to confer it on another. When freedom for one citizen is diminished, it is in the end diminished for all. It is not the "civil rights" of some but the civil liberty of all on which I take my stand.

Since coming to the Senate, Ervin had been several steps behind the Supreme Court. He saw this not as his shortcoming but the Court's. By his own estimate, he owned from 25,000 to 35,000 law books, and not a syllable in them—prior to the Court's sanctioning of the civil rights laws—suggested to him that the laws were constitutional.

Civil rights advocates criticized him for blistering the Court when he should, instead, have bowed to its rulings and accepted them as law. But Ervin believed it was his duty to comment fiercely on decisions in hopes that someday the Court would once again reverse itself.

Joseph L. Rauh, Jr., general counsel for the Leadership Conference on Civil Rights, brought a chart to the 1967 hearings on open housing legislation which showed how each one of Ervin's previous declarations about the constitutionality of bills had been shot down by the Court. Rauh said he was not asking Ervin to stop criticizing the Court, just to accept its rulings as to the meaning of the Constitution.

"Well, I am going to try to preserve the Constitution even against the Supreme Court," Ervin said.

"Sir," Rauh said, "I must respectfully, and I mean this respectfully, disagree with your right to save the Constitution from the Supreme Court. I believe it is your duty to follow the Constitution, as the Supreme Court interpreted it."

"Oh, no," Ervin shot back, "It is my duty to try to persuade the Supreme Court to follow the Constitution, not to follow after them when they go off under false skies."

At any rate, Ervin was convinced that any law telling a man to whom he could sell or rent his home flew squarely in the face of law and reason. Did not the Fifth Amendment say unequivocally that no person shall be deprived of life, liberty, or property without due process of law? But once again, the social need—to free black people from ghettos which are in part creations of the government—was deemed to be greater than the liberty of discrimination.

School desegregation, which had proceeded at a snail's pace during the early 1960's, hit a blinding speed by the end of the decade. In successive rulings, the Supreme Court said that freedom-of-choice plans were simply not ending segregated schools, that the job had to be done immediately, and that it could be done with the help of buses.

Ervin was not concerned about black and white children learning together in school. He could not accept the theory that children were denied the opportunity for equal education if they did not learn together. If he were black, he said, he would regard it as an insult to be told that his child could not learn to read or write unless seated beside a white child. Many blacks agreed.

Ervin peppered the Senate with bills that would sanction the right of children or their parents to select their school, to prohibit transportation for integration's sake, and to forbid the assignment of students to schools on the basis of their race. None of them passed, but toward the middle of election year 1972, the votes began getting closer and closer. Part of the reason was what was happening in the courts.

One of the most controversial court orders ever accepted for review by the Supreme Court was *Swann* v. *Charlotte-Mecklenburg Board of Education.* Federal District Judge James B. McMillan ordered the district to bus children from suburbs to inner city and from inner city to suburbs in a pattern that bordered on racial balance.

Acting as attorney for the Charlotte-Mecklenburg Classroom Teachers Association, Ervin entered the case as a friend of the court, writing a scholarly brief with some well-chosen words on a subject that was close to the hearts of southerners who knew there was precious little integration in the North.

Despite the fact that Charlotte and Mecklenburg County are in the South, Ervin said, whatever segregation there was existed as a result of residential patterns and was no worse than similar situations in the North. The distinction between the former legal segregation in the South and the actual segregation in the North was meaningless. To say, twenty years after *Brown,* that the South was still guilty and the North innocent was intellectually and legally dishonest. "The amicus curiae is confident that the Supreme Court will so adjudge. Indeed, it must do so if the United States is truly one nation under one flag and one Constitution."

But the Court upheld the McMillan decision and continued to maintain the artificial North-South distinction.

In late 1971, Ervin was able to stand virtually alone in the Senate and thwart a civil rights bill with a long history of House and Senate approval. He and James Allen of Alabama held the floor for three weeks, preventing consideration of a bill to give the Equal Employment Opportunity Commission (EEOC) the power to order companies to stop discriminating against blacks or women. The Senate, facing adjournment, was forced to give up. Ervin's opponents accused him of using "naked power." The following year, Congress passed an employment bill, but this one gave the EEOC far weaker powers. The agency would have to take discrimination cases through the courts, a much more time-consuming process.

By 1972, with massive desegregation beginning to be felt in the North, Ervin suddenly found himself with new allies. Years before, he had warned the Senate, "When the judicial activists and crusading bureaucrats reduce the South to a state of vassalage, they will not sit down like Alexander the Great and weep because there are no new worlds to conquer. They will turn their attention to the North, the East, and the West, take over and exercise the functions of their school boards, and herd their children like cattle and shift them about like pawns in a chess game."

An anti-busing bill was offered in the Senate that year that was in every respect similar to ones which Ervin had been proposing. Only this time its chief sponsor was not a southerner but Senator Robert Griffin, an erstwhile liberal from Michigan. Schools in Pontiac and Detroit were being threatened with court orders to desegregate, and Griffin and several of his Michigan colleagues in the House, having to face reelection, became instant converts.

Needless to say, it gave Ervin a great deal of pleasure to see this trend, and he was happy to step aside and allow Griffin to sponsor the bill. Tactically, it was better to have a northerner pushing a supposedly conservative bill.

The year before Griffin had not only voted against Ervin's amendment, but made a speech against it. Now, Ervin told Griffin, "I'm glad you've at last seen the light."

"Yes," he said Griffin replied, "they've gored my ox now just like you said they were going to."

The Griffin bill passed, at least temporarily, winning support for the first time in Senate history from all sections of the country. It was replaced, however, by a meaningless compromise. But it was a clear signal to Ervin that the end of the era of civil rights legislation was at hand. He had been fighting such bills for fifteen years.

The civil rights acts of 1964, 1965, and 1968 brought about the revolution Ervin had been trying to postpone. Between 1965 and 1970, close to a million blacks were added to the registration books in the South, and hundreds were elected to public office; hotels, restaurants, theaters, restrooms, buses, laundromats, and every other conceivable kind of public accommodation were shared alike by whites and blacks; industry, particularly the South's burgeoning textile industry, began hiring blacks in unprecedented numbers; and southern schools by 1971 had become the most integrated in the nation.

Much to everyone's surprise—integrationists as well as segregationists—these changes were accepted mostly with grace and dignity. And for many who fought out of blind southern pride, the end of the system of discrimination was greeted with a sigh of relief. The burden of intolerance was lifted from their shoulders, and they proved, without much resentment, that the South's respect for law was stronger than custom or habit.

Ervin was not sorry that he devoted so much of his time and energy to fighting civil rights legislation. Even though he gradually changed some of his beliefs, he thought he was still basically right. Someone had to stand up and warn the country that it was trading off some of its cherished liberties in order to compensate for the rights it had so long denied to black people.

By the beginning of the 1970's many young blacks who had not been involved in the civil rights struggles or remembered them dimly took a different view of Ervin than their predecessors had and even began looking to him as someone who would protect their liberties. "You know," a young black activist from Charlotte said, "if he runs again, I might just vote for that old honky."

I asked him one day in the spring of 1973, as he drove home to North Carolina, whether he thought, in spite of the problems he had with the laws themselves, that the South was better off than before. He considered the question for a long time. It was not easy to put aside the problems or to relax the legal posture he had maintained for so long.

"In many respects it's better off, yes," he said.

Then Sam Ervin, the South's legal defender, returned and quickly added how ridiculous it was for federal courts to be acting as local school boards.

Was he glad the battles were over and he could move on to other things?

"Oh, yes," he said, with a heavy note of sarcasm. "I'm glad that every civil rights law anybody could ever think of was passed. I'm glad it's out of the way."

11. *Civil Liberties*

The tides of fear are rising, and the
anchors of faith are dragging. It is in
such a time frightened humanity
needs freedom most. Since courage is better
than fear, and faith is better than
doubt, let us spurn fear, cherish faith,
and dedicate ourselves to this proposition:
Freedom is life's supreme value and
must be preserved for ourselves and our
posterity, cost what it may.

SAM ERVIN

THE BILL OF RIGHTS has been shaped by many hands in modern times. But with the possible exception of some of the great libertarian justices of the Supreme Court, it would be hard to find a single man in this century who has had more direct influence over the way basic American freedoms are enjoyed than Sam Ervin, the country lawyer from North Carolina.

Beginning with the first clause of the First Amendment to the U.S. Constitution and running down the list of commandments set forth by the Founding Fathers to protect individual rights, the document bears and will continue to bear for many years the imprint of that shy, witty man.

Freedom of religion; freedom of speech and the press; freedom to assemble and protest; the right to be left alone by government; the protection of life, liberty, and property; the right to a speedy trial before an impartial jury with the aid of legal counsel; freedom from excessive bail; and, generally, the power of the people—all have been strengthened, sometimes dramatically, by Ervin. If he had a fault, it was that he was less concerned with what government could do *for* people and more concerned about what it could do *to* people.

Ironically, but perhaps characteristically, Ervin arrived at the place where he could trip up the government largely by accident and for the wrong reasons. James Eastland, who took over the Senate Judiciary Committee in 1956, was looking for southern conservatives to put on the newly formed Constitutional Rights Subcommittee. The subcommittee's main function was to study civil rights bills, and Eastland wanted to load it with southerners who would fight them. He turned to Ervin, Johnston of South Carolina, and McClellan of Arkansas.

Under the leadership of the liberal Thomas C. Hennings of Missouri, the subcommittee began poking into wiretapping, criminal justice, and the rights of servicemen and the mentally ill. In 1960, to the horror of civil libertarians, Hennings died, and Joseph C. O'Mahoney of Wyoming, second-ranking Democrat on the subcommittee, retired. The filibustering, Bible-quoting North Carolinian moved up to become chairman. Forgetting what had happened with Joe McCarthy, many thought the cause of civil liberties in the Senate was dead. In some ways it had just come alive.

Ervin would have been perfectly content to sit out his Senate career on the Agriculture or Appropriations committees. But chance conspired to place him in the center of the greatest storm over individual rights in the history of the Republic.

He fought civil rights because there was a civil liberties position to fight them from. That made Eastland and the voters back home happy and it gave Ervin some stature as a constitutional lawyer. Then something strange happened: civil rights and civil liberties blended together, and Ervin suddenly appeared almost liberal. It was no sleight-of-hand trick, just that the old slogans did not work anymore. He could be a liberal and a conservative at the same time, and somehow it all seemed consistent. The Bill of Rights was the common ground on which liberals and conservatives could meet.

The Criminal Justice Act, which set up the federal defenders system, was designed to provide legal counsel for indigent defendants in criminal cases. The Bail Reform Act of 1966 made it possible for defendants who could not afford bail to be released from custody pending trial. As it happened, these two reforms have had the greatest impact on urban blacks, particularly in the District of Columbia, where a great many persons accused of crimes languished in jail because of crowded court dockets. Ervin wrote both laws. When he opposed the District of Columbia Crime Bill in 1969, black students gave him an award for trying to protect the rights of Washingtonians.

These efforts did not make him a civil rights champion or a liberal in the northern liberal sense. He was simply trying to uphold and defend the Constitution, and it did not matter to him who the beneficiaries were. Had Ervin been extra careful about appearing tough on law-and-order issues, he probably never would have done these things.

Ervin's constitutional sensitivities were offended when Congress responded to urban riots with an antiriot law making it a crime to cross a state line or to use the mail with intent to incite a riot (the "Rap Brown Law"). In a little-noticed appearance before the Judiciary Committee, Ervin said the only problem with the law was that it was unenforceable. He was right. "There may never be a conviction under the bill as drafted," he said in 1967, "for it would be virtually impossible to show beyond a reasonable doubt what existed in the innermost recesses of a man's mind as he crossed a state line." He suggested instead that the perfectly good laws already in existence be enforced.

When Ervin took over the Constitutional Rights Subcommittee in January, 1961, it was only six years old and had not yet begun to grow. At first it seemed that he wanted to rock along in the same way—like a sedate law firm, as a former staff member put it. But under pressure from an aggressive young staff, recruited by Chief Counsel William A. Creech, the subcommittee became more active.

During Ervin's first year, the subcommittee conducted public hearings, field studies, investigations, and background research in six major areas besides civil rights: wiretapping and eavesdropping; right to legal counsel; and the rights of the mentally ill, the American Indian, the military, and criminal suspects. During the next decade, major laws in all these fields were enacted.

Mental patients, as Ervin knew from having sat in judgment over many commitment proceedings, automatically lost a number of basic rights, including the right to manage their own affairs, maintain their marriages, and—all too often—receive treatment and return to society. In most states the patient had no legal right to correspond with persons on the outside, not even with an attorney. State legislatures were unwilling to spend the money for proper care, and the hospitals were little more than human warehouses.

"One of the paramount questions confronting us today," Ervin said during hearings in March, 1961, "is whether society, which is unable or unwilling to provide treatment, has the right to deprive the patient of his liberty on the sole grounds that he is in need of care." He said the evidence was "shocking and chilling." The laws assured the patient of only one right: "the right to be forgotten."

In 1964, Congress adopted Ervin's mental health bill for Washington, a model law which other states quickly copied. It encouraged voluntary hospitalization, attempted to remove the stigma attached to receiving treatment, and spelled out a patient's "bill of rights," including the right to treatment and periodic review.

Two months later, in May, 1961, a Philadelphia lawyer demonstrated how easily a tape-recorded conversation could be altered. The witness played first an original recording of his own voice and then a version of the same recording after it had been doctored by a professional tape editor.

"I have always been a great protector of the American way of life and an arch foe of Communism," said the first, taped voice of Samuel Dash. Then he played the second: "I have always been an arch foe of the American way of life and a great protector of Communism."

Ervin said he had heard conflicting views on the value of wiretapping. "Some think that the value of the interest of the individual in privacy is so much more important from a long-range viewpoint than that of bringing to justice the comparatively few who have been caught by wiretapping." Wiretapping went against Ervin's grain, against his deep-rooted feelings about privacy. But the Supreme Court consistently allowed it, while inviting Congress to restrict its use severely. Most of the bills proposed by the Kennedy and Johnson Administrations required investigators to obtain a search warrant for wiretapping—as they had always been required to do before searching homes—but they made an exception when investigating organized crime. Ervin was opposed. The enemy, he said, "can be destroyed without resorting to the enemy's tactics." Carefully controlled wiretapping was finally approved, with Ervin's endorsement, by the Crime and Safe Streets Act of 1968. Ervin was never comfortable with that law. His interests lay more in protecting the rights of individuals against the government—not the other way around.

With the help of Helen Maynor, a Lumbee Indian from Pembroke, North Carolina, and a member of the committee staff, Ervin became intensely concerned about the long-neglected rights of American Indians. Because the eastern band of Cherokee Indians resides just over the mountains from Ervin's home and because of the special federal status conferred on the original Americans by the Founding Fathers, Ervin was naturally drawn to their cause. Furthermore, the 500,000 Indians who lived on reservations were being deprived of basic constitutional rights by their tribal governments.

As a result of wide-ranging hearings, Ervin introduced legislation in 1966 to guarantee the same rights to reservation Indians that were enjoyed by other Americans. The bill passed the Senate but languished in the House Indian Affairs Subcommittee, a victim of indifference. That neglect inspired Ervin to pull off the biggest parliamentary coup of his career.

On March 8, 1968, when the Senate was considering the Fair Housing Bill, Ervin offered the "Indian Bill of Rights" as an amendment. "It gives the Senate an opportunity to show whether it believes in constitutional rights for red men," he said. It caught the Senate leadership by surprise, as well as civil rights lobbyists, who were convinced that it was a trick aimed at killing the housing bill.

Majority leader Mike Mansfield tried to talk Ervin into withdrawing the amendment, saying the House would surely give his bill prompt consideration. But Ervin knew that was highly unlikely. He could not resist taunting the Senate liberals again: "I did not think that anybody supporting a bill to secure constitutional rights to black people would be opposed to giving constitutional rights to red people. But I am apparently mistaken."

Mansfield then made the point of order that Ervin's amendment was not germane to civil rights, and Montana's Lee Metcalf, sitting in the chair, upheld him, saying Ervin's bill was too broad. The issue was drawn and Ervin struck the next blow.

"Mr. President, inasmuch as the ruling of the chair scalps the Indians, I appeal from the ruling of the chair and ask the Senate to reverse it," he said. Then, in back-to-back roll call votes, the Senate overturned the ruling 54–28 and approved his amendment 81–0. The amendment was accepted by the House-Senate conference committee and became law. The Cherokees made Sam Ervin an honorary chief for as long as the rivers run and the mountains are green. They also gave him a blow gun in case he ever needed it in the Senate.

Not all Indians were happy with Ervin's bill of rights, however, and some claimed that white man's law did not sit well with tribal customs. So the next year, Ervin, the Great White Father, spent a week in the hot New Mexico sun with the Navajos and the Pueblos, listening to their complaints, eating their hot, spicy food, and occasionally sampling their firewater. At one point, an enormous Navajo woman named Annie Waneka, who had boxed the ears of a legal service lawyer and was being sued under the Ervin Bill of Rights, looked as though she would box the ears of the bill's author and his aides. One of the aides, Rufus Edmisten, whispered in Ervin's ear, "If she comes after us, we're getting out of here." But Ervin only laughed.

Despite everything else that was happening in 1973, Ervin still found time to push a private bill for the relief of the Half Breed Kaw Indians, who had been run off their land by white settlers in Kansas and Oklahoma in the 1800's. He also received an award from the National Congress of American Indians.

Once the Constitutional Rights Subcommittee got into high gear, Ervin found himself like a child in a candy shop with a pocketful of pennies. The subcommittee had an almost unlimited scope and was beginning to put its feelers out in all directions. The office was flooded with suggestions from people who felt that their rights were being abridged and from professors at major law schools.

One of the most frequent complaints was that servicemen found unfit for duty were being discharged without a hearing or an appeal. Those suspected of homosexuality were simply given the axe, whether there was any proof or not. Dispensing with constitutional rights was viewed as necessary for retaining military discipline and efficiency, but Ervin had "an instinctive feeling that a man ought not to be condemned without a trial."

After six years of hearings and study, Ervin introduced his Military Justice Act. The Vietnam War was at its height, and close to 500,000 men were fighting without any assurance that they would find justice, if they needed it, in military courts. The bill extended the right of counsel to servicemen before court-martials, and also established a corps of military judges and a court of military appeals, both of which were insulated from control by the top brass. Ervin said it was time "to extend to servicemen the same rights they are defending." The bill became law in 1968.

In all three areas—Indians, servicemen, and mental patients—Ervin was basically invoking the rules of the game on behalf of neglected people, insisting that they were entitled to due process of law. The rules of society did not stop at the entrance to the reservation, the military base, or the hospital door. These interests in turn led him to discover another right that was being taken away without due process, the right to privacy. Ervin brought to this issue his own respect for privacy, as well as his reverence for the institutions of friendship and marriage. The frequency of intercourse, whether social or sexual, was nobody's business, nor was a person's financial condition. Before coming to the Senate he was asked to serve as an arbitrator in a strike, but he became so infuriated at a questionnaire concerning his personal finances that he sent it back to the government unanswered.

Nor did society have a right to pry into religious affiliations or beliefs or, indeed, into that most sacred right of all, the privacy of one's innermost thoughts. If the government could not enter a person's home, it certainly could not enter his mind.

But it had been attempting to do precisely those things, clumsily poking, probing, and analyzing both its employees and private citizens. Sensing that Big Brother was at hand twenty years ahead of time, Ervin went to the mat with the government in the mid-sixties. He became an ombudsman for the government's two and a half million employees and the untold millions being harassed by federal computers.

He was indignant over the psychological tests, the lie detectors, and all the other modern tools that government agencies were using as substitutes for common sense. As he told the Senate on September 13, 1967, "Do they not know how to evaluate a secretary for employment without asking her how her bowels are, if she has diarrhea, if she loved her mother, if she goes to church every week, if she believes in God, if she believes in the second coming of Christ, if her sex life is satisfactory, if she has to urinate more often than other people, what she dreams about, and many other extraneous matters?"

Furthermore, the agencies were recruiting college graduates, hooking them up to machines, and asking them such questions as:

When was the first time you had sexual relations with a woman?

How many times have you had sexual intercourse?

Have you ever engaged in homosexual activities?

Have you ever engaged in sexual activites with an animal?

When was the first time you had sexual intercourse with your wife?

Did you have intercourse with her before you were married?

How many times?

"What an introduction to American government for these young people," Ervin said.

The government's medical history questionnaire, which carried criminal penalties for failure to answer, was just as bad. And the one officials replaced it with after Ervin jumped on their backs was only a slight improvement. It was evidence to him that "hope springs eternal in the bureaucracy that it will someday, despite the best efforts of Congress, know all there is to know about a man."

According to subcommittee reports, one agency, the Department of Agriculture, required workers taking sick leave to surrender the confidentiality of their medical records; another, the Department of Health, Education and Welfare, held a blacklist of professionals involved in various social causes; most asked questions about religion, race, and national origin, and indoctrinated their employees with racial-encounter group sessions. Many conducted heavy-handed savings bond campaigns. Ervin saw all these activities as unconstitutional invasions of privacy.

Every year since 1966 Ervin has introduced a federal employee privacy bill only to have it die, after passing the Senate, in the House Post Office and Civil Service Committee. However, partly as a result of his nagging, reforms took place and employees' unions became more interested in pay raises and security than in privacy. But Ervin wanted the reforms cemented into law rather than being dependent on the temporary thawing of some bureaucrat's heart.

Not many people—not even some of those who have worked for Ervin or covered him as reporters—got overly excited about the privacy issue. Today we are more at home in the clutches of what we assume to be a benevolent government, with bigness and impersonal, antiseptic relationships, than a man of his era. The same pragmatic liberals who got us into Vietnam justified hooking us up to computers to make sure we were taking advantage of all the federal programs designed to guide us safely to the grave. It was, after all, for our own good . . .

With its growing computer technology, the government developed a tremendous appetite for "people studies." Most of them were conducted by the Census Bureau on behalf of other agencies. One that really frosted Ervin was a "voluntary" questionnaire sent to Social Security recipients. It wanted to know:

Do you have artificial dentures?

Do you—or your spouse—see or telephone your parents as often as once a week?

What is the total number of gifts that you give to individuals per year?

About how often do you go to the barber shop or beauty salon?

What were you doing most of last week?

Taking things altogether, would you say that you are happy, pretty happy, or not too happy these days?

Respondents were not told that they were not required to answer the questions. It was "a matter of rather subtle psychology," one of the officials said when interrogated by Ervin. The agency sent several follow-up questionnaires if the "target" old person did not cooperate, and then badgered him in person until he finally gave in.

Everybody got into the census act. Questionnaires were sent to lawyers and bus drivers, homeowners and farmers, veterans and owners of small businesses. The government wanted to know the drug habits of teenagers, the menstrual cycles of Alaskan women, and the bladder problems of institutionalized adults.

As outraged as he was, Ervin managed to find some grim humor in it all. He told the Senate in November, 1969 that he considered introducing a constitutional amendment to allow a computer to be elected President. "But I found that while it can make logical conclusions from information fed into it, it cannot draw illogical deductions from logical facts. For this reason, a computer can never be President."

He suspected that people all across the country were united in a common bond—they had either been harassed or victimized by a computer. "I received a check from the Social Security agency for $754.25 for lump-sum death benefits," he said. It was the ultimate triumph for a nineteenth-century man to be able to thumb his nose at a computer that had tried to do him in. "I returned the check with a letter saying I was happy to report that contrary to the computer's deduction, any indications that I had passed away were slightly exaggerated."

Ervin's suspicion of machines grew out of a long inability to make them do his bidding. In twenty years in the Senate, he never learned to use the intercom on his telephone. Maybe he did not want to learn. When he wanted to dictate to one of his secretaries, he walked out to his outer office and got her.

One of the pictures in my mind is of him fighting with a candy bar machine in a gas station off Interstate 95. Yielding to his craving for candy, he attacked the machine with a handful of dimes, inserting first one, then another, and each time pulling the candy lever before the dime settled to the bottom. When nothing happened, he frantically jerked on the lever until it responded.

Once Ervin, Don Quixote-like, attacked the Supreme Court with his car. It was not his fault. His old Plymouth simply rebelled one day, the brake failed, and it careened over the curb, across the lawn, and into the side of the building. Because of his occasional spats with the Court, Ervin was hard put to explain that he did not do it intentionally.

The greatest villain of all was the Social Security number. Indeed, the Department of Health, Education and Welfare had long been fascinated with the idea of assigning universal identifiers to newborn babies and establishing a national data bank. Ervin was convinced that "when the government reduces all of us to the status of a number, that number is going to be zero." Furthermore: "With this number on almost every government form and every private questionnaire, no man can be lost. And this is reassuring. But, similarly, no man can ever again be alone. And this is despairing."

The ultimate invasions of privacy are the external and internal body searches which customs officials sometimes inflict on Americans returning from abroad. One well-endowed English teacher from North Carolina was taken aside at Dulles International Airport in the summer of 1969 and made to strip to the waist because someone suspected that she might be smuggling something back into the country. "Are all full-bosomed women to be subjected to this sort of indignity?" she wrote Ervin, who in turn read her letter with great rage on the Senate floor.

To Ervin, it was the age of conformity, when few people

bothered to protest the various kinds of tyranny practiced by the government and by private industry. He believed that great things have been accomplished by nonconformists—his father was one of them—and that the computer age was pressuring people to fit their personalities to the image of the majority.

"When they cease to feel free to exercise their own intelligence, I think something very fine and most valuable goes out of all our lives and the life of our nation," Ervin said during his sensational hearings in early 1971 on computers, data banks, and the bill of rights.

A child in public school today may not know much about Ervin, aside from what he might have heard about the funny man who ran the Watergate hearings. But one of the main reasons that child does not recite a state-approved prayer each morning or bow during an official moment of silence is due to the efforts of that deeply religious man from the North Carolina Bible Belt. He stood up in the Senate on September 20, 1966 and turned around a swift tide of sentiment running in favor of a constitutional amendment to allow prayer in public schools. Many regarded it as his finest hour in the Senate, although not all of his constituents seemed to agree at the time.

The Supreme Court's rulings in 1962 and 1963 striking down state-sanctioned prayers in New York and Maryland were regarded as nothing less than the work of the devil by a substantial percentage of people in this country—perhaps a majority.

Ervin himself thought that the Court was wrong and said so shortly after the first decision in 1962. Mainly he felt the Court had left the question alone for one hundred and seventy-five years and should have continued to let it lie.

As few men do, he had the golden opportunity to tell the Court face-to-face what he thought about its rulings. Shortly after these decisions he accepted an invitation to be master of ceremonies at a Federal Bar Association luncheon for Nicholas

Katzenbach and Ramsey Clark. Seated at Ervin's right was Chief Justice Earl Warren, and several associate justices were in the audience.

Ervin was unable to resist telling Warren a favorite story about lawyers who, when they pray—which is seldom—do so with great sincerity: "A young lawyer went out to a revival service one night and was suddenly called upon by the minister to pray. And he prayed a prayer that came straight from the lawyer's heart. He said, 'Stir up much strife among thy people, oh Lord, lest thy servant perish.' " It was obvious, he said, that the Lord was using the Supreme Court to answer the young lawyer's prayers because so many of the Court's decisions, especially the divided ones, were stirring up much litigation and thus making plenty of work for lawyers.

The public furor over the prayer decision soon made the pressure on Congress almost unbearable. Senator Dirksen, author of the proposed amendment to allow prayers in the classroom, reflected perfectly the mood of the country when he complained to the Senate about modern educational theorems under which "almost anything can be taught in the schools. . . . They teach sex education today. In the interest of academic freedom, they teach communism today. They teach ballet dancing. You name it, and they have it. But do not mention prayer—the pipeline to the Almighty, to give one comfort in hours of distress and to assuage one's grief. What a strange thing."

Dirksen had missed the point. And few of the outraged mothers and fathers were ready to listen to intellectual arguments about the separation of church and state. They wanted Congress to do something and Congress was on the verge of acting.

Forty-one years had passed since Ervin kept the North Carolina legislature from making an unmitigated ass of itself by his ridiculing of the antievolution bill. He had been unhappy with the decisions of Hugo Black and Tom Clark, but the more often he read them and consulted with his advisors, the Founding Fathers, the more he began to agree. Like Ervin, Black understood the Constitution the way its authors had—with the full weight of British history on their shoulders.

Black could have been speaking to Ervin when he wrote in the *Engel* case that the First Amendment had been written to quiet citizens' fears because "governments of the past had shackled men's tongues to make them speak only the religious thoughts that government wanted them to speak and to pray only to the God that government wanted them to pray to."

Late one evening Ervin was sitting in his office with George Autry, the young subcommittee chief counsel. Autry had spent all day working on a statement that he hoped Ervin would use to explain his position. "Ervin didn't look at it, which was only somewhat unusual," Autry said in unpublished notes about his days with Ervin. "Instead he asked me to listen again to why he had originally opposed the Supreme Court's two prayer decisions." Ervin told Autry he had hoped the amendment would die in committee "so I wouldn't have to worry over it." He confessed he was searching for a way to support the Dirksen Amendment in good conscience and "put an end to all the controversy." But he could not vote for it and still be able to face the Religion Clause of the First Amendment. The next morning Autry helped Ervin carry towering stacks of notes, law books, and history books over to the Senate floor.

The chamber was pretty empty as the morning session began, although the public and press galleries were beginning to fill up. Ervin began the speech deliberately, pausing, at times, seemingly forever, to look up citations and historical quotations. He wanted to convince his colleagues—and the people back home who would be mad as hell—by explaining his own simple, strong beliefs.

"It is impossible to overmagnify the importance of faith in God," he began. "It is, in my judgment, the most potent force in the universe. Faith in God gives men and women the strength to face the storms of life and their consequences with the peace of mind that passes understanding. In times of greatest stress, faith in God has the miraculous power to lift ordinary men and women to greatness."

Autry sat in the chamber spellbound. It was the only speech he had ever known Ervin to deliver without using humor and one of the few in which he did not quote from the Bible. "Ervin is the last of those southern senators, maybe the last of the southern politicians, who either knows enough about the Bible or is not too embarrassed to quote it," he said.

The closest Ervin got to humor during the speech was a quote from a departed friend, Chief Justice Stacy of the North Carolina Supreme Court: "For some reason, too deep to fathom, men contend more furiously over the road to heaven, which they cannot see, then over their visible walks on earth. It would be almost unbelievable, if history did not record the tragic fact, that men have gone to war and cut each other's throats because they could not agree as to what was to become of them after their throats were cut."

Now here was Sam Ervin, former justice himself, the legal wizard of the southern block, the conservative constitutionalist, who had the day before delivered a thundering speech against open occupancy laws ("Freedom . . . entitles a man to his prejudices as well as his allergies") assuring worried liberals and befuddled southerners that it was all right to vote against the Dirksen Amendment. It did not matter whether or not they stayed to listen to the speech; Ervin's opposition meant a major realignment of votes.

He led the Senate through a history lesson on the Religion Clause. James Madison had said the belief of every man must be left to his conscience: "This right is in the nature of an inalienable right because the opinions of men, depending only on the evidence contemplated in their own minds, cannot follow the dictates of other men." What Madison meant, as far as Ervin was concerned, was that government must keep its hands off religion and religion must keep its hands off government.

Ervin returned, toward the end of his speech, to his personal religion and his God, who molded and shaped everything of beauty he had ever seen: "the lifegiving sun . . . the galaxies of stars, which twinkle in the infinite heavens . . . the majestic mountains with hills at their knees . . . the glory of the leaves and ripened crops of autumn . . . and the other beautiful things past numbering, which adorn the earth.

"I note with awe the order and regularity of the processes of life and nature as the tide ebbs and flows, as the harvest succeeds the seedtime, and the heavenly bodies move in their orbits without mishap in conformity with natural laws. I observe with reverence that, despite the feet of clay on which he makes his earthly rounds, man is endowed with the capacity to obey conscience, exercise reason, study holy writings, and aspire to righteous conduct in obedience to spiritual laws.

"On the basis of these things, I affirm with complete conviction that the universe and men are not the haphazard products of blind atoms wandering aimlessly about in chaos, but, on the contrary, are the creations of God, the maker of the universe and man."

It was undoubtedly Ervin's finest sermon, as well as one of his best speeches. He went where undoubtedly few have gone in speeches on the Senate floor—into his belief in life after death, his belief in a place "where tears never flow and rainbows never fade, where high hopes are realized and worthy tasks are accomplished, and where those we 'have loved long since and lost awhile' stay with us forever."

He asked the Senate to "preserve for all Americans of all generations the right to bend their knees and lift their voices to their own God in their own way.

"We can do this by standing by the First Amendment as it has been written and interpreted.

"I close with the prayer that the Senate will do exactly this and no more."

It is not certain how many votes Ervin may have influenced

by his dramatic opposition to the prayer amendment, but there is no doubt that his speech was the turning point. When it was finished J. W. Fulbright of Arkansas came up to Ervin and said he had intended to follow the line of least resistance and vote for the amendment. Speeches in the Senate seldom influence votes, but in this case that was not true, Fulbright said. "After listening to your speech, I couldn't vote for the amendment."

Ervin's beloved First Amendment survived its most serious challenge the following day as the Senate vote, 49–37, was short of the required two-thirds. The same morning *The Washington Post* called Ervin "an authentic hero."

The reaction back home was not as strong as many of Ervin's staff feared it would be. After all, North Carolina had some appreciation for religious liberty. Moreover, it did not hurt for Ervin to have several thousand copies of his speech—twenty-four pages of the *Congressional Record*—printed and sent to just about every minister in the state.

In late 1973, a new effort to adopt a prayer amendment was mounted, and Ervin found a good excuse to clear out some of the leftover speeches. He sent copies to scores of constituents with a brief letter explaining his stand once again: "The government must stay out of church affairs, and the church must stay out of government affairs . . . ."

Ervin did not always win good marks with professional civil libertarians. In fact, some, like Lawrence Speiser, former head of the American Civil Liberties Union, considered him often "out of step with the times"—an evaluation with which Ervin would be very comfortable. Speiser neatly summarized Ervin's performance in a November, 1970, interview with John Herbers of *The New York Times* when he said:

> When he's good,
> He's very, very good,
> But when he's bad,
> He's horrid.

Ervin was good on individual liberties, but bad, from the ACLU standpoint, on the rights of criminal suspects. Forgetting Ervin's record with the Criminal Justice Act, which provided legal counsel for indigent defendants, the Bail Reform Act, and his lonely opposition to the D.C. Crime Bill, Ervin's critics castigated him for trying to upset the Supreme Court's landmark decision in 1966. The Court, in its 5–4 *Miranda* ruling, declared that voluntary confessions were inadmissible when defendants were not advised of their rights to remain silent.

"Innocent men do not go around confessing crimes they do not commit," snorted Ervin, the former judge in him, the lenient judge who had freed many defendants because of the heavy-handed methods employed by policemen, popping to the surface. The pronouncement by the Warren Court, Ervin said on July 29, 1966, "certainly tilts the scales of justice unduly in favor of those accused of crime and against the prosecution." He proposed a constitutional amendment legalizing all voluntary confessions. He seemed more upset by the *Miranda* ruling than by any other Court pronouncement. Miranda had confessed to kidnapping and rape, but the Supreme Court freed him on a technicality. "Enough has been done for those who murder and rape and rob; it is time for Congress to do something for those who do not wish to be murdered or raped or robbed," he shouted to the Senate on May 9, 1968.

That summer, Ervin got his chance to reprimand the institution that had caused him so much grief. Lyndon Johnson nominated Abe Fortas, who had served on the Court for three years, for chief justice. During that time, Ervin said, the Court, with Fortas participating, had cast sound precedents of the past "into the judicial garbage can." When the Judiciary Committee took up the nomination in August, Ervin spent days lecturing the nominee about the sins of the Court.

The list of his complaints was substantial: Besides the *Miranda* rule, the Court had usurped legislative powers of Congress, thrown out an open housing referendum in California, permitted Communists to teach in public schools and work in defense plants, given unions the right to picket on private property, and a whole host of other supposed evils.

Even worse, in the spring of 1968, Fortas himself had declared in a speech at American University that the words of the Constitution "were not written with a meaning that persists for all time." The words, he said, "reflect light and shadow, they are modified by rain and sun, they are subject to the changes that a restless life brings upon them."

Ervin probably did not realize what he was doing when he interrogated Fortas for days on end. At least those who worked closely with him felt that he was acting strictly out of anguish with what the Court had done to the Constitution and wanted to put all its sins on record. He was exorcising the devil. What was happening, however, was that the storms that would eventually topple Fortas were gathering. While Ervin was reaching down into his great, fat briefcase for yet another example to dwell on during the hearings, Everett Dirksen leaned over and poked Jim Eastland as if to say, "Isn't that old bird something?" and the two of them leaned back in their chairs and chuckled at the ceiling of the judiciary committee room.

After *The Washington Post* attacked Ervin's performance, he spent several days writing a letter to the editor in response. While he was writing it, he read John Marshall's words in *Marbury* v. *Madison* for the thousandth time and recited them as if they had just been spoken from the bench. "This says it all right here," Ervin told an aide, then reading: " 'Why does a judge swear to discharge his duties agreeably to the Constitution of the United States, if that Constitution forms no rule for his government—if it is closed upon him and cannot be inspected by him? If such be the real state of things, this is worse than solemn mockery.' "

In May, 1969, under pressure because of his extra-judicial activities, Fortas became the first justice to resign from the court because of his conduct. Some believe that his defeat laid the groundwork for the Senate's subsequent rejection of Clement F. Haynsworth and G. Harrold Carswell. Once the idea that the Senate could successfully challenge the President had taken root, it could then move on to investigating the President himself and perhaps even entertain the idea of impeachment proceedings.

With the exception of the prayer amendment, Ervin's civil liberties battles had been essentially unopposed. The Indian Bill of Rights, the Military Justice Act, the District of Columbia Mental Health Act, the Employee Privacy Bill, and the Bail Reform Act were all badly needed reforms, and Ervin met with little resistance. But with the dawn of the Nixon Administration in January, 1969, Ervin saw his adversary face-to-face.

On January 31, Nixon made his first public statement on crime, calling for legislation to permit "temporary pretrial detention" of criminal suspects whose release on bail "presents a danger to the community." He thus let it be known that the Administration would seek to throw out a 172-year tradition that persons charged with noncapital crimes have an absolute right to be released on bail pending trial. It was time for a little law and order, with the emphasis on the latter.

The Administration had originally counted on Ervin to support this approach because he had been so outspoken against the Warren Court's crime decisions. What the Administration had not counted on was that Ervin was unwilling to attempt to correct one evil with another—the very thing conservatives were always accusing liberals of.

In a *Virginia Law Review* article, Attorney General John Mitchell said, among other things, that "the presumption of innocence is not a presumption in the strict sense of the term," and that due process of law "is not an absolute bar to official restraint of persons prior to trial and final judgment." Even so, the Justice Department, locked in a struggle between the hard- and soft-liners, took more than six months to produce the legislation.

Finally, after Nixon prodded the department into action, it came up with three separate bills, one dealing with public defenders, another with court reform in the District of Columbia, and a third with preventive detention in all federal cases.

Ervin's aides were not sure how strongly he would oppose preventive detention; he had acknowledged the need for some reform of the bail system and had been rather gentle with Administration witnesses during hearings in the spring of 1969. But when Lawrence M. Baskir, chief counsel of the Constitutional Rights Subcommittee, and Marcia MacNaughton, professional staff member, showed Ervin several places where they thought the bill tampered with the Constitution, Ervin showed them a number of others.

Much to the Administration's surprise and chagrin, at the House Judiciary Committee hearing on October 16, 1969, Ervin called the bill a "facile and desperate" device "which repudiates our traditional concepts of liberty." On October 27 he told the Senate that it was better to accept the risks of the bail system and remain a free society than it was to adopt "the tyrannical practice of imprisoning men for crimes which they have not committed and may never commit."

Ervin's opposition came as a blow to the Administration. Officials of the Justice Department decided that, rather than try the normal legislative route, they would go for an end run around him. Putting aside the national legislation temporarily, they went all-out for the District of Columbia bill, knowing it would go to the House and Senate district committees. John McMillan, chairman of the House District Committee, could always be counted on, they figured, and the Senate District Committee chairman, Joe Tydings of Maryland, was in deep political trouble and was ready to play the law-and-order routine to the hilt.

The Tydings Committee reported out a package of bills, including the badly needed court-reform and public-defender measures. At that time, Donald Santarelli, associate deputy attorney general in the criminal section, assured Ervin that the bills contained only "technical" changes.

Actually, buried in the 322-page court-reform bill, were some sweeping changes in criminal law, including one which would have practically wiped Ervin's mental health law off the books. Ervin was upset with Santarelli, but later assured him that he held no grudge. Meanwhile, the provisions Ervin objected to were removed and the bills passed the Senate easily. Then what Ervin referred to as a "fast shuffle" took place.

After only a few minutes of hearings, during which only the Administration testified, the McMillan Committee added what Ervin termed "literally a garbage pail of some of the most repressive, near-sighted, intolerant, unfair, and vindictive legislation" he had ever seen. The bill contained preventive detention, a new provision allowing police to enter the homes of suspects without knocking, and a provision for sentencing juveniles, upon their third conviction, to life sentences for such "crimes of violence" as purse snatching and tampering with gum machines. It sailed through the House and went to a House-Senate conference committee. Tydings caved in and the Senate was suddenly faced with an up-or-down vote on the "garbage pail" it had never had a chance to consider. The Administration had the Senate over a barrel.

Liberals like Tydings, who had fought so strongly for civil rights bills, ran for cover. They left Ervin standing virtually alone defending the rights of the residents of the District of Columbia, the vast majority of whom were black.

On July 17, 1970, Ervin treated the few senators in the chamber and the visitors in the galleries to a tour de force. Using small Senate envelopes on which he had scribbled page numbers of the Bible, the Constitution, and his favorite history books, he spoke extemporaneously for four and a half hours. He contemptuously took the legislation apart sentence by sentence, showing at each point where it did violence to the Constitution, hoping to draw attention to what the Senate was doing. Word got around that the old constitutionalist was on his feet, fighting the Administration's crime bill.

He said the no-knock statute would give policemen "the right to enter the dwelling house of citizens of the District of Columbia in the same way that burglars now enter those dwelling houses," and that preventive detention was "absolutely inconsistent with the policies that have prevailed in this nation since it became a Republic."

He scoffed at the term "necessity," which many of his fellow senators were using to justify the bill—in spite of William Pitt's warning. And he gave the Senate his simple prescription for living: "Mr. President, the supreme value of civilization is the freedom of the individual, which is simply the right of the individual to be free from governmental tyranny."

The District of Columbia provisions, he shouted, arms waving and voice trembling, "ought to be removed from this bill and transferred to the Smithsonian Institution, to manifest some of the greatest legal curiosities that ever have been evolved by the mind of man on the North American Continent."

Several hours later, still in a rage, Ervin implored the Senate "not to enact a bill which contains provisions that are absolutely hostile to the traditions which have prevailed in our country ever since it became a Republic." Once gone, the liberties which the bill threatened to destroy would be gone forever.

But it was a hopeless cause. The other side had too much going for it, and the bill passed and became law. Ervin, who probably was not aware of the racial implications of the bill, was praised as a champion of the rights of black people. Only one defendant was detained under the act and then released. A few policemen, suspected of being burglars, were shot trying to break into homes, and so were some of the occupants. The law was virtually abandoned as worthless. Tydings was defeated after all.

There was no doubt in Ervin's mind by this time that the Administration, reflecting the fears of many Americans, would attempt to abridge historic freedoms in order to gain some temporary security. It was, as he said in a number of speeches, "a time of doubt and fear."

If there was one doctrine that Sam Ervin had absorbed into his very being, it was the First Amendment's defiant command: "Congress shall make no law respecting an establishment of religion, or prohibiting the free exercise thereof; or abridging the freedom of speech, or of the press; or the right of the people peaceably to assemble, and to petition the Government for a redress of grievances." His total belief in the sanctity of those words separated him from the most recent occupant of the White House. The ramifications of this disagreement, which has to do with whether government is unafraid of the truth, helped explain the origins of Watergate.

On August 25, 1970, Tom Charles Huston, a White House aide who later figured prominently in planning for Watergate-related activities, recommended to H. R. Haldeman, Nixon's top aide, that they give serious consideration to an executive order expanding the activities of the Subversive Activities Control Board. The SACB, long moribund because of crippling Supreme Court decisions, had recently been refunded for $400,000 a year, and the Administration was urgently looking around for something it could do. "We cannot afford to let the Board sit idle or content itself with investigating old line Communist fronts which are largely irrelevant to our current problem," Huston said.

It took almost a year, but finally, on July 2, 1971, President Nixon issued an executive order granting the SACB vast new powers to investigate any group which appeared likely to engage in "treason, rebellion, or insurrection, riots or civil disorder, seditious conspiracy, sabotage, trading with the enemy, obstruction of the recruiting and enlistment service of the United States, impeding officers of the United States, or related crimes or offenses."

Nixon tried to give the SACB, which had done virtually nothing since he helped create it in 1950, authority that Congress had never intended it to have. The order was casually revealed when John W. Mahon, chairman of the SACB, attempting to justify its continued existence, told the Senate Appropriations Committee about its new-found authority. Several senators were intrigued and summoned Assistant Attorney General Robert Mardian to Capitol Hill to explain the executive order.

It was all perfectly legal, Mardian said, because of the President's "inherent" powers. Roman Hruska, an Appropriations Committee member and the ranking Republican on Constitutional Rights, told an aide, Malcom Hawk, "When Sam hears that he'll hit the ceiling."

Ervin, who had not been too concerned about the SACB before, did just that. William Proxmire had come before the Senate year after year, trying to get it to cut off funds for the agency, primarily because he thought the SACB was worthless. He got the usual thirty votes that liberals were able to muster on such occasions. When Ervin joined Proxmire the vote was a little closer, 47–41.

During the next year, Ervin wrote an epic speech on the First Amendment and delivered it dozens of times: "The First Amendment grants its freedoms to all persons within the boundaries of our country without regard to whether they are wise or foolish, learned or ignorant, profound or shallow, brave or timid, or devout or ungodly, and without regard to whether they love or hate our country and its institutions. Consequently, the amendment protects the expression of all kinds of ideas, no matter how antiquated, novel, or queer they may be.

"In the final analysis, the First Amendment is based upon an abiding faith that our country has nothing to fear from the exercise of its freedoms as long as it leaves truth free to combat error. I share this faith.

"To be sure, the exercise of First Amendment rights by others may annoy us and subject us at times to tirades of intellectual or political rubbish. This is a small price to pay, however, for the benefits which the exercise of these rights bestows on our country."

In 1972, Ervin co-sponsored the same motion with Proxmire and took the floor. He made great sport of the SACB's accomplishments: sixty-six identified Communists in over twenty years of investigating; five commissioners sitting in "big easy chairs," doing nothing but drawing their breaths and their $30,000-plus salaries; paying secretaries to assist them in doing nothing; and, during the previous year, "unlisting" one hundred and eleven groups that had ceased to exist some twenty years before.

"The Constitution of the United States gives a man the right to make a damn fool of himself and believe anything that he wants to," Ervin said. "I do not fear for the security of my country as long as my country only punishes people for the crimes they commit. However, I do fear for the continuance of my country as a free society when my country sets up a board which undertakes to tell people what thoughts they can think and what associations they shall choose."

The Senate passed the Ervin-Proxmire resolution 42–25; then its conferees gave in to the House and part of the agency's funds were restored. But not before Ervin again took the floor and got the Senate to agree that not a penny could be spent to carry out Nixon's executive order. Finally, without explanation, Nixon omitted the SACB's appropriation from his budget request for the following year, and the agency collapsed.

Ervin was no longer the child in the candy store. Instead of being free to select his issues, he found he was being irresistibly drawn into a confrontation with the Nixon Administration over the Bill of Rights. He was not, as his wife had accused him of doing, running out to meet controversy whenever he saw it coming. Controversy was landing in his lap.

During the summer and fall of 1971, a new and alarming pattern had been emerging: The Administration and its allies in Congress were waging an all-out attack on freedom of the press.

Although Ervin had taken his knocks from the press—he sometimes thought writers found warts he didn't have—he was virtually an absolutist on leaving the press unfettered. He was not entirely comfortable with Jefferson's startling suggestion that newspapers without government are far preferable to government without newspapers. Each needs the other, but democracy fails automatically without a vigorous and frequently abrasive press. "If we didn't have leaks," Ervin said, "I believe we'd have the most corrupt government in the world."

Whether or not the advent of the Nixon Administration had much to do with it, it was clear that, beginning in 1969, prosecutors all over the country were realizing that they could not only benefit by the investigative efforts of reporters but also make use of the reporters as primary witnesses. A growing number of reporters were being called before grand juries and asked to reveal the sources of their information and to turn over their notes, news films, and tapes to be used in evidence. By July, 1971, the practice had grown to avalanche proportions.

Congress nearly got into the act, too, when a House committee commanded cbs to turn over the "out-takes" of its controversial program "The Selling of the Pentagon" so the subcommittee could determine, in effect, whether the network had lived up to acceptable journalistic standards. Cbs refused, and the committee tried unsuccessfully to cite network officials for contempt.

In the Pentagon Papers trial, for the first time in modern history, the government attempted, and temporarily succeeded, to restrain newspapers from publishing stories that were based on classified documents. The Supreme Court upheld the press, but the decision was close and vague.

The Administration proposed a new policy of tying television license renewals to whether or not stations were "substantially attuned to the needs and interests of the communities" they served.

If official actions were not enough to put the message across, the vituperative attacks by Vice President Agnew against the press confirmed in most newsmen's minds that the Administration held freedom of the press in contempt and was bent on destroying or crippling its enemies in the media.

Chief Counsel Baskir and Assistant Counsel William Pursley began building a file on these events. They found Ervin receptive to the idea of holding exploratory hearings on the state of the media. The hearings, held in September and October of 1971, were deliberately inconclusive. Ervin and most of the witnesses agreed that the best policy was to tough it out and take their chances with the courts. The Supreme Court was about to take up the *Caldwell* case. Every indication was that the Court would uphold the *New York Times* reporter's right to refuse to reveal the sources of his stories on the Black Panthers.

In June, 1972, in one of its many 5–4 decisions, the Court shattered these hopes. Justice Byron R. White, writing for the slim majority, said reporters do not have "a testimonial privilege that other citizens do not enjoy." It was a bad case and a bad decision, but one the press and the public will have to suffer with until a better one comes along—if one ever does. Meanwhile, reporters will pay the price by losing stories and by going to jail for protecting their sources.

Appalled at the decision, Ervin held another round of hearings in early 1973 to determine whether some sort of "newsmen's privilege" was needed to shield reporters from the government. He still was not convinced that Congress ought to legislate any sort of press freedoms and risk the possibility that some future Congress, angry with the press, might try to take them away. The press might well have to fight its own battles.

"There is a way to resolve this problem which is more

difficult than legislation, but far preferable," he said when the hearings began on February 20. "That is to call upon the press to read its own courageous history. If reporters, editors, and publishers read this history, they would not come petitioning to Congress, but would win this point like they won the other elements of their freedom in times past. They would lay their personal freedom on the line. . . ."

But Ervin listened closely during the hearings, read everything he could on the subject, and slowly changed his mind. Hearings for him had always been an educational process. At one point he told a group of reporters, "My mind has not yet reached a majority on the issue." Soon, however, he became convinced that the press had suffered almost irreparable harm from the *Caldwell* decision and that prosecutors, by intimidating the press, were actually hurting their chances of catching criminals and cleaning up corruption.

Although he was not sure Congress would buy it, he offered a bill on March 8 asserting that newsmen may protect their sources by refusing to testify, except that, as in the past, they would be required to identify persons committing crimes in their presence.

Ervin received a dozen or so awards that spring for his tenacious devotion to freedom of the press. On May 4, when he was introduced at the annual banquet of the American Society of Newspaper Editors, newspapermen who had praised him, damned him, and ignored him in times past gave him a rousing ovation. As he stood in the ballroom of the Shoreham Hotel and waved his hand in salute, one of the guests at his table thought he saw a tear trembling in his eye. But maybe it was just a gleam.

In September, 1969 a small crowd gathered at the gates of Fort Carson in Colorado Springs for a demonstration against the Vietnam War. Most of the participants were college students, although there was another large group which somehow did not fit with the others: Men with cameras, notebooks and microphones—boom microphones that could pick up sound from a great distance. And several helicopters hovered over the speakers' platform.

It was probably one of the most extraordinary antiwar rallies in history. Considering the boasts that thousands would attend, it was not very well attended, at least not by demonstrators. Of the one hundred and nineteen persons at the rally, fifty-three were there to observe. Some were from the media, but the majority were military intelligence agents: Army, Navy, and Air Force spies on American soil, watching civilians engaged in lawful protests.

It was a classic case of spy versus spy. Some of the agents had come to observe how other agents observed a rally. Others were assigned to watch the men from the other services to be sure they could scoop them. The object was to be the first to get the information out on the teletype. Unfortunately, for those trying to monitor the speeches, all they could pick up on their sensitive microphones was the droning of helicopters.

Such was the testimony in February, 1971 of a former military intelligence officer. Needless to say, that kind of activity, comic though it was, tended to chill free and open expression by those attending the rally. The Defense and Justice departments agreed that it was probably bad form and impractical, but not an infringement of anyone's rights.

While Ervin and the subcommittee staff were developing their information about computers and data banks for hearings on government and private invasion of privacy, they received reports of a massive Army intelligence program. It had been initiated during the Johnson Administration to enable the military to be on the alert for possible urban riots. But after the riots cooled off, the military continued its monitoring, this time of the growing antiwar movement. From there it branched out to spy on practically any person or group of persons who did anything publicly, including politicians.

The Army list, according to witnesses in one city, contained the names of everyone with a peace symbol on his car; in another, every black person seen walking down a highway in a suspicious manner. It included those who signed petitions, made or listened to speeches, filed lawsuits, bought or read certain newspapers; church groups, ministers, college professors, students, labor unions, Quakers, Unitarians, Methodists, Jews; the NAACP, the Urban League, the John Birch Society; senators and congressmen, mayors, city councilmen, human rights commissioners; reporters, housewives, high school students, and taxi drivers.

It was an Orwellian nightmare come true. Ervin, a consistent supporter of defense spending and presidential war-making powers, went after the Defense Department with astonishing zeal. Its attack on the First Amendment was the most outrageous he could imagine, and he was determined not just to kill it but to find out who was responsible. He wanted to make sure it never happened again.

"Do you think it is logical and constitutional activity for Army intelligence agents, augmented by Naval intelligence agents, and augmented by Air Force intelligence agents, in large numbers to attend a student rally and have five or six helicopters flying overhead taking photographs? Do you think that is something that is sanctioned by the First Amendment?" Ervin asked at the hearings.

"I don't think it makes much sense from a management point of view," said Robert Froehlke, assistant secretary of defense. Then J. Fred Buzhardt, the department's chief lawyer, who later directed President Nixon's legal defense in the Watergate affair, said in his opinion "just watching somebody" did not violate the rights of the person being watched. Then this colloquy ensued:

ERVIN: Doesn't it have the tendency to deter a person from exercising his constitutional rights to participate?

BUZHARDT: Mr. Chairman, I would not be prepared to say that it did unless there was some specific evidence that someone was deterred. If it was unknown, the man wouldn't know it, so it could hardly deter his activities.

ERVIN: They would know there were five helicopters flying above them, wouldn't they?

BUZHARDT: As I said, I don't know in that particular case precisely.

ERVIN: I will be perfectly frank. If I had five helicopters flying over my head and I had gone out to make a speech on a subject, and I was a public servant, I think it would deter my freedom of speech very much for the Army to have five helicopters flying over my head and to have fifty-three agents, law enforcement officers, and press there watching me talk to a crowd that didn't number more than seventy, when you count only the demonstrators.

FROEHLKE: If the facts are as you allege, I think we will all agree at the very minimum that it was inappropriate.

Ervin said the intelligence gatherers did not gather intelligence on people like him (he was wrong, they did). They would not catch him at an antiwar demonstration, either, because he felt that a strong national defense was imperative to the survival of the nation. "But I also think it is imperative to the survival of basic American freedoms for the military to engage in combat against the enemy and not in surveillance of civilians whose only offense is that they are exercising their First Amendment rights, no matter how unwisely they may be exercised."

With the help of articles written by investigative reporters, Ervin uncovered the vast network of military snooping, in which well over a hundred thousand civilians and groups were placed under surveillance. The Defense Department informed Ervin almost immediately that it was disbanding the operation. It persistently refused, however, to permit the generals, those who knew how the whole thing got started, to testify. Ervin threatened to subpoena them and finally got the information he was seeking.

During the hearings, Deputy Attorney General William Rehnquist told Ervin that the practice of spying on civilians "is undesirable and should be condemned vigorously, but I do not believe it violates the particular constitutional rights of the individuals who are surveyed."

In the spring of 1972, Rehnquist sat on the Supreme Court while arguments were being heard in *Tatum* v. *Laird,* an Army surveillance case. Ervin assumed he was just observing, since he had been so closely associated with the government's position.

Ervin himself was a very active participant in the case. Appearing as a friend of the court, he declared: "If these allegations do not state a cause of action in which judicial relief can be granted . . ., 'The Star Spangled Banner' lies when it says that our country is the land of the free. I believe our country is the land of the free."

Ervin at first refused to believe that the Court had, by a 5–4 decision, thrown out the *Tatum* case, saying the plaintiffs had suffered no legal harm. Rehnquist had participated. Ervin issued a statement saying the Court "ignored the very serious harm that military surveillance has caused and continues to cause to the liberties of Americans."

Meanwhile, the Army was disbanding its intelligence system and turning the responsibility over to the Justice Department. It was temporarily absorbed by Robert Mardian's Internal Security Division. What happened then is not clear. The department was reported to have an even greater civilian intelligence operation than the Army had at the height of its activities. At the time of the transition Nixon approved the creation of a special unit to carry out clandestine intelligence activities, including the use of illegal methods such as breaking and entering.

Ervin tried repeatedly to learn what the Administration was up to but could never get an answer. He may have been on the track of the Watergate affair long before the burglars broke into the headquarters of the Democratic Party.

In an interview during the Watergate hearings, Ervin brought up the Army spying business. He could not understand why a Republican administration tried so hard to obstruct his efforts to dig up the truth about misdeeds put into operation by a Democratic administration:

"I would expect the Republicans to be glad for the committee to bring out this evidence of how the Democratic administration permitted the Army to spy on civilians. I could not understand it. But now I do, since the revelations of these things were right in harmony with the spirit of these plans of 1970."

12. *Against the Tide*

> The injury which may possibly be done by
> defeating a few good laws will be amply
> compensated by the advantage of
> preventing a number of bad ones.
>
> ALEXANDER HAMILTON

ERVIN MAY HAVE BEEN insensitive to many of the movements and currents that swirled about him in the Senate and swept the country off its feet. Men of great vision, as well as those with keen herd instincts, sensed them and responded with far-reaching reforms. But sometimes they only built atomic mousetraps. Ervin seldom saw a trend he liked or a fashion he quite approved of. All too often it was a trend to do away with personal liberty, however painless the initial loss. He looked beyond the transient, flesh-and-blood problems to the abstractions of history and "the everlasting things"—truth, faith, courage, duty. Knowledge of these principles, he said during commencement exercises at a women's college in the spring of 1960, gives people "the vision of seeing life steady and whole."

He reached inside himself for the answers, rarely responding to pressures, whether from his colleagues in the Senate, his constituents, or the press. He said those constituents who took the trouble to write letters were usually possessed by one extreme or another, while the majority in the middle expected him to make up his own mind and forgave him when he was wrong. He agreed with the judge who once told him, "When I want to know what the people think, I go in my office, shut the door, sit down at my desk and communicate with myself." About the only thing Ervin was really susceptible to was argument. Except perhaps for civil rights, most of his reactions were not from the gut. He listened and studied harder than anyone else. He went to the Senate library—in fact he was the only member of the Senate to go there regularly—and soaked up the law. Once he made up his mind, almost nothing, certainly not a stampede by others in the Senate or a storm of angry letters, could change his mind. He had a Scotch-Irish affliction, he said, that would not permit him to follow a multitude to do evil.

Once he had decided, there was no use arguing the merits of an issue with Ervin. He had marshalled his arguments and his strategy and would fight in the face of the most persuasive opponents. He often seemed not to be listening and would reply with a well-worn story or quotation tested and polished by time. The mere sight of Ervin walking into the Senate with his arms full of books was occasionally enough to cause the Senate leadership to withdraw legislation.

There was nothing complicated about Ervin's principles. He went into combat with the subtlety of Edgar Guest's verse—which he recited at the drop of a hat:

> I have to live with myself, and so
> I want to be fit for myself to know,
> I want to be able, as days go by
> Always to look myself straight in the eye;
> I don't want to stand with the setting sun,
> And hate myself for the things I've done.

In 1972 *The Congressional Quarterly* said that Ervin was the most independent member of the Senate. He frequently swam against the tide, voting 31 percent of the time against bipartisan majorities, both against legislation that passed and for legislation that failed.

There were two major ideas, it seemed, whose time had come in 1970: direct popular election of the President and equal rights for women. Loathing that overworked phrase of Victor Hugo's, Ervin decided he would try to postpone, if not blot out, their appointed hour. He did so with all the tactics he had mastered in the old battles, including the filibuster, the obfuscating amendment, delay, confusion, and tough-minded logic.

The popular election proposal was a direct result of the 1968 election, in which George Wallace got almost enough votes as a third-party candidate to throw the contest between Richard Nixon and Hubert Humphrey into the House of Representatives. If that had happened, the argument went, Wallace would have been able to pick the winner; he would control enough votes in the House to hand the presidency to the one who whistled Dixie the louder.

Senator Birch Bayh's Subcommittee on Constitutional Amendments had been holding hearings on electoral reform for four years, but the 1968 election brought the issue alive. On May 26, 1969, the subcommittee reported out a resolution proposing a constitutional amendment ending the electoral college system and awarding the presidency to the candidate with the largest popular vote.

It sounded simple and fair, Ervin conceded, but added that because of its unknown potential for mischief, "it is like John Randolph of Roanoke's rotten mackerel—it both shines and stinks by the moonlight." He was afraid it would put an end to the two-party system and lead to the beginning of a splinter-party system. He believed that simple majoritarianism was not what the Founding Fathers had in mind when they established a federal republic, and that with popular elections state boundaries would be further obliterated.

Nevertheless, the amendment had overwhelming support. It had passed in the House 330–70, and the identical version in the Senate had forty-six sponsors. A national poll showed that more than 80 percent of the public favored changing to direct elections.

None of these figures impressed Ervin, who felt that those

who favored it probably had not thought it through. He and his top legislative aide, Robert Bland Smith, Jr., a young lawyer from eastern North Carolina, looked around for some way to slow it down. Smith, one of the best behind-the-scenes operators in the Senate, developed the fine art of "crossquotesmanship," lining up prominent liberal opposition to issues which seemed conservative. Articles by liberal columnists opposed to busing or to changing Senate filibuster rules, for instance, were widely circulated among unsure senators. Harvard Law School professors, brought down as witnesses, always made an impression on Ervin's northern opponents.

Although Bayh had already compiled over two thousand pages of testimony from more than a hundred witnesses, Smith and Ervin decided to hold their own hearings. It was no problem getting Eastland to let Ervin chair meetings of the full Judiciary Committee, or lining up anti-amendment witnesses, or keeping Bayh in the dark. Bayh was not told until late one Friday night that the new hearings would be held the following Wednesday.

While the first witness, Alexander Bickel of Yale, waited to begin his attack on the amendment, Bayh let his slow fuse burn through to the powder. "I do not think I have ever made this kind of statement before," Bayh said after Ervin's long opening remarks. Bayh said the hearings had been organized with "the most blatant disregard for senatorial courtesy I have experienced in eight years in the Senate." He had not been told about the hearings, and when he finally saw the witness list, he found it was stacked. "I want to say to our distinguished acting chairman that this procedure is so contrary to his normal sense of fairness that . . . I am of the opinion that he himself was not aware of this until about the same time I was." Then Bayh turned to Smith and shook his finger at him while Smith looked back innocently. "Whoever on the staff was responsible for this calculated effort to try to prevent direct election from having a fair hearing, I want the record to show that here is one member of the Senate who is not going to be silent while this type of practice is followed by this committee."

Ervin replied, "I am not going to let my sweet disposition turn sour at all," and then reminded Bayh that he had forced the committee to vote on the amendment by threatening to filibuster to prevent a vote on G. Harrold Carswell, Nixon's ill-fated choice for the Supreme Court. If Bayh wanted to play rough, Ervin would too. Nevertheless, the resolution to accept the Bayh amendment was approved by the committee, and when it went to the Senate floor, Ervin led his own filibuster. He held the floor, refusing to allow the Senate to take up any amendments to the resolution, not even his own. He knew they would all be defeated and that would build momentum for the original resolution. That was how it had passed in the House.

Ervin's own proposed amendment would have taken a partial step, eliminating the presidential electors but retaining the unit rule whereby states award all their electoral votes to the candidate who gets the most votes. But he was not going to let the Senate take it up and take him off his feet. The leadership tried a couple of times to invoke cloture but failed. Finally, under the press of business, the resolution was withdrawn. Bayh was furious. He said some people, referring of course to Ervin, were willing to use parliamentary tactics to thwart the will of the majority. That is exactly what Ervin was doing. As much as he hated to make enemies, he believed in the two-party system. He felt it had produced great presidents. He did not want to see the system or the office subjected to an uncertain and potentially dangerous fate.

Ervin was fighting on a dozen fronts at this point in his career, taking on the Army here, the White House there, the privacy invaders, the enemies of the press, the school-busing advocates, the witch hunters, and, on a fairly regular basis, the Senate itself. His capacity to take on so many battles was partly due to his own considerable energies, but also to a group of devoted young lawyers and investigators, both men and women, who worked for him. Their backgrounds ranged from Brooklyn, New York to the mountains of North Carolina, but they shared the same dedication to Ervin and his causes.

Ervin became chairman of three Judiciary subcommittees— Constitutional Rights, Separation of Powers, and, one of the smallest and most obscure in the Senate, Revision and Codification. Instead of revising and codifying, this hip-pocket operation, headed by Smith and later William E. Pursley, served as Ervin's legislative attack base. Ervin relied heavily on his young assistants to handle the details and develop the issues. While they battled, often with each other, for his attention, he seemed to float above it all like a hawk, swooping down now and then to snatch up a bill or an issue. After a day or two of study, he would master the issue, know more about it than anyone else, and make it his own. Staff aides wrote many of his speeches, but the best ones he wrote himself.

The power of Ervin's intellect could be seen in the influence he had over those who worked for him. Conservatives became more liberal and liberals more conservative. The liberals sometimes cringed when Ervin launched one of his lost causes, but they found his logic perfectly consistent with libertarianism, and pitched in to help. Conservatives were dumbfounded at Ervin's Bill of Rights liberalism and quietly cheered him on. The effect was a moderating influence on almost everyone he came in contact with.

Ervin did almost exactly the same thing with the women's rights issue as he did with direct elections. He upstaged Birch Bayh's Constitutional Amendments Subcommittee hearings and held his own, again as acting chairman of the full Judiciary Committee. And then he went into the Senate and harangued the galleries and the nearly empty chamber for hours about the functional physiological differences between the sexes.

He argued that women were well protected by the Equal

Protection Clause and the Civil Rights Act, that every form of discrimination they were seeking to rectify had been abolished by law, particularly where it really mattered—jobs, promotions, and salaries. But a constitutional amendment was a potential blunderbuss that might destroy all the legal rights of women who did not want to bare their breasts and wrestle with men.

"If the militant supporters of the House-passed equal rights amendment could obtain their hearts' desire without having their sisters robbed of their necessary legal protection, I would keep silent," he said in a Senate speech on August 21, 1970. "If such were possible, they would merely reap the fate of those mentioned in this verse of the Apocrypha: 'They digged a well, and made it deep, but fell themselves into the pit which they prepared.' "

Women's liberationists characterized Ervin as a male chauvinist pig and worse. But more conventional groups, such as "Females Opposed to Equality," dubbed him "American Father of the Year." A small plaque with that inscription was hung in his office.

Some of the women who descended on him were, as he informed the Senate, well beyond the draft age (almost "as ancient as I"), and yet they insisted that women were willing to fight wars alongside men. This is his version of what he told them: "Ladies, I have always tried to be a gallant gentleman. I have made it a practice all my life never to refer to a lady's age. But looking at you I am compelled to conclude that, despite your very youthful appearances, you are at least a month above the draft age. If you want to persuade me that women want to be drafted and sent out like the men to face the bullets of the enemy and to have their fair forms blasted into fragments by the enemy's bombs, you are going to have to send some of the sweet young things within the draft age up here to persuade me on that point."

There were plenty of sweet young things who would gladly have argued that point with Ervin. In fact, one of his nieces complained to her aunt that it was not fair to men that their studies and careers were interrupted by the draft while women were not called.

Ervin mischievously got the Senate to adopt his amendment to the equal rights resolution forbidding the drafting of women. It hopelessly tied up the House and Senate, and the whole issue was dropped for the rest of the year. When Ervin again threatened to wage war on the Equal Rights Amendment the following year, it was again withdrawn. But by 1972 the momentum behind the issue was so strong—even most of the South was for it—that Ervin stepped aside. It passed 84–8, with only Ervin, Stennis, and six conservative Republicans voting against it. The proposed amendment promised that "Equality of rights under the law shall not be denied or abridged by the United States or any state on account of sex." The following spring the North Carolina General Assembly declined by one vote to ratify the amendment. It was only in 1971 that it had gotten around to ratifying the Nineteenth Amendment, which gave women the right to vote!

Ervin has explained on numerous occasions that he did not consider either sex superior to the other. Just different. And the differences were complementary, equipping men to provide food and shelter and women to nurture, care for, and train the children, who enter the world in a state of utter helplessness. Without this arrangement, he firmly believed that human life could not continue. As if this were not enough to infuriate the women's movement and its allies, he was fond of quoting the Jewish proverb: "God could not be everywhere, so he made mothers." Mrs. Ervin, however, saw it his way: "I like things the way they are," she has said. "I don't like for men and women to be exactly alike because they can't be."

His position would have been much more assailable if he had practiced discrimination against women. But in fact he has had more women working for him in high positions and at considerable salaries than any other member of the Senate, including all the champions of women's rights. They included not only secretaries and receptionists but also professional staff and lawyers, and an administrative assistant who in 1973 was making $36,000 a year.

Ervin's first act as chairman of the Government Operations Committee was not to engage the Nixon Administration in a colossal wrestling match, but to thwart the passage of legislation designed to protect consumers against gouging by both industry and the government.

Ervin refused to bury the bill in committee—a practice followed routinely by many committee chairmen—and failed to cripple it with amendments. It went to the Senate with powerful public support, intense consumer-group backing, and ardent champions within its chambers. And there it died.

The trouble was that the consumer advocates had demanded too much and the bill, as reported by the committee, gave the proposed consumer protection agency vast powers to monitor and harass the activities of businesses and other government agencies. In the guise of protecting consumers from fraud and deception, it attempted to turn the government against industry and against itself.

Ervin again led the opposition, a rag-tag group of southerners and midwestern Republican conservatives. They took the floor and in speech after speech tied up the Senate. Liberals had their own filibuster going against an anti-busing bill, another Ervin creation, and the two wildly unrelated issues killed each other off. With the election only a month away, both liberals and conservatives surrendered their prize goals for the year. For a time, at least, both of these issues seemed to go away.

As popular as the consumer protection issue was, Ervin felt it was the ultimate tyranny over the individual—over both the businessmen and the consumers themselves. It was more than just an extension of the civil rights argument that businessmen were being denied the freedom to be thoroughly disreputable if they chose. The public was also, in a sense, being robbed of its freedom by a new bureaucracy that, with the best of intentions, wraps the individual in a protective cocoon, gives him a number at birth, feeds him, clothes him, shelters him, and smothers him with benevolence. Nurture a man and you own his mind.

13. *In the Catbird Seat*

You do not have the power to compel me
to come up here if the President directs
me not to and even if you would attempt
to compel me, I would not come here.

WHEN HE WAS PRACTICING LAW, Sam Ervin had a client who had been caught red-handed with one of the sweetest little copper stills you ever saw running full blast right in his home. There wasn't much the young lawyer could do except enter a guilty plea for the old moonshiner and pray for the mercy of the court.

But the prosecutor, sensing he was on the trail of the supplier of the still, pressed Ervin's client, a mountaineer named Benton, relentlessly. Benton, equally stubborn, kept replying, "I ain't gwine ter tell you."

The prosecutor finally appealed to the judge to make the man talk, but the judge refused, recognizing that the defendant, however mean his profession, had a certain code of ethics that would not allow him to rat on an associate. Nevertheless, hoping to smooth things over with the prosecutor, the judge said, "Mr. Benton, I imagine you would prefer not to give him the information as to where you obtained the still."

"Yes, your honor," Benton replied, "that's what I mean to say, but I ain't gwine ter tell him nohow."

Ervin told the story many times to illustrate his arguments, whether he was talking about judicial wisdom, ethics, or the reluctance of witnesses to provide information. But old man Benton had never been compared to a president of the United States until Sam Ervin began delving into secrecy by the executive branch.

It was no such code of ethics, Ervin felt some forty years later, that prompted President Nixon to declare that he had a right, in fact a duty "rooted in the Constitution," to prevent his aides from appearing before committees of Congress. It was, instead, self-protection on the part of a man who bore all of the traces of guilt, who had been caught making political white lightning in the executive mansion. "Executive privilege," Nixon called it.

"Executive poppycock," thundered Sam Ervin. "Divine right went out with the American Revolution." Then, in one of the classic bluffs of all time—he claimed he was perfectly serious—he threatened to arrest any White House aide who refused to appear before his committee. There was no such right inherent in the President's office nor was there even a hint from the Founding Fathers that one was implied, Ervin contended.

The showdown over official secrecy was quickly over-shadowed in the spring of 1973 by events which followed in rapid succession and, for a time, virtually paralyzed the government. But it emerged once again—in crystal-clear form—in the controversy over the Watergate evidence. Could the executive thwart the legitimate investigative role of Congress by refusing to provide it with information bearing on criminal activity? This issue was far more important in Ervin's concept of "the everlasting things" than whether or not the President or his aides were guilty of wrongdoing. It was the difference between democracy and monarchy.

After Nixon's landslide election in November, 1972, and the moves he had begun to make, it looked like monarchy. It was not only the withholding of information, but a whole range of actions by the White House, that threatened to reduce Congress to an empty shell, a less-than-equal branch of government. Actually, Congress may have deserved being kicked around. But in the bleak, early days of the second Nixon Administration, it seemed powerless to kick back.

On the one side was the mighty executive branch, with its new supercabinet, its vast public-relations apparatus, its army of economists and lawyers, and its solid clout with white, middle-class America. In the opposite corner—wearing the baggy trunks—was the slow-moving, tradition-bound legislative branch, ill-equipped, and lacking the nerve to assert its authority, much of which had already been surrendered.

It was no accident that the Senate and, in effect, the entire Congress turned to the aging, loquacious southerner for help. As he had been in the struggle over civil liberties, this enormously energetic man was well prepared to step into the ring with the President. He was the right man for the times.

With a sparkle in his eye that was part pleasure and part the grim anticipation of mortal combat, Ervin told me on January 24, 1973, "It's time for a confrontation with some of those folks."

He had been alarmed at the growing might of the executive branch ever since coming to Washington. President Eisenhower conceived the principle of "executive privilege" to keep Joe McCarthy from hounding Army officers. It quickly blossomed into a standard device for keeping secrets from Congress, and Ervin, during his first year in Washington, suggested that somebody ought to look into it. "I have been appalled," he said in a 1958 speech at Little Rock, Arkansas, "by the practice which the present administration adopted during the Army-McCarthy hearings and has pursued ever since—withholding information concerning what the executive branch is doing."

It was not until 1966, however, when Everett Dirksen got boiling mad about the school prayer and reapportionment decisions, that Ervin got his chance. Dirksen proposed the creation of a subcommittee on separation of powers to study the extent, if any, to which the three branches of government were encroaching on one another. He was looking for a forum from which the Senate could take on the courts and recommended that the Senate's leading constitutional authority, Sam Ervin, head it. It was carved out of the Senate Judiciary Committee the following spring.

Ervin had ideas of his own about what the important separation-of-powers issues were. Even so, it took him a long time to get them off the ground. He hired as consultants the best constitutional lawyers he could find, including Alexander Bickel of Yale, Philip Kurland of the University of Chicago, and Arthur S. Miller of George Washington University, and began plodding along in rather academic fashion.

Among the subcommittee's early issues were congressional pork-barreling, the role of the Supreme Court, the quasi-judicial powers of the National Labor Relations Board, the independence of federal judges, and the procedures for holding a constitutional convention. Its findings aroused only great yawns from Ervin's colleagues and the press. He got the same reaction when he began delving into hotter issues, such as executive privilege, the pocket veto, and impoundment of funds. Very few bills emerged from the subcommittee, and those that did were quietly buried.

"At that time we couldn't interest anybody in those issues," said former Chief Counsel Paul L. Woodward. "That was the academic period," said Rufus L. Edmisten, the most recent chief counsel.

Then along came Richard Nixon.

Shortly after taking office, Nixon assured Congress that his Administration was "dedicated to insuring a free flow of information to the Congress and the news media." On March 24, 1969, he issued a memorandum to all department heads saying that all executive privilege claims must be cleared through him. He would invoke the privilege "only in the most compelling circumstances and after a rigorous inquiry into the actual need for its exercise."

On November 11, 1969, J. W. Fulbright, chairman of the Foreign Relations Committee, asked Secretary of Defense Melvin R. Laird if his committee could take a look at a seventeen-volume history of the decision-making process in Vietnam. A month later Laird replied that the study, which later became known as the "Pentagon Papers," contained data "of the most delicate sensitivity," and refused to turn them over.

Again and again Fulbright asked Laird either to change his mind or to make a formal claim of executive privilege. Neither was ever done. As Fulbright told Ervin during the first hearings on executive privilege in July, 1971, the study "didn't have a lot in it. It just fills out what I have gotten from other sources, but I am offended by the idea that they would refuse to make it available."

Ervin sympathized with Fulbright because he, too, had been getting the runaround from the Defense Department over details he was seeking about the Army's surveillance of private citizens. Laird told Ervin that the release of the documents would be "inappropriate." J. Fred Buzhardt, the department's general counsel, informed Ervin that "no useful purpose would be served" by making the information public.

"These practices reflect a certain contempt for Congressional requests for information and an apparent disdain for the right of the American people to be informed fully about the operation of their government," Ervin said.

He admitted it was at least partly the fault of Congress. "In all candor, we in the legislative branch must confess that the shifting of power to the executive has resulted from our failure to assert our constitutional powers." Ervin could see that this condition invited the ultimate tyranny, "a government of men, not of laws."

He held hearings in early 1971 on the increasing tendency of the White House to sit on money that Congress said by law should be spent. Whenever Congress voted substantially more funds for a program than Nixon had called for in his budget message, the President simply directed his Office of Management and Budget to freeze the additional money. He was stealing the power of the purse from Congress on the theory that Congress did not know how to wield it. It was his duty, he said, to hold down the budget.

Nixon's critics said that was nonsense, that he was lavishing the government's money on military hardware at the expense of housing and education. But hardly anyone was listening.

The Administration was on the attack in other ways, challenging the independence of members of Congress. All it needed was a test case, and on June 29, 1971, it found one. On that date, in the midst of the court battles over publication of the Pentagon Papers, Mike Gravel of Alaska hastily convened a midnight meeting of the Public Works Subcommittee on Buildings and Grounds and began reading extracts from the papers into the public record.

Ervin felt Gravel's action was unwise and perhaps stupid, but also courageous and lawful. When the Justice Department went before a federal grand jury in Boston and asked to subpoena Gravel's aide—Gravel had hired him on the spot the day he read the papers—Ervin became Gravel's most ardent defender.

The two men were not close friends and were miles apart in age and ideology. In fact they probably did not even like each other very much. But Ervin considered the Justice Department's action to be as grave a threat to freedom of speech in Congress as the attempted gagging of newspapers was to freedom of the press.

It was an attack on the very plain words of the Constitution that protected members of Congress from any inquiry about what they say in speeches or debates in either house. If the Administration succeeded in calling either Gravel or his aide, the independence of the legislative branch would be gone forever.

A lot of people who supported Nixon's Vietnam policy had a hard time understanding why Sam Ervin, whom they considered a consistent war hawk, got so excited about the Gravel affair. But Ervin was not one who would say, sure, we defend your right to say things we disagree with, but only as long as it doesn't threaten us politically. Was that what Voltaire meant by "to the death"?

Those who did not know Ervin could have mistaken him for a flaming liberal when he told the Senate on September 20 that the Administration was attacking Gravel because he dared oppose the war. "If the Administration were to have its way, we must remain in total ignorance of what has transpired in Vietnam, and anything else the government does, unless it chooses to tell us. By suppressing this information, the executive branch has tried to keep the Congress in total ignorance." His voice trembling and his arms waving, Ervin shouted to the puzzled Senate galleries that the Administration was attempting to harass Gravel and silence him and its other critics inside the chamber and out.

In April, 1972, Ervin marched over to say a few words to his next-door neighbors, the justices of the Supreme Court. On the way over, he noticed how green the grass growing around the Capitol grounds looked and told the nine justices that they and officials of the executive branch "must keep off this legislative grass."

Ervin was appearing on behalf of the Senate. "Even though Senator Gravel may have violated Senate rules and even though he may have acted improperly, that is a matter for the judgment of the Senate," he said. Congressmen were "among the earth's most timid creatures," and nothing would come closer to scaring them to death than to have the courts or a powerful administration holding them accountable for their conduct. "That would absolutely destroy the independence of the legislative branch."

The only leverage the Senate had against Nixon were the periodic scandals that had begun to haunt his Administration. The ITT affair broke just as he was changing attorneys general. That allowed Ervin and others on the Judiciary Committee to hold up the nomination of Richard G. Kleindienst and force the reluctant Peter Flannigan, a presidential aide, to appear.

Ervin said at the time the only reason the committee was able to work its will on the White House was because "we've got the executive where the wool is short," meaning, he explained later,

"When the wool is short on lambs, they're much more susceptible to being firmly seized and that means you can get a man at a disadvantage, like catch a man with his pants down."

Like Chinese firecrackers, events were beginning to explode all around Sam Ervin. But he seemed to stay just above the commotion while those about him were consumed by it. The Senate was headed inevitably toward a major clash with the man in the White House.

While the White House was attempting to muzzle free expression in Congress, it was also gradually eroding the powers of the Senate in the field of foreign policy, supposedly a shared power. Nixon had already avoided much of his accountability in foreign policy by stripping the State Department of authority. And, as his predecessors had done, he relied less and less on treaties with other nations and more and more on executive agreements, often made in total secrecy.

Neither South Vietnam nor Cambodia was a signatory to the SEATO treaty, yet it was assumed that some kind of commitment existed that obliged the United States to intervene in Southeast Asia. Ervin thought we should never have made that mistake.

In a dialogue with former Secretary of Defense Clark Clifford in April, 1972, Ervin said, "Some time ago I attempted to make a study of the way we got involved in Vietnam, and it is a long story. I was astounded to find that on several occasions our presidents made statements which the people of that area could only interpret as a commitment by the President of American protection." He added, "I sometimes think we sort of talked our way into our present involvement in Southeast Asia largely through remarks made by Presidents for which there was no authority outside of a proclivity to talk." Ervin authored legislation giving Congress a voice in the signing of executive agreements.

The next month, while Ervin was resting quietly in Morganton, the Supreme Court startled him with its 5–4 decision in the

Gravel case, saying that legislative "errands" performed for constituents and speeches made outside the halls of Congress were not immune from prosecution. Ervin called it "a clear and present threat to the continued independence of Congress." The new "activist" majority on the court, four of the five appointed by Nixon, "has tinkered with the very heart of the Constitution," he said, and opened the door to intimidation of Congress by the other two branches.

In a *Virginia Law Review* article, Ervin said the Court's opinion that the "Speech or Debate" clause did not protect a legislator who attempts to acquire and publish information about the government "is a dangerous double blow to the concept of the separation of powers and to the governmental process. The court not only cut off the Congress from the executive, but it has cut off the people from the Congress."

It was time for Congress to act. Perhaps, Ervin felt, it would have to write new laws, prohibiting the executive from keeping any information from Congress that was vital to its oversight function, perhaps restricting the federal courts from harassing members of Congress who attempt to inform themselves about what the executive is doing. Something had to be done before the two branches declared "open warfare" on each other, a state which Woodrow Wilson had warned would be fatal to the country.

In spite of all of Ervin's efforts on behalf of civil liberties and the constitutional rights of Congress, he had no real power. Whatever influence he had was the result of his persuasion and wit, the admiration of others for his hard work, and his impressive knowledge of the law.

Then fate intervened. Allen Ellender of Louisiana, chairman of the all-powerful Appropriations Committee, died, creating a void that resulted in major shifts of power. Ervin was not even on the Appropriations Committee or next in line anywhere else, but nevertheless the power shift went in his direction.

John McClellan was next in seniority on Appropriations, and had to give up his chairmanship of the Government Operations Committee in order to move over. About the only thing that keeps the old warlords in Congress from becoming absolute dictators is the rule that they cannot hold two major chairmanships at one time. Henry Jackson held the second spot on Government Operations, but he wanted to keep his influential position as head of the Interior Committee. So he willingly stepped aside, and the plum fell to Sam Ervin.

By August, 1972, it was apparent that Ervin was going to become chairman of the Government Operations Committee, and that was when things began to happen. The committee had a tremendous potential for a man with a consuming interest in checking the growing power of the federal government. The job did not require any shifting of gears for him. He could move his issues over to this committee, gather in the support of its influential members—men like Jacob Javits, Charles Percy, Edmund Muskie, and Henry Jackson—and ram his bills through the Senate. He already had the prestige; now he had the power. He could still use the expertise and the investigative abilities of his subcommittees and let the full committee write and pass the very legislation that Congress needed to regain its standing as a co-equal branch of government.

"Senator Ervin's accession to this post is an unusually apt merger of personal concerns and committee jurisdiction," *The Washington Post* said that year. "The senator from North Carolina, with his unique grasp of the Constitution, his country-lawyer eloquence and his talented staff, has established himself as a champion of congressional prerogatives, a kind of de facto solicitor general for the legislative branch." The newspaper, understandably cool toward him in the past, said that Ervin, "with his long list of grievances and proposed remedies, is now in the catbird seat."

Ervin needed all the power he could muster. Nixon won the

election on November 8 in a landslide and believed it gave him a mandate to carry out his policies. Ervin felt that was a mistaken interpretation. It did not show that the electorate loved Caesar more, but Brutus less.

Ervin was not at all happy in January, 1973, when Mike Mansfield asked him to head the Watergate investigation. Ervin felt he had more important things to accomplish and that time was closing in on him. But he accepted, hoping it would not take much of his time from important matters. He did not realize the investigation would do more than all of his bills to soften up the White House and strip it of its power.

He was snowbound in Morganton at the end of the first week in January when I phoned him. As usual, he answered the phone as though greeting an intruder in his bedroom. The grumpy edge to his voice disappeared when he began talking about the coming year. "I've got more irons in the fire than a man could get around to," he said. "It seems that everything I've been working on since I went to the Senate is coming to a head this year."

It was the beginning of Ervin's most prodigious year in the Senate, a year in which the delicate system of checks and balances would be dramatically restored. Ervin would be the driving force behind the congressional revolt, making move after move to counter the thrust of presidential power. Some, like historian Arthur M. Schlesinger, Jr., were alarmed that Ervin wanted to cripple the executive and bequeath to the country "a generation of weak presidents." Actually, that was not Ervin's intent at all. A look at his stand on the War Powers Act will attest to that. He was as much an admirer of Hamilton as he was of Jefferson and was concerned only insofar as the President acted within the limits of the Constitution. If some of his proposals seemed rather drastic, it was because the times called for drastic action. The political process would take care of the refinements.

Nevertheless, Schlesinger was taken with Ervin as one who made the Constitution of 1787 "superbly alive and fresh." "No one for a long time," he said in *The Imperial Presidency* (1973), "had done so much to educate the American people in the meaning and majesty of the Constitution."

That document gave Ervin all the authority he needed to act at the dawn of the second Nixon Administration. For starters, he joined in a lawsuit with the State of Missouri against the Nixon Administration for impounding highway funds. The courts eventually ordered the money released. It was the first shot fired over the bow of the new Administration.

Then he made a move that was as audacious as it was doomed. He walked into the Senate on January 23 with a bill to require Senate confirmation of the director and deputy director of the Office of Management and Budget, including the two men who were already occupying those jobs. Ervin had the signatures of the chairmen of all seventeen standing committees, the majority leadership, and fifteen others.

Roy L. Ash, the cocky ex-president of Litton Industries, which was embroiled in a huge cost overrun fight with the Navy involving multimillion-dollar nuclear submarine contracts, had just been chosen by Nixon to run the OMB. The director's position had become one of the most powerful jobs in the country. Under Nixon, the former Bureau of the Budget had acquired a Scroogelike image along with vast new powers to run the government.

Ervin was not out to get Ash, although there were plenty of staff investigators on Capitol Hill who would have loved to work him over during confirmation hearings. It would have provided a rare look at the inner workings of the military-industrial—now military-industrial-executive—complex. Ervin merely thought that any official with more authority than a member of the cabinet, who would in fact be a "deputy president," ought to stand inspection before Congress.

The bill passed overwhelmingly, and was of course vetoed by Nixon. The Senate overrode the veto, but the House succumbed to White House pressure and sustained it. "Gutless wonders,"

Ervin muttered to an aide—an uncharitable but accurate assessment. He had failed his first test with Nixon, but it served as a strong message to the White House that the Senate was ready to fight back.

There was a certain spirit of revolution in the air. One could almost smell the gunpowder from the muskets as the first shots were fired.

In January, the U.S. Judicial Conference, headed by Chief Justice Warren Burger and other members of the Supreme Court, proposed new uniform rules of evidence for federal courts. They included provisions to eliminate the doctor-patient and husband-wife testimonial privileges and to allow the government to invoke executive privilege before the courts whenever it felt it was not in the public interest to divulge "state secrets and other official information." This latter bit of hocus-pocus, which was included, according to Ervin aides, at the request of Attorney General Kleindienst, would have radically altered the federal justice system. The new rules would have gone into effect ninety days after being submitted to Congress if Ervin had not blocked them. He introduced a bill on January 29—it was signed into law a few weeks later—requiring specific approval of Congress before the rules could take effect. Congress stripped the provisions from the new rules of evidence.

The next day, January 30, Ervin assembled an ad hoc subcommittee on impoundment of funds and began grilling Ash and a number of other Administration witnesses about the President's budget-juggling act. When two of the witnesses cancelled their appearances at the last minute, Ervin threatened to subpoena them. They came quietly a few days later.

Ervin was feeling his oats. During the five days of hearings he chuckled and guffawed and skewered the witnesses with his favorite stories and his sharp-edged constitutional sword.

The President, he said, was clearly entitled to give Congress advice about the budget. "But I submit, the Congress should have the same power as the old lady who came to see me in my

law office many, many years ago and asked my advice on a point
of law. I took down the law book to enlighten myself as to what
her legal rights were, and what she ought to do. She got up and
started out of my office and I said, 'Wait a minute, you owe me
five dollars'.

"She said, 'What for?'

"I said, 'For my advice.'

"She said, 'Well, I ain't going to take it.' "

Congress, he said, could totally ignore the President and
write its own budget, but it never did. Ervin had voted against a
lot of appropriations bills because they spent money the country
did not have. And he would gladly sustain presidential vetoes on
the same grounds. That was the legal, proper way to do it. But
the President had no grounds for suspending programs that were
already signed into law. After all, William Rehnquist had said
impoundment "is supported by neither reason nor precedent."
Nixon, Ervin crowed, "thought anybody who could define the
law with such efficiency and wisdom ought to go to the highest
tribunal in the land."

Deputy Attorney General Joseph T. Sneed, former head of
the Duke University Law School and one of the smoothest
lawyers in town, received a full dose of Ervinisms after losing a
constitutional debating match with him. Sneed said the President had the power to freeze funds irrespective of the Constitution. When it came down to a collision with Congress, he said, it
was a "political question" justified by past practice and congressional acquiescence.

ERVIN: I am reminded of the story of the deacon who desired to preach.
The deacon went to the board of deacons and wanted to know why they
fired him, and he asked the chairman, "Don't I arguefy?" He said, "Yes, you
arguefy, yes." He said, "Don't I sputify?" The chairman said, "Yes, you sure
do sputify." He said, "What's the trouble with my preachin'?" The
chairman said, "You don't show wherein." I wish you would show wherein
there is any provision, other than the veto power, that the President has the
right to ignore any provision of Congress.

SNEED: There is no explicit veto power of impoundment.

ERVIN: The power has to be either expressed or implied. Now, tell us where it is implied. If you can tell us where it is, it will facilitate this.

SNEED: We have to go, as far as the Constitution is concerned, to article II in sections 1 and 2 and 3.

ERVIN: Well, the only thing I see in there that anybody has invoked so far is that the President has the power to ignore an act of Congress, either in whole or in part, in the exercise of his power to see that the laws are faithfully executed. I cannot reconcile that conclusion with what the words say. If there is any other provision of the Constitution which provides that power. . . .

SNEED: Senator, I have done my best to contribute to this discussion.

ERVIN: Somebody told me once when I was representing a case; he said, "You put up the best possible defense for a guilty client."

Ervin's Impoundment Control Bill would have required affirmative approval by Congress in order for the President to freeze appropriated funds for more than sixty days. The bill passed the Senate overwhelmingly four times, but the House wanted a much weaker bill and it died for want of an acceptable compromise. However, a number of court rulings commanding Nixon to spend the funds may have made legislation unnecessary.

Ervin knew full well that Congress could not carp about the President's unilateral budget cuts unless it did something dramatic about its own serious habit of bouncing checks off the walls of the U.S. Treasury. In October, 1973, in the midst of the second phase of the Watergate hearings, he introduced—with impressive bipartisan support—a revolutionary bill to reform the budget-making process of Congress.

It provided for ceilings on federal spending and the national debt, budget committees in each house, and a congressional office of the budget that would allow Congress to compete with the OMB. If it continued to allow the Administration to run budgetary circles around it, he said, "Congress will drift toward becoming a meaningless debating society and our liberties could suffer the consequences."

Ervin, who had the habit of scribbling furiously during hearings, sometimes with an extra pen clenched between his teeth, then asking questions as though he had been listening all along, was working with single-minded determination during the impoundment hearings. He had thought out the issue in his sleep the night before and came up with S. R. 60, a resolution to establish a select committee "to conduct an investigation and study of the extent, if any, to which illegal, improper, or unethical activities were engaged in by any persons, acting individually or in combination with others, in the presidential election of 1972, or any campaign, canvass or other activity related to it." The resolution authorized the most sweeping powers ever given to any investigative committee in history. It was unanimously approved by the Senate one week later.

The confrontation with Nixon was growing daily.

Ervin played a part in the Judiciary Committee's decision to hold up the confirmation of L. Patrick Gray as director of the FBI. Again it was an effort to pressure the White House into allowing an aide to testify. This time it was the President's counsel, John W. Dean III. Ervin wanted to know why Gray had turned over FBI files to Dean and allowed him to sit in on interviews with White House aides in connection with the Watergate affair.

That prompted the White House to abandon Gray and, in the elegant words of John D. Ehrlichman, "let him hang there. Let him twist slowly, slowly in the wind." Gray's nomination was abruptly withdrawn.

Ervin escaped from Washington one brisk weekend in March. One thing he had not given much thought to was whether to run for reelection to the Senate in 1974. He would be seventy-eight then and entertained no illusions of immortality. He needed to get back to North Carolina and see what the folks at home thought about it.

On the way down, sitting in the back seat of his dusty-blue Chrysler with his wife, he unfurled a copy of the *Wall Street Journal* and read aloud an article about a man who regretted having retired. He laughed with approval at the writer's observation that there was a difference "between not having to do anything and not having anything to do."

Ervin would have plenty to do. He desperately wanted to get back home to his library, to do some research and writing, and even to try a few more cases in court. But on the other hand there was so much to be accomplished in Washington. And who was going to keep an eye on Nixon?

If he made up his mind that weekend after rubbing elbows with hundreds of Democratic politicians in Raleigh, he kept his decision a secret. But he had given Miss Margaret enough hints that they were not going back to Morganton for her to say, "If there were two Sam Ervins, one who ran and one who didn't run, I'd keep the one who refrained from running."

As if his mind were already back on the tangled web of Watergate, Ervin changed the subject. He noticed a motorcyclist passing in the twilight on the country road and said, "That must be Diogenes with his lights on, looking for an honest man."

Things were beginning to come unglued in Washington. Suddenly, the issue that Ervin had been so irate about, the use of executive privilege to keep witnesses and information from Congress, had become *the* crucial Watergate issue. What had been a rather academic question was now becoming intimately linked with the guilt or innocence of the President of the United States.

Nixon declared at a press conference that he had an absolute right to prevent his aides from appearing before the Ervin committee. But after Ervin threatened to have the aides arrested, a negotiating process began. The White House said it would allow Dean, who was supposed to have conducted an investigation for the President, to meet privately with committee members.

In a rare press conference of his own on April 2, one of the best attended ever on Capitol Hill, Ervin put on a virtuoso performance. "I'm not going to let anybody come down like

Nicodemus by night and whisper something in my ear that the public can't hear," he said. "Shakespeare asks in one place, 'What meat doth this our Caesar eat that he's grown so great?' There's a lot of talk about meat these days. I just wonder what meat these White House aides eat that makes them grow so great."

In mid-April, a month before the opening of the Watergate hearings, Ervin conducted some more hearings on executive privilege. Attorney General Kleindienst demonstrated that the Administration was digging in its heels. He expounded the fantastic doctrine that any of the two and a half million federal employees could be kept from appearing before Congress merely at the request of the President. That was Administration policy, he said, and if Congress didn't like it, it could impeach the President. In a few weeks Kleindienst was looking for another job, and impeachment was a wide-open topic of conversation. Executive privilege was a myth without constitutional foundation, and Ervin sought to restrict its use by giving Congress authority to order officials of the executive branch to testify. The bill passed the Senate in December.

Later in the hearings on executive privilege, Ervin gave consumer advocate Ralph Nader his favorite lecture on George Washington, remonstrating about the tendency of public officials to abuse power. In his farewell address, Washington said the way to change the Constitution was by amendment, not by usurpation, "a customary weapon by which free government is destroyed."

Nader cheered Ervin on. "Now you are putting it on the line, Senator. Like Washington had his Cornwallis, you have your Nixon."

Ed Muskie put in, "I might say that George Washington won over Cornwallis."

"But he had to fight seven years to win," Ervin said, exploding with laughter.

14. *Watergate*

Something was rotten in the Committee
for the Re-election of the President.

SAM ERVIN

SAM ERVIN WAS UNCOMFORTABLE with the suggestion
that he compare himself with Richard Nixon. Holding himself
up to anyone, especially a President with whom he was engaged
in mortal combat, was not quite proper. It was June 8, 1973, in
the thick of the hearings which dramatized the grim struggle
between the great independent branches of government. The
future course of the Republic was at stake. Somehow, in that
incredible year of 1973, it seemed that the contours of that course
would be determined by the clash between those uniquely
different personalities.

"I wouldn't want to express my opinion about him," Ervin
said, sitting in his office that Friday afternoon. But then he
ventured something about himself which struck the comparison
neatly. "I would say this: I have a tendency to trust people. My
experience has been, with the average man, the average woman,
I think they try to do right, that they're trustworthy, that they'll
do the best they know how. I think very few people merit distrust.
I think the overwhelming majority of human beings I've ever
known are people who can be trusted.

"There's an old story I always liked about the blacksmith
shop along the trail that people used in the old days, frontier
days, moving to Kentucky. The blacksmith had a lot of work to
do there because the wagons would break down and their horses

and mules would need shoes. The story goes that these people that were moving from Virginia to settle over in Kentucky would get in conversations with the old blacksmith. And one of the things they mentioned the most, they'd ask about what kind of neighbors they'd have when they got over to Kentucky. And the old blacksmith would say to them, 'What kind of neighbors did you have down in Virginia where you came from?' If they said they had fine neighbors, generous neighbors, the old blacksmith would say, 'Well, you'll find the same kind of neighbors over in Kentucky.' If they said they had mean, ornery neighbors, the old blacksmith would say, 'Well, you'll have the same kind of neighbors over in Kentucky.'

"So, I think a person has a tendency to find people like he anticipates they're going to be. If you're good neighbors, you're going to have good neighbors; if you're a bad neighbor, you'll probably have bad neighbors. And if you distrust people, they'll probably distrust you."

Ervin, the libertarian, had a childlike, and perhaps somewhat naive, faith that people could work out their problems and live together, as Jefferson said so often, in "perfect harmony." Protest was sometimes good for the government and nearly always therapeutic for the protestors. Lawlessness could be dealt with by firm application of existing law but was not an occasion for surrendering basic freedoms to obtain temporary security.

Nixon, the authoritarian, reacted to challenges to his authority by firing everyone in sight. When protestors demonstrated against his policies, he responded with stern, repressive measures that trampled on constitutional rights. Apparently believing himself surrounded by enemies, he built an impenetrable wall around himself and delegated authority to automatons.

"I think," Ervin said, referring to Nixon and his strong men, "they were unable to accept the risk that people should exercise freedom for themselves. The First Amendment was written giving the rights of freedom of speech and freedom of thought, freedom of the press and freedom to protest to government, to make America a free society. This illustrates a disbelief in the wisdom of having a free society and the fear of a free society.

"I think one of the unfortunate things which have arisen in recent years is that too many men in power have too little commitment to freedom and actually fear the exercise of freedom by other people, especially people whose actions or thoughts are displeasing to them."

The theme, fear of freedom, runs through the written and spoken words of Sam Ervin all during the long siege by Richard Nixon on fundamental liberties, beginning when Nixon entered the White House in 1969. This "climate of fear" led irrevocably to the "White House Horrors," as John Mitchell called them, and to Watergate.

On June 5, 1970, Nixon met with Tom Charles Huston, a new White House aide who had been hired to draw blueprints for the Administration's response to the country's growing restlessness over the war. It was shortly after the invasion of Cambodia and the deaths at Kent State University. Antiwar sentiment was at a fever pitch. Believing, as he once said, that the public prefers order to liberty, Huston drew up a forty-three page plan for White House–directed intelligence operations that was unprecedented.

Among other things, it called for lifting restrictions against surreptitious entry. "Use of this technique is clearly illegal: it amounts to burglary," Huston wrote in a summary of the plan. "It is also highly risky and could result in great embarrassment if exposed. However, it is also the most fruitful tool and can produce the type of intelligence which cannot be obtained in any other fashion." The plan contemplated intensified electronic surveillance and wiretapping against "groups in the United States who pose a major threat to the internal security." It also recommended tampering with suspected mail, which, again, was flatly illegal, but, in the equation that tantalized the White House, "the advantages to be derived from its use outweigh the risks."

Defending his action on the grounds that it was essential for national security, Nixon approved the plan in July, only to abandon it when it ran into opposition from FBI Director J. Edgar Hoover. However, the intelligence activities that took place shortly afterward, including burglarizing the office of Daniel Ellsberg's psychiatrist, indicated that the methods, if not the plan itself, were put into operation.

At the same time, the White House was putting pressure on the Internal Revenue Service to take action against activist organizations, and conferring on the Subversive Activities Control Board fantastic authority for investigating all sorts of unconventional groups. A siege mentality, indeed, a climate of fear, pervaded these actions.

In mid-1971, the White House began compiling what it variously referred to as its "opponents" or "political enemies" list, and by that time opponents and political enemies had become synonymous. The list included newsmen, businessmen, entertainers, members of Congress, and joiners of peace groups, all of whom were assumed to be against Nixon. Every effort was to be made, in the poetic language of Nixon's counsel, John W. Dean III, to "screw" these enemies by enlisting the full cooperation of the federal bureaucracy: take them to court, audit their tax returns, withhold grants—the whole gamut of persecution and revenge.

These activities reduced the Nixon Administration to such a low moral plane that it was but a few steps to breaking into the Democratic National Committee headquarters, installing bugging devices and stealing documents, spying on Nixon's likely opponents, disrupting their campaigns, and attempting to destroy all but the weakest of them.

The burglary was discovered and the connection made between the burglars' finances and the Committee for the Re-election of the President. But instead of launching a thorough investigation, the White House began an all-out campaign to hide it, to limit the scope of the FBI's inquiry, to destroy evidence and withhold it from federal prosecutors, to commit perjury, to provide support money for the defendants and promises of executive clemency if they agreed to remain silent and plead guilty. All these activities were paid for in cash out of political contributions given to help reelect Richard Nixon.

The cover-up was a success. Federal prosecutors looked no further than the five men caught inside the Watergate offices and their two accomplices. Only these seven were indicted. The White House was saved from being directly implicated. Nixon was reelected. It looked as though he and his closest aides had been spared. Everything was fine—except it was apparent to anyone who kept his eyes open that everything was rotten.

The Senate turned, in its hour of gloom, to one of the few of its membership without presidential ambitions—Sam Ervin. "Sam is the only man we could have picked on either side who would have the respect of the Senate as a whole," said majority leader Mike Mansfield.

Ervin was not overly excited about spending one of his last years in the Senate examining the entrails of political corruption. He was much more concerned with curtailing the abuses of presidential power, which, at the time, seemed far more threatening to the country. "I wish to God I'd never agreed to take this thing," Ervin grumbled to an aide at one point during the hearings. "But it was my duty. I had to take it."

The job had its consolations. It had become apparent by the spring of 1973 that Watergate was the symptom of everything that was wrong with the Administration and indeed with the office of the president. It went to the roots of executive arrogance, high-handed policies, political corruption, domestic intelligence activities, and official secrecy. Ervin had been struggling all of his Senate career with the growing might of the executive branch. Liberal Democrats were as much at fault as anyone for creating the so-called "strong presidency" that Nixon inherited, along with the doctrine of implied powers—those powers which are not in the Constitution but which presidents believe ought to be.

This doctrine led the President to claim the right to impound congressionally authorized funds, invoke executive privilege to prevent Congress—and thus the American public—from finding out what the executive branch was doing, and transfer the power of cabinet officers to unaccountable White House assistants. It added up to the most stunning assertion of presidential power in history, overrunning fundamental constitutional laws that are supposed to protect ordinary citizens.

James Madison said the accumulation of judicial, legislative, and executive powers into one branch of government was the very definition of tyranny. Ervin had been saying that for years, but hardly anyone paid attention. Now it appeared that an administration run by corporate executives had decided, after receiving one of the most impressive mandates in history, to carry out its policies without help from Congress or the benefit of constitutional sanction. It could undo the delicate balance the Founding Fathers had achieved after throwing off imperial rule. By the time Ervin picked up the gavel on May 17 and marched into the hearing room, the Administration was in a shambles and the balance was well on the way to being restored.

Ervin felt much of the credit for uncovering the Watergate scandal and thus stopping the presidential power grab went to U.S. District Judge John J. Sirica for insisting on an honest prosecution of the case, and to *Washington Post* reporters, Bob Woodward and Carl Bernstein, for doggedly pursuing the story in the face of harsh White House criticism and stony silence from most of the rest of the media. It was evidence that the most autocratic government could be made accountable by a free and courageous press and judiciary.

What was needed most now, more than pointing the finger of guilt, was public education, not only about the facts of Watergate but also about the traditions of constitutional law and ethical behavior. The hearings would also show the American people that the system could examine itself without fear and correct its faults. Sam Ervin, righteous but quick to forgive, gentle but capable of indignation, eloquent but not too smooth, seemed right for the central role as Teacher.

"In pursuing its task, it is clear that the committee will be dealing with the working of the democratic process under which we operate in a nation that still is the last, best hope of mankind in his eternal struggle to govern himself decently and effectively," Ervin said in his opening statement.

"We will be concerned with the integrity of the governmental system designed by men who understood the lessons of the past and who, accordingly, established a framework of separated governmental powers in order to prevent any one branch of government from becoming dominant over the others. The Founding Fathers, having participated in the struggle against arbitrary power, comprehended some eternal truths respecting men and government. They knew that those who are entrusted with power are susceptible to the disease of tyrants which George Washington rightly described as 'love of power and the proneness to abuse it.' For that reason, they realized that the power of public officers should be defined by laws which they, as well as the people, are obligated to obey, a truth embodied by Daniel Webster when he said that 'Whatever government is not a government of laws is a despotism, let it be called what it may.' "

The evidence of wrongdoing that had surfaced, Ervin said, "has cast a black cloud of distrust over our entire society." He was determined to disperse it with the winds of truth. "The aim of the committee is to provide full and open public testimony in order that the nation can proceed toward the healing of the wounds that now afflict the body politic." He was not exaggerating when he concluded, "The nation and history are watching us. We cannot fail our mission."

Ervin approached his mission, as he had most others, with a rich blend of humor, philosophy, and constitutional wisdom. This time he went a little heavier on the philosophy and lighter on the humor. In fact, he told fewer stories in confronting the witnesses at these hearings than he ever had. Watergate triggered a series of entirely different responses. The old Calvinist doctrines of good and evil, right and wrong, the biblical and poetic wisdom learned at his father's knee, from the church pulpit, and in the college classroom came back vividly in this twentieth-century morality play.

The Kind Judge felt sorry for the Honest Policeman who said he participated in the cover-up out of loyalty to the President. John J. Caulfield admitted early in the hearings that he had met convicted Watergate burglar James W. McCord at an overlook on the George Washington Parkway and promised him executive clemency in return for silence.

"Well, it is proof of what my old philosophy professor told me," said Ervin, "that the greatest trials we have in this world are when we are compelled to choose between different loyalties, some of which are conflicting. And you were trying to protect the President, you were trying to aid a friend, and you were trying to carry out a mission which you accepted somewhat reluctantly from the man that you knew—that is, John Dean—whom you knew to be the President's counsel and who you knew would be actuated by the desire to protect the President against any scandal?"

"Absolutely correct, Senator," said the penitent Caulfield.

When Gerald Alch, McCord's former lawyer, mentioned that his client wanted to write a book about Watergate, Ervin was reminded at once of the Bible and Sherlock Holmes. "The Scriptures say, 'Much study is a weariness to the flesh and of making books there is no end.' It seems that everybody who gets into jail today wants to write a book about it." Then he added, "I might say if Mr. McCord wanted to write a book about Watergate, he could make A. Conan Doyle turn green with envy."

G. Gordon Liddy, the former counsel to the Nixon reelection committee and Watergate mastermind, was said to have other bizarre ideas, such as hiring a woman to appear at the Democratic National Convention wearing a McGovern button and disrobe in living color. At that point, Ervin leaned over and whispered to Howard Baker and Deputy Counsel Rufus Edmisten, "That's what I call uncovering the cover-up." Liddy, Ervin commented, was like the Lord in one respect, since he "moves in mysterious ways his wonders to perform."

Hugh W. Sloan, Jr., treasurer of the Nixon committee, was the first witness to say he had refused to lie to federal prosecutors. Looking almost as though he would embrace him, Ervin said—with help from Alexander Pope—"I think you have strengthened my faith in the old adage that 'an honest man is the noblest work of God.' " Then, for good measure, he threw in a little Sir Walter Scott. "I will also meditate for a moment on the old saying, 'What a tangled web we weave, when first we practice to deceive!' "

Then, when former campaign deputy director Jeb S. Magruder confessed to having committed perjury, Ervin gave him and his wife a benediction that was enough to mollify the daytime soap-opera fans who had missed their programs. "I was very much encouraged by your statement that you are not going to let this keep you from going ahead and living a useful life," he said, "and I would recommend to you, go get the poem by Walter Malone called 'Opportunity' which tells of 'Each night I burn the records of the day. At sunrise every soul is born again,' and I think it is the most encouraging set of words ever put together by man. And despite your very unfortunate state at the present time, you have got about the greatest asset that any man can have, you have a wife who stands behind you in the shadows and where the sun shines, so I wish you success in your future endeavors."

Normally, such sentiments from a politician sound mawkish, but Ervin meant them and they came across that way. Much to his horror, Ervin, the loather of fads, quickly became a fad himself, one of the most colorful figures in American politics. At least three books on his wit and wisdom were assembled, and his stories and readings, including "The Night before Christmas," were stamped into long-playing, unbreakable plastic. Sam Ervin posters, buttons, and T shirts were distributed by his fan club.

He was not just the lovable Bible-quoting storyteller to his followers. He was also a formidable interrogator. He went into the hearings with an impressive grasp of the fiendishly complex details of the great political fiasco. He had salted down the facts by absorbing several six-inch-thick notebooks of information. Then, unlike the other committee members, he went into the hearings cold. He shunned the witness summaries based on hours of staff interviews. As a judge he had never known what witnesses were going to say, and he wanted to be able to listen with a fresh ear, without the daily crib sheet. The result was the constant surprise on Ervin's face and his frequently startling observations. His questions, except when he wasn't listening, were crisp and spirited, sometimes too spirited for Nixon partisans.

He could not understand why former Secretary of Commerce Maurice H. Stans decided to destroy records of campaign contributors a few days after the break-in unless he meant to hide something. Stans contended that the break-in and the shredding of records were totally unrelated, and since the old campaign law did not require him to keep records of contributions made before April 7, 1972, he was free to destroy them. Ervin obviously did not believe him and went after him with rare fury.

It was "rather a suspicious coincidence," he said. Stans indignantly replied that he saw nothing suspicious about it, that he did it on advice of counsel. Ervin inquired if this counsel was none other than G. Gordon Liddy, the Watergate plotter. Stans acknowledged that it was, but refused to see the humor in that.

Stans was having to reconstruct the records of contributions, and that seemed to Ervin a lot of bother when they could have been saved in the first place. "It's very simple," Stans started to explain. Again, Ervin, with low-key mockery, speared the one-time big game hunter. "It's too simple for me to understand, really," he said.

Stans said it was all perfectly legal. And it was, strictly speaking. It just did not look very good. "Well, Mr. Stans, do you think the men who have been honored by the American people, as you have, ought to have their course of action guided by ethical principles which are superior to the minimum requirements of the criminal laws?" Have such men, he asked, fulfilled their duty to the American public "as long as they keep on the windy side of the law?"

Senator Edward Gurney of Florida, the committee's openly pro-Nixon backstop, had had enough. "I, for one, have not appreciated the harassment of this witness by the chairman in the questioning that has just finished," Gurney protested. Gurney had inadvertently given Ervin a golden opportunity.

"Well, I'm sorry that my distinguished friend from Florida doesn't approve of my method of examining the witness," Ervin drawled. "I'm an old country lawyer and I don't know the finer ways to do it. I just have to do it my way."

The South is one of the few places in America where it is still a virtue to act and sound like one of the boys, to retain, no matter how impressive one's education, every bit of the old rough mannerisms and, above all, the accent. To lose that is to lose one's spiritual ancestry; and so Ervin, with all his worldly attainments, refused to take on any airs.

The simple country lawyer did not understand, or simply refused to understand, double talk. He believed that words spoken in his mother tongue, like the words of the Constitution, meant what they said. He knifed through oceans of sophistry like a great gull diving for prey.

As crimes went, it was fairly simple to Ervin: five burglars were caught "red-handed"—he always threw that in—in the headquarters of the opposition political party with money in their pockets belonging to President Nixon's reelection campaign. Reasonable men would have taken immediate steps to clean house and, if the blame was partly theirs, taken their lumps. Only those with prior knowledge of a crime, or those incapable of taking responsible action after the crime became known, would have permitted a massive cover-up to follow.

Erwin did not like being placed in the position of accusing or even confronting the President of the United States. A "peace-loving man," he wanted to spread the facts on the table and let the public decide who was guilty, let public pressure rather than the courts force the evidence into the open.

His questions betrayed his contempt.

He was intrigued, he told Dean, about a White House statement that "the President was concerned that all the available facts be made known." If he was so concerned, he wanted to know, what action had he taken to make them known? Neither Dean nor any of the other witnesses was able to tell him.

Article II of the Constitution says the President "shall take care that the laws be faithfully executed." It was clear that he thought Nixon failed to do so. "Do you know anything that the President did or said at any time between June 17 and the present moment to perform his duty to see that the laws are faithfully executed in respect to what is called the Watergate affair?" Even the loquacious Dean asked to be excused from answering that question.

"Don't you agree with me," he prodded John Mitchell, "that any person, whether it's a president, or a senator, or a hod carrier, or anybody else, who gives the impression to the public that he's withholding information within his power is putting himself in a bad light?" The unusually subdued Mitchell agreed.

Ervin dredged up a 1968 Nixon campaign speech and read part of it with great sarcasm: " 'Let us begin by committing ourselves to the truth—to see it like it is and to tell it like it is—to find the truth, to speak the truth and to live the truth.' " "Now, do you have any reason," he belabored Mitchell, "to think that between that time and 1972 that President Nixon had changed his position, his fidelity to the truth?" The President, Mitchell said, hadn't changed.

Then the crucial questions: "Did you at any time tell the President anything you knew about the White House horrors?" "Did the President at any time ask you what you knew about Watergate?" The answer to both questions was no.

"Well, if the cat hadn't had any more curiosity than that," Ervin scoffed, "he would still be enjoying his nine lives, all of them."

Mitchell's excuse for not telling Nixon what was happening was that he was sure Nixon would "lower the boom" on those responsible, and that might jeopardize his reelection chances.

"You know," said Ervin, "I have a high opinion of the American people. I think if the President had lowered the boom and had come out performing his constitutional duty to take care that the laws were faithfully executed, I think he would have made his election more sure than ever."

He might also have saved himself a tremendous amount of grief. He certainly would have saved Ervin from a distasteful and difficult job that diverted him from his real interests and cost him dearly in his private and intellectual life. He had to request an unlisted telephone in Washington and take his name off the directory in the lobby of his apartment building, making him more of a non-person than he cared to be. He hated having his phone silenced. "I've always felt that a public official ought to be accessible to his constituents. I've been called on very sad missions late at night." Now, most of his calls were coming from crackpots and newsmen. "You almost have to protect yourself," Ervin said, still amazed that this could happen.

The ultimate indignity was having a bodyguard assigned to him. But it was becoming nearly impossible for him to appear anywhere near the hearing room without being accosted by some strange person. "Like this black woman who wanted to talk with me, and I said, 'Who are you?' and she said, 'I'm your stepdaughter.' And then later she tried to follow me into an elevator when I was going over to the Senate to vote. She said, 'Don't you want to talk to me?' And I said, 'No, I don't.'

"I've always decided I'm not immortal and I think if somebody wanted to take a pot shot at you or something, I don't think a security guard would stop it. And I'm enough of a Presbyterian to believe that whenever your time's come, it's here. I'm not that fatalistic, but I don't think there's much you can do about things like that."

By July, 1973 it was becoming increasingly clear that the White House was going to make it very difficult for the Ervin committee to obtain the information it needed to find out how Watergate happened. It claimed executive privilege in refusing to provide papers documenting the charges of high-level White House involvement. When Ervin asked Nixon by letter for the papers and Nixon refused, the committee began to push Ervin into a confrontation with him.

Meeting in Ervin's office on July 12, the committee members urged him to call the President and ask for a meeting to talk about the documents. Ervin said he would rather make the call in private but the others did not want to be left out. So Ervin, with senators and staff staring intently at him, placed a call to Nixon. Edmisten got the President's secretary on the line and said, inadvertently, "Ma'am, the Senator wants to get the President."

Ervin finally reached Nixon at his residence in the White House. Nixon was ill with pneumonia and left later in the day for Bethesda Naval Hospital. On the phone his voice was unusually strident, according to some in the room with Ervin, who could hear it several feet away. Ervin refused to comment on what Nixon told him, but others are certain they heard the President say, "You people are out to get me." Ervin quickly replied, "Mr. President, nobody's out to get you."

They had a lengthy conversation, about seventeen minutes, each strongly disagreeing with the other about the scope of executive privilege. Finally, they agreed to meet at a later date to discuss the release of the papers.

The meeting never took place. It was overshadowed four days

later when former White House aide Alexander P. Butterfield produced one of the biggest surprises of the hearings: Nixon had secretly tape-recorded all conversations and phone calls. The proof of whether or not he had been informed of the cover-up, had congratulated those who were conducting it, and had said that raising a million dollars in hush money was no problem—all charges made by John Dean—could be right there on tape.

Thus began one of the great legal battles of all time. Both the Senate committee and Archibald Cox, the newly appointed special Watergate prosecutor in the Justice Department, asked Nixon for the tapes.

Then, on July 19, it suddenly appeared that the impossible had happened. Just before the lunch break, Ervin was told by a breathless aide that Secretary of the Treasury George P. Shultz was calling with an important message. Ervin took the call in a phone booth tucked away behind one of the huge Corinthian columns at the back of the hearing room. The committee staff could tell it was good news because they could see Ervin flapping his arms about excitedly in the glass booth and hear him shout into the phone: "Oh, that's fine; that's just wonderful. Tell the President he's performed a great public service and that he's cut the committee's work in half."

The hearings recessed for lunch before Ervin, bursting with the news, stepped from the booth. He went to lunch with his family and kept the secret in his breast the whole time, not bothering to tell the staff lawyers. The only one who found out about the apparent White House peace gesture was Howard Baker, but only a few minutes before the hearings resumed. Ervin opened the afternoon session and stated proudly: "I am pleased to announce that Secretary Shultz has called me and advised me that the President has decided to make available to the committee tapes of conversations which may have been with witnesses before the committee which are relevant to the matters which the committee is authorized to investigate."

Ervin had been the victim of a hoax. The identity of the

caller—it certainly was not Shultz—was never discovered, but he couldn't have picked a more gullible person on whom to try such a fiendish prank.

The announcement caused momentary heart failure at the White House, where it was well known that the President had no intention of surrendering the tapes. There was a flurry of activity on the part of various staffs, and then Ervin talked with the real Shultz, after which he announced with pained embarrassment that he had been the victim of a cruel hoax. "It is an awful thing for a very trusting soul like me to find that there are human beings, if you can call them such, who would perpetuate a hoax like this." His father had warned about telephones. "My trust in humanity," he said, "has been grossly abused."

In spite of the public humiliation, Ervin consoled himself that evening by laughing until his sides hurt. His grandchildren, who had come up just in time to see their grandfather fooled, kidded him about mysterious callers and Ervin laughed away whatever anger he might have had.

There was no time for reflection on the wickedness of men. A few weeks later, on July 23, Nixon informed the committee that he would fight for possession of the tapes, even though, he said, they exonerated him. He said, in a letter to Ervin: "The fact is that the tapes would not finally settle the central issue before your committee. Before their existence became publicly known, I personally listened to a number of them. The tapes are entirely consistent with what I know to be the truth and what I have stated to be the truth. However, as in any verbatim recording of informal conversations, they contain comments that persons with different perspectives and motivations would inevitably interpret in different ways." No useful purpose would be served, Nixon said, in meeting with Ervin.

The battle lines were drawn. In closed session the same day, the committee decided unanimously to issue a subpoena for the tapes, and its chairman returned to the hearing room full of fight.

There was a fine edge of contempt in his voice as he said,

"Well, at long last, I have got something I agree with the President on in connection with this matter. If the President does not think there is any useful purpose that can be obtained by our meeting together, I will not dissent from that view. So I will not ask for the privilege of visiting the White House."

Nixon's letter was "rather remarkable," Ervin said. "If you will notice, the President says he has heard the tapes or some of them, and they sustain his position. But he says he's not going to let anybody else hear them for fear they might draw different conclusions."

There was laughter at this point from the largely anti-Nixon audience, but it quickly subsided. The spectators could see that Ervin was not kidding. His blue eyes seemed to darken and his normally chaotic eyebrows were placid.

"I love my country," Sam Ervin said. "I venerate the office of the President, and I have the best wishes for the success of the incumbent of that office, because he is the only president this country has at this time."

It was a lecture on the duties of the President, delivered straight to Nixon. The sometimes tremulous voice was surprisingly clear as the old judge reminded Nixon that he was supposed to be doing more than just carrying out the laws. "But beyond that, the President of the United States, by reason of the fact that he holds the highest office in the gift of the American people, owes an obligation to furnish a high standard of leadership to this nation and his constitutional duties, in my opinion, and undoubtedly his duty of affording moral leadership to the country, place upon him some obligation under these circumstances."

This obligation, Ervin said, included coming forward with any and all evidence that would tend to explain why those men who were caught in the act of burglary had the President's campaign funds in their pockets. "And I don't think the people of the United States are interested so much in abstruse argu-

ments about the separation of powers or executive privilege as
they are in finding the answer to that question."

Then Ervin, the student of history, the son of parents who
knew the hurt of a country wrecked by war, placed the
Watergate affair—not just the burglary but the crisis that was
gradually enveloping the country—in historical perspective. "I
deeply regret that this situation has arisen, because I think that
the Watergate tragedy is the greatest tragedy this country has
ever suffered. I used to think the Civil War was our country's
greatest tragedy, but I do remember that there were some
redeeming features in the Civil War in that there was some spirit
of sacrifice and heroism displayed on both sides. I see no
redeeming features in Watergate."

In terms of what Watergate symbolized, in terms of the
aggrandizement and corruption of power in the executive branch
and the subsequent peril to the American system of government
and to human liberties, Ervin's cataclysmic assessment may have
been accurate. It had to do with men who, as Senator Lowell
Weicker said, almost stole America.

Still, Civil War historians, who would gladly trade that
calamity for Watergate and all its ramifications, thought Ervin
went a bit overboard with his hyperbole. Ervin was always
looking for historical parallels and tended to exaggerate, for
rhetorical purposes, the significance of modern-day events. Thus,
there have been many "tragedies," many "greatest" judges,
statesmen, and poets, and many "wisest words ever spoken."

He was not kidding, however, about the redeeming aspects of
the Civil War. Unlike most dyed-in-the-wool southerners, Ervin
found courage and high motives on both sides of the war.
Dedicating a national battlefield park in Richmond fourteen
years before, he had said: "The men of the North fought to
preserve the Union, and the men of the South fought to preserve
the states. As a consequence, all Americans have inherited a

country whose Constitution contemplates 'an indestructible Union composed of indestructible states.' "

The redeeming thing about Watergate is that the system worked, however imperfectly. It was a close call, but the fact remains that largely as a result of the efforts of three men—two reporters and one judge—the press and the courts performed their appointed roles. And Ervin, presiding over the public inquisition, was living proof that the greatest governmental system in the world could heal itself.

His greatest fears for the government were personified by such men as John D. Ehrlichman, the deposed domestic adviser to Nixon, who, denying all wrongdoing and seeking to justify burglary of psychiatric records, told the committee that the ancient right of people to be free from government intrusion in their homes "has been considerably eroded over the years." He contended that even if he or Nixon had ordered the burglary, it would have been perfectly legal to have done so in the name of "national security."

Ervin seized on the Ehrlichman testimony as an opportunity to get a few things off his chest. The hearings could not end without Ervin's relating two of his favorite historical examples illustrating the central issues raised by Watergate.

"The concept embodied in the phrase 'every man's home is his castle' represents the realization of one of the most ancient and universal hungers of the human heart. One of the prophets described the mountain of the Lord as being a place where every man might dwell under his own vine and fig tree with none to make him afraid."

Ervin always found the very best poetry to illustrate his convictions, whether it was contained in the Bible, in literature, or in the words of great statesmen of the ages. William Pitt the Elder had said all that needed to be said on this subject before the American Revolution. Ervin recited it:

The poorest man may in his cottage bid defiance to all the forces of the crown. It may be frail, its roof may shake, the wind may blow through it, the

storm may enter, but the King of England cannot enter. All his force dares
not cross the threshold of the ruined tenement.

Then, bridging two hundred years of history, he said, "And yet
we are told here today, and yesterday, that what the king of
England can't do, the President of the United States can."

Ervin went from there to a discussion of the Supreme Court's
decision in *ex parte Milligan*—"the greatest decision the Supreme
Court of the United States has ever handed down in my
opinion." It involved a civilian who was tried for treason by a
military court during the Civil War and sentenced to be hanged.
The government argued that although he would normally have
the right to be tried in a civilian court, the President had the
right to suspend that principle in time of war. The Supreme
Court overturned the conviction in a decision that has become a
milestone in the rights of man.

Those words by Justice David Davis, spoken the year after
Sam Ervin's mother was born, flowed from the center of Ervin's
being as though they were his own:

> The good and wise men who drafted and ratified the Constitution
> foresaw that troublous times would arise, when rulers and people would
> become restive under restraint and seek by sharp and decisive measures to
> accomplish ends deemed just and proper, and that the principles of
> constitutional liberty would be put in peril unless established by irrepealable
> law.
>
> And for these reasons, these good and wise men drafted and ratified the
> Constitution as a law for rulers and people alike, at all times and under all
> circumstances.
>
> No doctrine involving more pernicious consequences was ever invented
> by the wit of man than that any of its provisions can be suspended during
> any of the great exigencies of government.

"And notwithstanding that," said Ervin, "we have it argued
here in this year of our Lord, 1973, that the President of the
United States has a right to suspend the Fourth Amendment and
have a burglary committed just because he claims that the

records of a psychiatrist about the emotional or mental state of his patient, Ellsberg, had some relation to national security."

How Ellsberg's mental history bore any relation to the nation's security, Ervin scoffed, "is something which eludes the imagination of this country lawyer."

The hearings often dragged because of the long-winded answers from witnesses and the unwillingness of the senators to surrender their turns as Perry Mason before the cameras. Rather than bluntly telling everybody to move things along, Ervin, during the rambling Ehrlichman sessions, quoted from Longfellow's "A Psalm of Life":

> Art is long and time is fleeting,
> And our hearts, though stout and brave,
> Still, like muffled drums, are beating
> Funeral marches to the grave.

On July 26, Nixon rejected the subpoena. The crisis had begun. Both the committee and Archibald Cox decided to go into court to force the President to release the evidence. It was a dramatic move by the committee, made by unanimous show of hands during the open, televised meeting. Ervin thought it was too hasty and harbored doubts that the federal courts would take sides in an argument between the White House and the Senate. He was not anxious to engage in a constitutional confrontation with Nixon. He wanted the confrontation to take place in the court of public opinion and in the minds of reasonable men, who could surely resolve their differences amicably.

He took his case repeatedly to the public. He had to. Nixon was on the attack during August while Congress was in recess, blaming many of the country's problems on "the backward-looking obsession with Watergate" and urging the committee to turn the investigation over to the courts.

"We're not going to continue the investigation until the last lingering echo of Gabriel's horn trembles into ultimate silence, but we are going to continue until we get the truth," Ervin told a news conference in Shelby, North Carolina, during the August recess. "It is really absurd to say the Constitution empowers a President to impede a search for truth."

That same evening in Shelby, which is just a short drive down the winding road from Morganton, it was obvious that, in spite of the strong criticism Ervin was receiving from hard-core conservatives back home, he was not without considerable honor in his own state. Thousands turned out for a free barbecue dinner in the auditorium and gave him a hero's reception. Four generations of people, black and white, crowded around him as he sat in the bleachers nibbling on a barbecue sandwich. They waited on line to reach for his twisted hands and kiss his soft cheeks. He signed autographs on the T shirts bearing his smiling, jowly profile, as the afternoon sun blazed through a far window and caught him in a warm orange spotlight. It was good to see a man like Ervin, a man of experience and wisdom, instead of the cool, sexy, now-generation types, basking in such adulation.

It was late August. I had driven down to see Ervin in hopes that, by that time, he would have had a chance to recover from the murderous punishment Watergate had inflicted upon him. Unfortunately, rest was not possible for a man who had become, in many minds, President Nixon's chief antagonist. Ervin's Nemesis—like the Greek goddess who meted out punishment— was the telephone. At the instigation of hundreds of reporters, committee lawyers, and constituents, it hounded him from morning till night. And yet, like a fatty with an obsession for chocolate candy, he could not resist picking it up when it rang. While he writhed in agony on the phone, caught for at least twenty minutes by a promoter who said he had dreamed up a new Watergate song, I poked around his immense library. Among the volumes of Dickens, Scott, Brooke, Shakespeare, the Bibles, the law books, and the biographies of all sizes, was Carl Sandburg's *Lincoln, The War Years*, autographed by Mrs. Sandburg. It was lying on its side, with a bookmark stuck in at the account of President Lincoln's surprise appearance before a congressional committee looking into charges that Lincoln's wife was spying for the Confederacy. Lincoln had "an almost inhuman sadness in his eyes" and communicated to committee members "an indescribable sense of complete isolation."

After Ervin freed himself from his tormentor, we talked about the Watergate episode in its historical context. He spoke quietly, deliberately, and it seemed as though he had pulled down one of the books from his shelves and was reading from one of its chapters.

"Unfortunately, I think the President took his mandate too seriously," he said, "and after his mandate, he undertook to exercise powers denied him by the Constitution. And as a result of that, it took a sort of languid Senate—part of it that was willing—to confront him and demand recognition of the rights given them by the Constitution. I think history is going to record this as a rather unfortunate episode in which some men in high government positions thought that what they conceived to be a desirable end justified the use of any means to obtain it. You had members of the Committee for the Re-election of the President and White House staff members who were willing to violate the laws of the land and to violate their obvious moral duties to society in order to accomplish the reelection of the President.

"The attitude that's been manifested in Washington is in such a different contrast with what Grover Cleveland said; he said 'a public office is a public trust.' Apparently many of these people thought a public office was something to be perverted from its true purpose in order to further political ends and, in some cases, personal ends. Also, Grover Cleveland said, as he lay dying, 'I have tried so hard to do the right'; and there's certainly been very little effort among the people connected with the campaign to do what was right. I just think it's an awfully sad commentary on the moral attitudes of the people upon whom the President conferred great political and governmental power."

The hearings resumed in September, delving into the "dirty tricks" that were employed against Nixon's Democratic opponents. A wide variety of political sabotage—"rascality on a national scale," Ervin called it—was carried out, including the sending, on letterhead stationery stolen from Edmund Muskie's campaign office, a letter falsely accusing Henry M. Jackson and Hubert H. Humphrey of sexual misconduct, and apparently another letter accusing Muskie of slurring Canadian-Americans.

Ervin was just as perturbed about unethical behavior as he was about unconstitutional behavior. They were illustrations of the same sickness in the body politic. Thus, when the alleged perpetrators of political rascality appeared before the committee —this time not on daytime television—Ervin went after them like a vengeful angel.

Michael McMinoway, known, for some unfathomable reason, as "Sedan Chair II," told the committee, as the others did, that he was not practicing fraud and deception when he planted himself as a spy in three different presidential campaign headquarters, that he was performing legitimate intelligence services for the Republican Party.

"Well, did you tell the truth when you gave a false name?" Ervin said.

"I wasn't under oath at the time," McMinoway said.

Ervin was flabbergasted. "Well, do you think it is all right to lie when you are not under oath and practice fraud and deception just when you are not under oath?" The witness persisted in his innocence. They could sit there all winter and talk about ethics and religion, he said smugly, "but these things are not relevant to my particular operation." At this point, Edmisten, prodded by Baker, whispered to Ervin that his ten minutes were up, but Ervin was so exercised by the young man's reckless disregard for political morality that he pressed on with a question which was not quite within the committee's jurisdiction to investigate, but which, for Ervin, was the ultimate question.

"You are swearing upon your oath that you believed that everything you did as revealed by your diary was righteous conduct?"

McMinoway's lawyer objected to the question, saying it was not material, but Ervin ordered the witness to answer it.

"From my interpretation, yes, sir," the witness said.

Baker was so uncomfortable with Ervin's question that he gave the committee chairman a long lecture about it. "I am not one of those who believe that anything is fair in love, war, and politics. But I am concerned for how the committee goes about an orderly examination of the political mores or the habits, patterns of conduct, and activities that have grown up in the American political system."

The lecture had little effect on Ervin. Instead of sitting there penitently, he clamped a pen in his mouth and one in his hand and began writing furiously. As he had done so often during the hearings, he was catching up on one of the many things he had to write. In this case, it was a resolution allowing him to appear, if necessary, at the trials of John Mitchell and Maurice Stans. Their lawyers had successfully served him with a subpoena a few days before, and he was furious about it. But he did not want to appear, like Nixon, unwilling to provide evidence. At other times, while listening with one ear, he wrote his Christmas cheese list, several other resolutions, and a number of speeches. There just was not enough time for everything.

On October 3, he delivered a speech to the Senate, hammering away at Nixon for withholding the tapes. "I deeply deplore President Nixon's action. It obstructs the select committee in the performance of its constitutional task, and, in addition, is calculated to induce multitudes of people to believe that he withholds the tapes and memorandums because their contents are adverse to him.

"In closing, I make this pledge to the people of our land: As long as I have a mind to think, a tongue to speak, and a heart to love my country, I shall deny that the Constitution confers any arbitrary power on any president or empowers any president to convert George Washington's America into Caesar's Rome."

Later in October Ervin went to Tulane University to make a

speech and wound up lecturing to several classes on constitutional law. On the 19th, while waiting at the New Orleans airport for a flight to Charlotte, he was told there was an urgent call from the White House. It was Fred Buzhardt; the President wanted to see Ervin as soon as possible. He flew immediately to Friendship airport in Baltimore, where he was met and whisked to the White House. There was no time to notify anyone on the committee or staff. Ervin and Baker, who had also been summoned without notice, went, after a few minutes of conferring with White House lawyers, directly in to see Nixon.

They were told, according to Ervin, that they would receive exact transcripts of the taped conversations, after the contents were verified by Senator John Stennis. They were not told, however, that Special Prosecutor Cox had already turned down the proposed compromise. Both Ervin and Baker agreed to the proposal because the committee's suit had been thrown out of court, and they believed chances were slim that they would ever hear the tapes.

Unable to get a commercial flight, Ervin was flown home that night by military plane. He was quite pleased by his visit to the White House. As he said later, "I thought the President was at long last doing what was the responsible thing to do, not only from the country's standpoint, but from his own standpoint as well."

The next day, Cox announced that he could not accept the compromise, and that night, the "Saturday night massacre" took place. Cox was fired, and Attorney General Elliot Richardson and Deputy Attorney General William Ruckelshaus were forced to resign. Cox was supposed to be independent of the White House, but it appeared that he was doing his job too well, coming too close to Nixon and his friends. For the next few days, the country was rocked with talk of impeachment.

There was something fishy about the tape "compromise." Ervin said he was promised word-for-word transcripts of the relevant conversations, yet the President announced that what Ervin and Baker had agreed to was a summary which Nixon himself would prepare. Why did Nixon fire Cox? Because Cox refused to accept an offer that was so reasonable that the two senators accepted it. It looked as though Ervin had been had—or, as they say back in North Carolina, "canigled"—by the President of the United States.

I saw Ervin two days later in Hot Springs, Virginia, where he had gone to make a speech and escape from Watergate. But Watergate was inescapable. Ervin had been shadowboxing with Nixon over the subject for nearly a year and was now seventy-seven years old; yet the issue was far from being resolved. He was tired of it. Why couldn't Nixon, if he was so innocent, hand over the evidence and get on with the business of the country? It would spare Nixon, Ervin, and the country months of grief.

"Nothing would give me more pleasure than to be able to say in all sincerity that the President was not involved in any way with the Watergate affair," he said.

He said if he were Cox he would have done the same—refuse the offer and accept the consequences.

"I think it's a great tragedy for the President to do anything to make the people feel that he is superior to the law," he said. "I so strongly believe in government by laws. I don't think the occupant of any office is above the Constitution or above the law. If you don't have a government of laws, the only alternatives are anarchy on the one hand or tyranny on the other; I don't think there is any middle ground."

The events of the weekend had done nothing to shake Ervin's conviction about the place of Watergate in the nation's history. "I don't think there has ever been anything like it. There have been mistakes before, but never anything of this nature."

As it turned out, Nixon agreed to surrender the tapes—what there was of them—to the courts. And finally, he began the long and painful attempt to explain himself to Congress and the public. Many people thought it was too late; that the damaged presidency of Richard Nixon could never be restored, certainly not to the heights of power and prestige it once enjoyed.

With or without the tapes, there were some conclusions about Nixon's role in the whole tawdry affair that were inescapable. If the President did not know what was going on around him, he should have found out pretty quickly, even, as Ervin said, if he had to raise "pluperfect hell" and call in John Mitchell and Maurice Stans and demand an explanation. Instead of traveling on leaden feet, justice would have been swift. But hiding the evidence until the courts finally ordered him to turn it over tended to convict Nixon in the eyes of the American people. As Ervin said, "It's a rule of evidence; it's a rule of common sense; it's a rule of psychology; it's a rule of human nature."

Americans have nearly always been skeptical of politicians, usually with justification. With Watergate this cynicism seemed at a nadir, a point beyond which the country could not go and survive as a government of the people. It became a question of whether the public would instantly disbelieve any candidate, any officeholder, any government official. A president had permitted the suspicion of criminal wrongdoing to stand against him for more than a year without clearing himself, and Spiro T. Agnew, the man to whom he had entrusted the vice presidency, had resigned in disgrace. It had to have a devastating effect on the country.

That is the reason the Senate investigation was so important. As Ervin said before the hearings began, it did not matter so much that a number of men might be sent to jail, but that the American people be told the complete truth, whatever it was; a nation founded on truth could only survive on truth. It helped to have a man in the middle of that committee table who took his stand by truth.

Nixon understood this. That is why he tried to make his

goal-line stand in the courts rather than before the bar of public opinion. He had closed down "Operation Candor" in January, 1974 and informed Ervin again that he would not surrender his tapes. "I can only view your subpoena," Nixon said, "as an unconstitutional usurpation of power." Ervin replied that there was nothing in the Constitution that gave the President the power to withhold information concerning illegal activities. We seemed to be back on square one, except that the clock was ticking and time was running out.

Ervin was pleased to find, as he made the rounds of college campuses in the winter of 1973, that there seemed to be a new appreciation among students of the basic principles of American government and the Constitution, and he was flattered by those who said he embodied those principles. "I think the faith of young people in our system has been largely reestablished," he said, optimistic as usual.

Those principles were as much or more concerned with morality and ethics as with the letter of the law. Few men in public life could have said what Ervin said, during the summer, to one of the witnesses and be believed. Ervin was not speaking for the Senate or for the Watergate Committee, but for himself—and that was his duty, as Teacher in that morality play—when he said:

"The evidence thus far introduced before this committee tends to show that men upon whom fortune had smiled benevolently and who possessed great financial power, great political power, and great governmental power undertook to nullify the laws of man and the laws of God for the purpose of gaining what history will call a very temporary political advantage."

Then Ervin, who believed every word of it, added: "And I think that those who participated in this effort to nullify the laws of man and the laws of God overlooked one of the laws of God, which is set forth in the seventh verse of the sixth chapter of

Galatians: 'Be not deceived. God is not mocked; for whatsoever a man soweth, that shall he also reap.' "

It was probably one of the few times in history that men and women stood up in a public place and lustily applauded a quotation from the Scriptures.

15. *Beyond Watergate*

OUR PERSPECTIVE is much too limited to permit an assessment of the meaning of Watergate and all that it has come to symbolize in our national life or of the man whose career seemed to reach a climax because of it. We cannot predict what judgments history will render on either the events or the man. But Ervin's place in history does not depend solely on Watergate. He will certainly be remembered for the moral example and leadership he gave us in this time of deepest trouble, but even more important are the contributions he made in shaping our laws and revitalizing our liberties throughout his senatorial career. He was a man with large flaws and impressive virtues, a maverick perhaps, but he was no average man and no average senator. I personally believe that history will see him as one of the great men of the Senate.

Ervin himself was modest about his place in history, but also, I believe, deeply concerned. "I would hope," he said, "that history would reach the verdict that although I may not have done the right in all my official actions, I did what I thought was right in the light of the circumstances as they appeared to be at the time I was compelled to act. I would hope that history would reach the conclusion that I have not sold the truth to serve the political hour."

It was a cautious self-evaluation from a man frequently given to extravagant praise of others. He set very high standards for himself. Where others have aimed for power or money, he sought to live by personal codes of morality and self-discipline. Applying his own standards, it did seem that he believed in the actions he took during the twenty years from McCarthy to Watergate. As far as it was possible for a person in public office to act without regard to the political consequences, Ervin somehow managed to do it; and if he had any strength at all, he said many times, it was due to that ability.

In a way it was fortunate for the country that Ervin had a constitutional case against the civil rights bills; he would not have opposed them on any other grounds, and without the opposition he undoubtedly would not have remained in the Senate. If he had somehow fallen in with the other side on those issues, he would not have been in the Senate in 1973 when the system seemed to be falling apart; in 1972 when freedom of the press was under attack; in 1971 when the Army's civilian intelligence operation was exposed and the SACB was marked for extinction; in 1970 when preventive detention was offered as a substitute for due process; in 1968 when the Indian Bill of Rights rode through Congress; in 1966 when the prayer amendment was defeated and the Bail Reform Act came into being; even, indeed, in 1954 when McCarthyism breathed its last.

It is probably a good thing there were not a hundred Sam Ervins in the Senate during the civil rights years. Because he was unique his voice was valuable, even to those who so passionately hungered for change. He played by the rules, amended what laws he could, and accepted defeat. At the same time he reminded the country of what liberties it was suspending in order to right long-standing wrongs—even if they were the liberties of the most bigoted restaurant owner, school official, or voting registrar.

There were always enough votes against Ervin and his southern allies to pass any civil rights law whose time really had come. The others probably did not deserve to be passed, at least not in the harsh, vindictive form in which they were presented. Some of the bills were improved, either by his amendments or because of grudging concessions to his opposition.

Lastly, Ervin lent a certain dignity to the southern cause, introducing restraint and decorum where these qualities had not always been present.

On the other hand, Ervin brought his southern brand of libertarianism to Capitol Hill and, after years and years of scholarly debate and at times ringing speeches, hooked a lot of his colleagues on it, even the part about people being truly free only if they accept responsibility for their own lives. His integrity and mental gravity pulled others toward him from all parts of the political universe and changed them.

His finest hours in the Senate were not those spent in the Watergate hearings, but those given in defense of liberty. Ervin watchers agreed during the hearings that if he decided to retire in 1974, he would surely rather go out fighting the newly rejuvenated school prayer issue—which several liberals were ducking and even supporting—than in finding all the answers to Watergate.

Ervin reacquainted people with the heady principles of liberty at times when they seemed willing to give them up in exchange for order and security. They were principles that had been tested and proven so long ago that most Americans seemed unaware of their existence. Freedom of speech and the press were not very popular concepts with presidents or kings during wartime or domestic instability. In times of stress the right to assemble and protest was viewed with alarm by those in power, and the rights of criminal defendants were easily forgotten when people feared to walk the streets.

Ervin changed with the times, but gradually, so that to others who were drifting in and out with the tide he appeared to be standing still. He tried to slow the rate of change, with some success, hoping that when his adversaries had a chance to reflect after their passions had cooled, they might see things his way.

But when the times proved him wrong, he quietly went along. One could say that the country, rather than Ervin, changed. Actually, they met each other halfway.

His confrontation with Richard Nixon on the issues of executive versus congressional power might have been lost if not for Watergate; as it was, it was a spirited contest instead of the bone-crunching defeat it was expected to be. Aides said he got more pure pleasure out of threatening the White House into making concessions on executive privilege than from anything else that happened during the hearings.

For many in public life, history has a way of walking away just when they are getting ready to make their mark on it. It walked right into Sam Ervin's corner, mainly because he waited patiently for it. In fact, he probably did not think in these terms because he was too busy worrying about the state of the Constitution. In spite of his age, he was remarkably fit for the fight, with all his marbles and plenty of vinegar.

What Ervin dreaded more than anything else was the waning of his mental powers. There have been many in Congress who stayed past their time and made fools of themselves, nodding off to sleep during committee meetings, losing their nerve and their grip, and, in the end, being defeated. He wanted no part of that. If he sought another six-year term, he wanted the assurance—and who could honestly say for sure?—that he could give it all he had.

The question of retirement was a profound dilemma during the year of Watergate. He desperately needed time to think the matter through, but he could never find it. Many of his friends and members of his family told him he owed it to himself to call it quits.

He told me he did not think he was exceeding the bounds of modesty to say that his friendships, his experience, and his seniority—in short, his power—put him in a position to do more for his state and country than he had ever been able to do before.

There was the Democratic Party to think of and the prospect—perish the thought—that another Republican would appear on the scene. He was not overjoyed with the potential candidates from either party. What bothered him most was the prospect of surrendering his Senate seat to someone who lacked sensitivity about the Constitution.

On the other hand, he would be seventy-eight when the 1974 election took place, and he would have to ask the voters to trust in his durability beyond his eighty-fourth birthday.

"There's one inescapable reality that no man can ignore and that is that time takes a terrific toll which is of an increasing nature with respect to those who live many years, and I would hate to be in the Senate and have to, in Kipling's words, force my heart and nerves and sinew to serve their turn long after they're gone." One of his mistakes in life, he said, was that he had worked too hard.

"And I'm frank to state that I would love to read and do a little historical research and go fishing and watch the sunset over here in all its indescribable glory behind Table Rock and Hawks Bill Mountain and be here among the people who've known me best and, I think, love me most; with my wife. So it's not an easy thing to decide."

Even though he had always felt it was better to wear out than rust out, "at the same time I'd love to slow down to a trot instead of having to run at full tilt."

That conversation was in August, 1973. When I saw him in October in Washington, he was in the middle of a classic duel on the telephone with a high-ranking HEW official. Ervin was trying to get him to bend the regulations because of an honest error by a school for deaf children in Morganton in getting its application for funds to Washington before the deadline. Ervin pleaded with him for almost half an hour, even reciting a poem about forgiveness, but the man refused to budge. Finally, Ervin gave up in utter frustration. "That's the damndest bureaucrat I've ever heard of," he said as he hung up.

Ervin had not finally made up his mind about his future, but on that day, he sounded very close to it. "Frankly, I'd like to quit," he said. He looked tired, as though the constant struggle with so many problems that seemed never to resolve themselves completely was finally getting to him. He could no longer handle the issues on his own terms. They had become his master and taken away his own liberty.

There were many things he could do. He was intrigued by the college lecture circuit. A lot of young people had told him that he had helped restore their faith in the system. That pleased him tremendously because in those young people lay the hope for the country's future.

He wanted to be able to travel. He wanted to lie in the sunshine and let it soak up the aches and pains of his arthritis. He wanted to be able to sit and read books he had never gotten around to and not have to worry about appointments. "If I don't do it now," he said, "I'll never do it. So there it is. It's the most difficult decision I've ever had to make. As far as I'm concerned, I've had whatever honor there is in it, and I've done the best I could."

Still, it was hard to let go. There were so many things yet to be done; he was as full of himself as he had ever been: full of pep, full of spirit; the Senate had become his life; the country was desperately in need of leadership; issues of constitutional rights and constitutional government were still unresolved; there was the lengthening shadow of Watergate.

It seemed during those gloomy winter days that he would change his mind, or that events would change it for him. The White House had angered him by hinting that his income tax records might contain the same kinds of inconsistencies and apparent violations that the President's contained. But, of course, whoever planted that one in the press could not have been more wrong. On December 14 Ervin placed his entire 52-page tax return in the *Congressional Record*. It was the handiwork of a fiendishly meticulous Scotch-Irishman, showing virtually every penny he had earned and spent during 1972. Just to make sure he was right, he had deliberately overpaid his taxes and demanded a refund so that his return would be automatically audited. He was furious at having to reveal his private finances, so much so that Mrs. Ervin feared he might decide to run again.

He had a hankering, he told one of his aides, to try it. But the prospect of spending the better part of his seventy-eighth year on the barbecue circuit instead of looking after the Constitution turned him cold. Allen Ellender had died that way. No one was going to give him the election; he had stirred up too much enmity for that. The time had come to reckon with old age.

On December 19, the day he had signed subpoenas for hundreds of White House tapes and documents, he called a press conference in his office and got it over with. He was close to tears as he told reporters that his old friend Albert Coates had called earlier in the day to remind him of a story about their former college president, Edward Kidder Graham. Graham asked his janitor whether or not he should take a wife, and the janitor replied, "Well, whichever you do, you're likely to be disappointed."

He read a brief statement that he had written out in longhand a few days before, saying that "intellectual honesty compels me to confront this inescapable reality: If I should seek reelection in 1974, I would be asking North Carolinians to return me to the Senate for a term which would extend beyond the 84th anniversary of my birth.

"Since time takes a constantly accelerating toll of those of us who live many years, it is simply not reasonable for me to assume that my eye will remain undimmed and my natural force stay unabated for so long a time."

As triumphant as it might have been for a man to leave public life at the height of his powers, Ervin looked afterwards like a lost child. It was one of the few times people could remember seeing him truly dejected. He moped around the office until late that afternoon, then put on his old gray overcoat and walked home.

There would still be another full year in Washington, time

enough perhaps to nail down some of the things that had come loose. It promised to be an epic year for Ervin and a crucial one for the country, and the good thing about it was that he would be uncommonly free to act. It would not be so if his name were on the ballot.

Sam Ervin had been kind to history and history was kind to him in return. It gave him the chance to end his career in politics with a blaze of glory instead of the humiliation of impotency and defeat.

He brought the stern values of another age into the latter half of the twentieth century at a time when unprincipled men had been permitted to flourish by chicanery and the arrogant abuse of power. He found that those older values were more valid than ever during the Watergate era and that people like himself, who were schooled in them, were in great demand. Many in the nation reached out for his guidance and in doing so reached out for the guidance of the Founding Fathers.

As often as he had lighted candles to the memory of those men, Ervin was probably just as fond of a good story as he was a classic statement of freedom. His crackling wit and vast mental library of quotations helped lighten the leaden moments of 1973.

Ervin was a new "Uncle Sam" to many who were turned off by the soap-flake media politics of 1972 and thirsted for "real" images. Many of us saw in Ervin—and some of Ervin's contemporaries—a grandfather figure: honest, unpolished, principled. By restoring our respect for history and the values which it handed down to us, by renewing our appreciation for those who had seen a little of life, Sam Ervin put us in touch with our past—and thus with ourselves.

SOURCES

Interviews for this book with Senator Ervin, members of his family, and his associates were all conducted during 1973.

Chapter One

Most of this material is based on the writer's observations during the Watergate hearings, interviews with Ervin, and excerpts from his speeches.

Chapter Two

References to Ervin's parents appear throughout his Senate speeches; this one to his father was made on December 11, 1959, and the discussion of his ancestors occurred on September 20, 1966. His family history is detailed in *North Carolina, the Old North State and the New* (1941) and *The Ervins of Williamsburg County, South Carolina* by Sam Ervin.

The travails of John Witherspoon Ervin were chronicled in the *South Carolina Historical and Genealogical Magazine*, July, 1945. Dr. Jean C. Ervin lent me her grandfather's poems and her father's reminiscences. Jean, Eunice, Hugh, and Sam Ervin provided many of the details from which the character of the town and the personalities of their parents were pieced together. The letters to the editor by S. J. Ervin had been neatly folded and stuffed into two brown envelopes; the dates of births and deaths were found in a family Bible. I interviewed Mrs. Tillet at her home in Charlotte.

The legacy of Reconstruction was described by W. J. Cash in *The Mind of the South*. Newspaper articles from the period are on microfilm at the Burke County Library and the North Carolina Room at the University of North Carolina Library. The town's balmy climate was described in *Western North Carolina—Historical and Biographical* (1890).

Chapter Three

Besides the many clues to the past that still can be found about the campus of the University of North Carolina, other useful sources were Thomas Wolfe's

The Web and the Rock and *Look Homeward, Angel,* Albert Coates's *What the University of North Carolina Meant to Me,* and Robert Watson Winston's *Horace Williams, the Gadfly of Chapel Hill.*

Williams' classroom comments come from three sources: Winston's book, Williams' *Logic for Living, Dialogues from the Classroom,* and Floyd Crouse's notebooks. President Graham's chapel talk was described in an interview with Coates. All the dialogue involving Ervin comes from his own recollections.

Chapter Four

Ervin's war experiences were told during an hour-long interview on April 20, 1973; additional help came from Jean and Eunice Ervin, his sisters, and Margaret Ervin, his wife. S. I. Parker, eighty-one at the time, spoke to me at his home in Concord, North Carolina, on April 18.

Chapter Five

The Harvard and General Assembly stories were told during interviews in Raleigh and Morganton on March 24, April 20, and August 24. Both of Chafee's books on freedom of speech were invaluable, as were Frankfurter's *The Case of Sacco and Vanzetti* (1927) and Morison's *The Oxford History of the American People* (1965).

I spoke with Mrs. Ervin in mid-August while her husband was presiding over the Watergate hearings. He referred to her as wife and ministering angel during a speech, "The Everlasting Things," to her alma mater, Converse College, on May 30, 1960.

Part of the background on the evolution bill was provided by Secretary of State Thad Eure; other information was found in *Preachers, Pedagogues and Politicians* (1966) by William B. Gatewood, Jr., wire service stories in *The Charlotte Observer,* and George B. Tyndall's *The Emergence of the New South.* I also spoke with Judge Higgins by phone at his home in Raleigh.

Chapter Six

The country lawyer stories were told during interviews with Ervin on March 23, April 21, and August 23. His sister Jean helped recreate the old law building, and his daughter Laura told me about his habit of singing while driving. The other material comes from Riddle and Franklin, whom I saw on another visit to Morganton in mid-June.

Chapter Seven

Ervin told me of his experience as a judge during the March 23 and April 21 sessions.

The section dealing with Ervin as a father combines interviews in Morganton with Sam J. Ervin III on April 19 and Laura on June 20, and in Orange, New Jersey, with Leslie on August 4.

The story of Joe Ervin was told by his brother Sam, his widow, Susan Graham Williamston, and by the men whose tributes to their former colleague appear in the *Congressional Record* on January 14, 1946. Ervin's votes and speeches are taken from the *Record* for 1946.

Chapter Eight

. Much of the material comes from the *North Carolina Reports* (1948–54), the collected opinions of the North Carolina Supreme Court, and from interviews with Ervin on April 21 and August 23, and Adrian Newton and Justice Sharp on June 22. Ervin's story about Justice Denny appeared in the *Congressional Record,* January 12, 1967.

Umstead's comments on the *Brown* decision appeared in *The Ordeal of Desegregation* (1966) by Reed Sarratt, Carlyle's in Coates' booklet, *Talks on the Rule of Law and the Role of Government in the Cities, the Counties and the State of North Carolina.*

Chapter Nine

The McCarthy material comes from news stories, an interview with Ervin on March 23, the hearing record, transcripts from "Meet the Press" and the *Congressional Record.*

The Rackets Committee section was written from news stories, the records of the hearings, and an interview with Ervin on August 23.

Chapter Ten

The civil rights years were discussed in numerous interviews, including March 23 and August 23. I talked with Clarence Mitchell in May in Washington and Terry Sanford in June in Durham, and also with present and former aides on dozens of occasions. I personally observed Ervin for three years during this final, anti-busing phase. This section also includes excerpts from dozens of speeches and committee hearings. The Kilpatrick editorial appeared in *The Ordeal of Desegregation* by Reed Sarratt, 1966.

Chapter Eleven

This material is taken from thirteen years of hearings and Senate speeches. The questions about employees' sexual habits were read during a speech on

August 29, 1967, and those dealing with the personal lives of social security recipients in one given on November 10, 1969. The Huston memo on the SACB was made public at the Watergate hearings.

Background was obtained from interviews with MacNaughton, Baskir, Smith, Woodard, Autry, Pursley, and Speiser.

Chapter Twelve

The sources for this chapter were the hearings and speeches on direct elections and women's rights in 1970, consumer protection in 1972, and interviews with Mrs. Ervin and committee staff.

Chapter Thirteen

This material comes from hearings on impoundment, executive privilege, and executive agreements; Ervin's speeches and briefs in the Gravel case; my own notes from hearings and press conferences; and my trip with him to Raleigh in March.

Chapter Fourteen

Ervin's part in the Watergate hearings is recorded in the committee's official record. The record also contains copies of the White House memoranda that were introduced as evidence.

I interviewed Ervin at length about Watergate on June 8, then as part of wide-ranging interviews on August 23 and October 17, and again on October 22 after the firing of Cox.

Chapter Fifteen

My conversation with Ervin in Morganton took place on August 24, and the one in his office occurred on October 17.

INDEX

DATE DUE

GAYLORD			PRINTED IN U.S.A